HORMONES

The Woman's
Answerbook

Books by
LOIS JOVANOVIC AND GENELL J. SUBAK-SHARPE

Hormones: The Woman's Answerbook 1987
Living with Diabetes 1985

Books by
LOIS JOVANOVIC, M.D.

Controversies in the Field of Diabetes and Pregnancy 1987
The Diabetic Woman 1987
Diabetes in Pregnancy: Teratology, Toxology, and Treatment 1986
Contemporary Issues in Nutrition 1985
The Diabetes Self Care Manual 1984

Books by
GENELL J. SUBAK-SHARPE

*The Columbia University School of Public Health's Guide to
  Health and Well-Being over 50* (with Robert J. Weiss, M.D.) 1987
The Cancer Book (The American Cancer Society; editor) 1986
*The Columbia University College of Physicians and Surgeons Complete
  Home Medical Guide* (editorial director) 1985
The Physicians' Manual for Patients (editor) 1984
Freedom from Menstrual Cramps
  (with Kathryn Schrotenboer, M.D.) 1981
Frontiers in Medicine (with James V. Warren, M.D.)
  Breathing Easy 1987
  Overcoming Breast Cancer 1987
  Controlling Hypertension 1986
  Living with Diabetes 1985
  Surviving Your Heart Attack 1984

HORMONES

The Woman's Answerbook

Lois Jovanovic, M.D.
and
Genell J. Subak-Sharpe

Fawcett Columbine • New York

A Fawcett Columbine Book
Published by Ballantine Books
Copyright © 1987 by Lois Jovanovic and Genell J. Subak-Sharpe

Library of Congress Catalog Card Number: 87-91394

ISBN: 0-449-90304-4

This edition published by arrangement with Atheneum Publishers, an imprint of
Macmillan Publishing Company.

Cover design by James R. Harris

Manufactured in the United States of America

First Ballantine Books Edition: September 1988

10 9 8 7 6 5 4 3 2

This book is dedicated to our mothers
and to all women who may, at times,
feel they are ruled by inner forces
they do not understand.

Acknowledgments

The writing of any book involves many people, and this one has been no exception. Indeed, space does not permit even listing the scores of people who have lent their insight and assistance in bringing the book to fruition. Still, there are some whose contributions cannot be overlooked. We want to extend special thanks to Jane Margaretten-Ohring for her meticulous fact checking and research, and to Susan Ginsberg, our editor at Atheneum, for her thoughtful guidance. Dr. Kathryn Schrotenboer has shared her medical experience and knowledge, as has Dr. Charles Peterson (who also came up with the book's title). Beth Anne Willert provided the medical illustrations, which give so much added meaning to the text.

Above all, the understanding and support of our respective families have helped carry us through from beginning to end. To Kevin, Larisa, Boyce, Gerald, David, Sarah and Hope go our love and very special appreciation.

Contents

Introduction

MOST OF US GIVE VERY LITTLE THOUGHT TO HOW OUR bodies work until something goes wrong. For example, we often hear that we are ruled by our glands, yet very few people have even the haziest notion of what this means. Most of us know that glands produce hormones and that in some way, hormones make women different from men. But most people, including many doctors, lack a clear understanding of just how important hormones are or what they do.

Why, you may ask, is it important that women learn about a complex area of medicine? There are many good answers to this question. A knowledgeable, informed patient is better able to participate intelligently in important health decisions. Potential problems often can be avoided by knowing how to recognize warning signs. Simply knowing that a troubling symptom is a variation of what is normal and shared by millions of other women is, in itself, reassuring.

And there's a special reason for women to learn more about how their bodies work. A few years ago, at the height of the women's movement, a well-known physician and presidential advisor asserted that women were unfit to hold high political office or other positions of authority because their natural hormonal surges made them unreliable. Predictably, feminists immediately denounced the insinuation that women are prisoners of "raging hormones," while anti-feminist forces seized upon the notion as justification for keeping women in "their place"—at home, safely tending house and children. The more recent attention to premenstrual syndrome and the fact that, in some women, the symptoms can be quite pronounced, has added further fuel to the debate. The truth is, however, that hormones govern almost every facet of life for both males and females of all ages, and that by understanding the role of these vital substances, we can better adapt to lead more productive, harmonious lives.

This book, by specifically focusing on the role of hormones in controlling the way the body functions, is intended to clear up many common misconceptions. We also hope to give women the information they need to make informed health decisions—on everything from treating acne and dieting to deciding on a method of contraception or whether to take estrogen supplements following menopause.

At the outset, it is essential to understand a few basic medical terms and concepts. Patients often complain that they don't know what their doctors are talking about, largely because medicine has its own language. Following are some of the more important terms; others are defined throughout the text and also in the Glossary.

Glands

A gland is any organ or structure that produces secretions. Some are familiar to virtually everyone—the sweat glands that produce perspiration or the salivary glands that secrete saliva. These are *exocrine* glands—by definition, glands that have ducts to carry their secretions externally. In this book, we are specifically concerned with the finely tuned network of *endocrine* glands—ductless glands that secrete dozens of different chemical compounds, or hormones, directly into the blood stream. The thyroid, pituitary, pineal, parathyroid, thymus, adrenals, gonads (the ovaries in women and the testes in men) and pancreas all are examples of endocrine glands. A number of organs also secrete important hormones: an area of the brain, kidneys, lungs, heart, and intestinal lining, among others.

Hormones

Hormones are chemical messengers that control scores of vital processes and act on virtually every cell of the body. When people say "we are controlled by our glands," they really are referring to hormones produced by glands. The various glands work in concert with each other and the nervous system, through a finely tuned "feedback" network, to release specific hormones that carry messages to other parts of the body and set in motion specific responses.

To envision how this works, let's look at what happens when a hungry baby begins to breast-feed. The baby's sucking sends a message along the mother's nerves and spinal cord to the hypothalamus area of her brain. The message, which is transmitted in only a fraction of a second, signals the hypothalamus to instruct the pituitary (often referred to as the body's master gland) to release a hormone called oxytocin into the blood. In a few seconds, the oxytocin reaches the milk ducts in the breast, causing them to contract and release a stream of milk. During the process, the pituitary releases another hormone, prolactin, which also is essential in the production of milk. Sometimes just the sound of a hungry, crying baby provides enough stimulation to send the message to the mother's brain.

Although this is an over-simplified description of a complex but marvelously fine-tuned interaction of the endocrine and nervous system, it illustrates the vital role of hormones in a basic body process.

Virtually every bodily function and response depends, at least to some extent, upon hormones. Hormones control or influence growth, sexual development and desire, metabolism, muscular development, mental acuity, behavior and sleep cycles. They enable us to respond quickly to a dangerous situation, and are instrumental in maintaining the proper internal chemical and fluid balances.

Some hormones act directly on an organ to produce a desired effect. Oxytocin is an example of such a hormone; it not only stimulates the flow of breast milk, but it also induces labor by causing contractions of the uterus in pregnant women.

Some hormones have no direct impact on their own; instead, they prompt other endocrine glands to go into action. These are referred to as *trophic* hormones, and include thyroid-stimulating hormones which stimulate the thyroid gland to secrete its hormones, and the gonadotropins, which stimulate the ovaries and testes to produce their respective hormones.

Endocrinology

The branch of science and medicine devoted to the endocrine system is called endocrinology. An endocrinologist is a physician who specializes in disorders of the endocrine system. Within endocrinology, there are several subspecialties. A reproductive endocrinologist, for example, deals specifically with problems related to conception and infertility. A pediatric endocrinologist treats various hormone-related growth disorders, such as premature puberty, dwarfism or giantism.

Even though there are so many different hormones and so many body functions that depend upon them, the endocrine system is remarkably stable and endocrine disorders are relatively rare. Frequently, a health problem may be attributed to a glandular disorder, but careful medical examination often disproves this. For example, a sluggish, underactive thyroid may result in weight gain. Thus many obese people blame their weight problem on a thyroid disorder, and will ask their doctors for thyroid hormone supplements to help shed pounds. More often, however, laboratory studies will confirm that the thyroid is functioning normally and the weight problem is caused by poor eating habits, faulty appetite control or some other factor.

Even though serious endocrine disorders are relatively uncommon, it is still important that women gain a better understanding of the system because even normal hormonal fluctuations influence the way we feel and act. Knowing how and why, for example, the monthly fluctuations of female sex hormones can cause the mood changes and other symptoms related to premenstrual syndrome makes it easier to cope with this problem. Young girls, often alarmed at the bodily changes that herald the onset of puberty, can forestall unwarranted anxiety with knowledge.

In the last few years, women have become more attuned to the importance of taking steps to prevent osteoporosis—the thinning of bones that afflicts millions of older women. By understanding the important role of estrogen in calcium metabolism, women can make informed decisions about the need for estrogen therapy following menopause. There are hundreds of other examples—many of which can literally change your life and the way you perceive yourself and your womanhood.

In the following chapters of Part I, the various endocrine glands and their hormones will be described in greater detail. Part II is devoted to the role hormones play in a woman's life-stages, from childhood to old age. Part III describes the various hormone-related disorders and how they are treated.

Part I

Hormones: How They Rule Your Life

Chapter 1

The Endocrine System—
An Overview

IF YOU HAVE EVER SPENT MUCH TIME WITH A YOUNG CHILD, you undoubtedly have been asked scores of difficult, if not "unanswerable," questions about what makes us different from each other. Why is Daddy different from Mommy? Why are some people tall and others short? What makes me fall asleep at night and wake up in the morning? Why does Jimmy get mad so often? Why is Johnny's voice getting deeper? Why does Mommy have breasts and when will I grow mine?

The answers to these and thousands of other puzzling questions can be found in studying the endocrine system. This system, working in close cooperation with the nervous system, keeps us "in tune" with ourselves and our environment. It also produces the hormones that help make each of us a unique individual.

To a large extent, hormones determine whether we will be tall or short, fat or thin, calm or nervous, even-tempered or irritable, fast-moving or slow. The endocrine system enables us to adapt to a constantly changing environment, to cope with the stresses of daily life and to reproduce and fulfill our biological functions as human beings. Many of these processes take place without any conscious thought or action; both the endocrine and nervous systems have messengers that are responsible for thousands of different automatic responses and, working in concert, both regulate and integrate body functions.

The nervous system is somewhat analogous to a telephone. Messages are conducted by electrical impulses along a network of specialized cells, called neurons, to a specific receptor—in a manner similar to the transmission of your voice over a telephone line to a person on the receiving phone. Neural responses are virtually instantaneous—if you touch a hot stove, the sensory nerves in your fingers immediately send out a pain message and your hand is automatically jerked away before you even have time to think about it.

In the endocrine system, the messengers are chemical and travel via the bloodstream to the receptors, specialized cells in the various organs or body tissues that are specifically programmed to receive them. These chemical messengers are, of course, hormones, and they are produced by endocrine glands, the hypothalamus area of the brain, and tissues scattered throughout the body. Working through an elaborate, exceedingly sensitive and fine-tuned communications system, the various glands secrete hormones as needed to regulate or integrate body functions. Since hormones, in effect, travel by water instead of the electrical impulses used by the nervous system, their responses are somewhat slower than neural reactions.

THE ENDOCRINE GLANDS

The major endocrine glands are pictured in Figure 1. Hormones are also manufactured in glandular tissue located in other organs such as the intestines, lungs and heart.

Every now and then, researchers discover a heretofore unidentified hormone, and new things are constantly being learned about previously identified ones. It is highly likely that there are many more hormones awaiting discovery. Each finding is hailed as a new milestone, since the more we

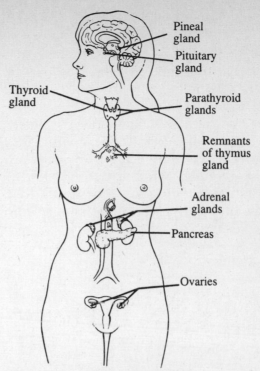

The Female Endocrine System

learn about the endocrine system and its interaction with the nervous system and other organs of the body, the more we learn about ourselves and what makes us who we are. To give a clearer picture of just how important the endocrine system and its hormones are, here is a brief description of the major glands, their hormones and their myriad functions.

THE PITUITARY

The pituitary is located deep inside the head, behind the nasal cavities and just below the hypothalamus. The hypothalamus is part of the forebrain, or diencephalon. This is often referred to as the "old," or original, brain and is the seat of primitive instincts—hunger, thirst, sleep, procreation, self-defense—needed for survival of a species. As humans evolved, new areas of the brain developed—specifically, the cerebral cortex, which is the seat of intelligence. The hypothalamus links this thinking part of the brain and the pituitary gland.

The pituitary is sometimes referred to as the body's master gland because, together with the hypothalamus, it produces many of the hormones that control other glands. (See Figure 2.) The pituitary is divided into two parts, or lobes: the foremost part, or anterior lobe, is made up of glandular tissue; the back, or posterior, lobe is actually an extension of the hypothalamus and is more nervelike in makeup.

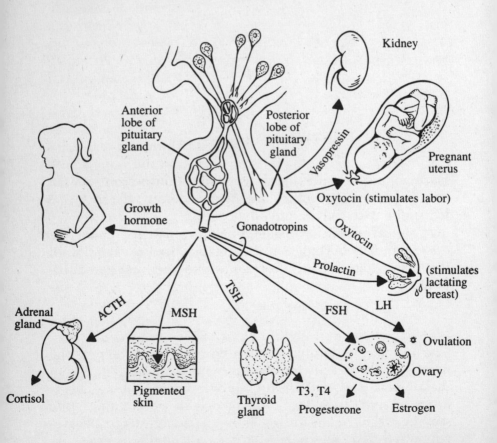

How the Pituitary Controls Other Endocrine Glands

Hormones produced in the pituitary's anterior lobe are mostly trophic hormones, meaning that they stimulate other glands or organs to go into action. For example, hormones known as gonadotropins are produced here. In a woman, these include FSH (follicle-stimulating hormone), which prompts the ovaries to ripen an egg each month, and LH (luteinizing hormone), which stimulates the ovarian follicle to release the ripened egg. In males, these hormones are called FSH and ICSH (interstitial cell-stimulating hormone); the latter stimulates the testes to produce male hormones.

Other anterior pituitary hormones include: growth-stimulating hormone, or somatotrophin, which is responsible for a child's growth; ACTH (adrenal-cortex-stimulating hormone), which stimulates the adrenal glands to produce their hormones; TSH (thyroid-stimulating hormone), which stimulates the thyroid gland to produce its hormones; and prolactin, which stimulates the breasts to produce milk.

Two hormones are secreted from the pituitary's posterior lobe: vasopressin, which controls the muscle tone of blood vessels and is also an antidiuretic hormone that helps the kidneys conserve water and maintain the body's fluid balance; and oxytocin, which promotes uterine contractions during labor and also stimulates the breasts to "let down" their milk.

The hypothalamus regulates and coordinates many endocrine functions, especially through its control of the pituitary gland. (See Figure 3.) Its nerve cells also produce hormonelike substances that are released directly into the blood. These are poorly understood, but it is thought that many symptoms or disorders rooted in psychological or emotional causes are related to the interaction between the hypothalamus and pituitary. For example, the body's appetite control center is in the hypothalamus and the source of some eating disorders, such as anorexia nervosa or bulimia, may be here. Also, women who are under tremendous emotional stress sometimes stop ovulating or experience menstrual irregularities.

The relationship between the brain and physical health

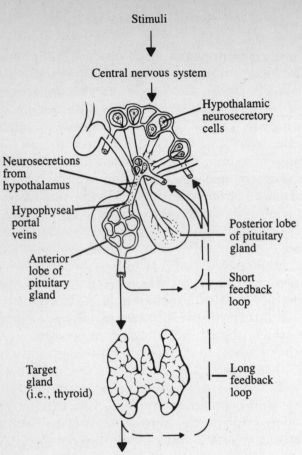

Stimuli

Central nervous system

Hypothalamic neurosecretory cells

Neurosecretions from hypothalamus

Hypophyseal portal veins

Anterior lobe of pituitary gland

Posterior lobe of pituitary gland

Short feedback loop

Target gland (i.e., thyroid)

Long feedback loop

Thyroid hormones to target tissues

A Typical Hormone Feedback System

is still poorly understood, but many researchers believe that a number of psychogenic ills may have their origin in the close relationship between the brain and the pituitary gland.

Given the pituitary's variety of hormones and functions, it is understandable that disorders of the hypothalamus and pituitary can have profound effects throughout the body. Too much growth hormone, for example, can result in giantism; too little, in dwarfism. If the hormones that prompt the ovaries or testes to go into action are released too early, premature sexual development will result. Conversely, a failure to produce the proper gonadotropins at the time of puberty results in a failure to mature sexually; this also may be a cause of infertility in women. Too little vasopressin may result in diabetes insipidus, a condition marked by excessive thirst and over-production of urine. Abnormal production of breast milk and failure to menstruate may be caused by over-production of prolactin.

Destruction of the anterior lobe of the pituitary—fortunately, a rare occurrence—can have a devastating effect. Consequences can include a shrinking of the genitals; impotence in men and infertility and lack of menstruation in women; low blood pressure, slowed heart rate and lethargy; difficulty in fighting off infections; poor tolerance of cold temperatures; premature aging; and, eventually, increasing disability and death. Many of these effects can be avoided or minimized by replacing the missing hormones.

THE THYROID

Moving down the body, the next major endocrine gland we encounter is the thyroid, a butterfly-shaped structure that lies over the windpipe and just below the larynx. Normally, the thyroid weighs only an ounce or less. Its hormones are essential to proper metabolism and a failure of the thyroid can affect virtually every organ and system in the body.

The thyroid secretes three hormones—triiodothyronine and thyroxine, which control metabolism by increasing the oxygen consumption of cells, and calcitonin, which is instrumental in calcium metabolism. Triiodothyronine and thyroxine, commonly referred to as thyroid hormones, or T_3 and T_4, are instrumental in the normal growth and development of the brain, muscles and bones, as well as the functioning of other endocrine glands and organ systems. A baby born with a thyroid deficiency is in danger of developing cretinism, a severe, irreversible form of mental retardation. Too much thyroid hormone causes speeded metabolism, characterized by a rapid heart beat and a number of other symptoms; too little results in a slowdown of almost all body processes. A goiter, or swelling of the thyroid gland, may develop in both hyper- and hypothyroidism.

The thyroid needs iodine to manufacture T_3 and T_4. Today, iodine deficiency is relatively rare in this country, thanks to the addition of the mineral to salt and the increased availability of iodine-rich foods, particularly saltwater fish and seafood. Iodine deficiency can lead to an underactive thyroid, or hypothyroidism, which also may be caused by a failure of the pituitary gland to produce enough thyroid-stimulating hormone or by destruction of all or part of the thyroid gland itself from inflammation, infection, radiation or other causes. While hypothyroidism in infancy results in cretinism, it is characterized in older children by slowed growth and delayed sexual development, although mental function may be relatively normal.

Hypothyroidism in adults is marked by a slowing down of almost all body functions. The skin, fingernails and hair become dry and brittle due to a slowdown in growth of these normally fast-growing tissues. Intestinal activity also slows down, resulting in constipation. Other symptoms include a slow heart rate, fatigue, lethargy, intolerance of the cold, puffiness of the legs and ankles from accumulation of body fluids, muscular soreness and leg cramps. Menstruating women may notice that their periods are heavier and more frequent; this is caused by a failure of the ovaries to produce an egg each month and the resulting excess buildup of the uterine lining.

THE PARATHYROID

The parathyroid glands are small, disk-shaped structures that normally lie on the back and side of each thyroid lobe. Most people have four of these tiny glands, but the number varies. Parathyroid hormone raises the amount of calcium circulating in the bloodstream while calcitonin (produced by the thyroid) lowers it.

The role of calcium in building and maintaining bones is well known, but many people are surprised to learn that calcium has a number of other vital functions. Small amounts of calcium are needed in order for muscles and nerves to function properly; it is also essential for proper metabolism and normal clotting of blood. Calcium is by far the most plentiful mineral in the body—the average adult has about 2.4 pounds of it. Most of this calcium is stored in the bones and small amounts also circulate in the blood. When the amount of circulating calcium falls, parathyroid hormone is secreted to prompt the bones to release some of their stores into the blood. The hormone also increases the action of vitamin D, which is needed in order for the body to absorb calcium consumed in the diet. In response to parathyroid hormone, the kidneys increase the excretion of another mineral, phosphate, which increases the amount of calcium circulating in the blood.

Parathyroid hormone deficiency can cause tetany—severe muscle spasms that make it impossible to move the affected body part. Sometimes these spasms affect the larynx. If untreated, suffocation may occur as a result of obstruction of the windpipe due to laryngeal spasm.

A rise in circulating calcium signals the parathyroid glands to stop secreting their hormone and instead, the thyroid releases calcitonin. The exact function of this hormone is unknown, but it is thought that it stimulates the bones to increase absorption of calcium; it also may affect calcium excretion from the kidneys. Too much circulating calcium may result in kidney stones, mental changes or irritability.

THE THYMUS

The thymus gland, which lies behind the sternum, or breastbone, is another gland whose function still is not fully understood. It is made up mostly of lymphoid tissue and is instrumental in the production of lymphocytes—cells that are essential to the immune system. Babies are born with a large thymus; the gland continues to grow during childhood, reaching its largest size just before puberty. It then starts to gradually shrink, and is quite small in older people or people who have prolonged, severe infections or are subjected to unusual stress.

The thymus is therefore instrumental in the body's rejection of foreign tissue. For example, young animals whose thymus glands are removed accept grafts of skin, kidneys and other organs without the usual rejection response. Injecting these animals with extracts of thymic tissue stimulates the production of lymphocytes and thus prompts rejection of the foreign-tissue grafts.

THE ADRENALS

The adrenals are triangular-shaped glands that rest atop the kidneys. Each gland is divided into two parts—the cortex, which makes up the outer layers, and the medulla, which is the inner portion. The adrenal cortex produces a group of hormones commonly referred to as steroids, which are divided into three categories according to their function: (1) the mineralocorticoids, which control the body's fluid balance by regulating the kidney's reabsorption of sodium and potassium; (2) the glucocorticoids, which help regulate the metabolism of glucose (blood sugar) and other nutrients, maintain blood pressure and enable the body to respond to physical stress; and (3) the sex hormones (androgens and estrogens) that function similarly to those produced in the ovaries or testes.

The adrenal medulla produces a group of hormones referred to as catecholamines, which include the stress hormones epinephrine (adrenaline) and norepinephrine. Catecholamines are produced by other body tissues; therefore, a person can get by without an adrenal medulla. The cortex and its hormones are more essential, however, not only for their own vital functions but also because they are involved in intricate feedback systems that prompt the release of certain pituitary hormones.

Aldosterone is the major mineralocorticoid produced in the adrenal cortex. Its major role is to help the kidneys conserve sodium and thereby maintain the body's balance of fluids. Its secretion is related to a complicated feedback system involving ACTH (from the pituitary gland) and the blood levels of sodium, potassium and angiotensin II (a substance instrumental in the regulation of blood pressure). An overproduction of aldosterone—a condition referred to as hyperaldosteronism—leads to excessive sodium retention, resulting in high blood pressure, and a depletion of potassium, which can cause irregular heart beats, muscular weakness and cramps. Most instances of hyperaldosteronism can be traced to the growth of a tumor producing the hormone—a situation that can be treated by removal of the tumor. If the problem is caused by an overactivity of the adrenal gland itself, drugs to counter this may be prescribed.

Cortisol is the most abundant of the glucocorticoids in humans; corticosterone (which also has some mineralocorticoid function) is produced in lower quantities. The liver can metabolize cortisol into cortisone, a steroid that is used to treat allergic disorders, such as asthma. It also may be given to counter the inflammation of arthritis and other inflammatory conditions.

The glucocorticoids affect metabolism in several ways. Cortisol has an anti-insulin effect and is instrumental in transforming protein and fats into glucose, or blood sugar—the body's major fuel. The adrenal glands increase cortisol production following any stress or injury—a process that is related to the body's so-called "fight-or-flight" response and our ability to counter the effects of injury or infection. The instant the danger is perceived, the brain signals the pituitary gland to produce ACTH, which in turn tells the adrenals to pump out extra cortisol, as well as catecholamines.

Cortisol production is also influenced by our internal biological clocks. Even in the absence of stress, the pituitary secretes spurts of ACTH throughout the day. But these spurts are more frequent during the predawn hours and become increasingly less frequent throughout the day. These normal fluctuations explain our sleep/wake patterns and also account for our jet lag when we travel across several time zones; the clock on the wall may say it is time to get up, but our internal biological clock needs time to adjust and will continue to operate on its own "time" for a few days.

The importance of our ability to produce extra cortisol on short notice is especially evident among people whose adrenal glands have been damaged, particularly by prolonged steroid therapy. Frequent administration of steroids causes the body's own steroid-producing glands to shrink and become sluggish. If the steroid drugs are then abruptly stopped, a person may die of a relatively minor illness or injury because the adrenal glands simply cannot rally and produce the cortisol needed to overcome the emergency.

Addison's disease—a relatively rare disorder in which the adrenal glands are gradually destroyed, usually by an autoimmune disorder or by other diseases, such as tuberculosis—is one that comes to mind. This disease is characterized by a variety of symptoms: fatigue, abdominal pains, lack of appetite, nausea, dizzy spells or fainting, a darkening of the skin and increased susceptibility to infection or physical stress. A minor injury or operation may quickly lead to shock and death. Fortunately, Addison's disease can be treated with drugs to replace the cortisol and also aldosterone.

Cushing's syndrome is another disorder related to glucocorticoids; yet, in this disease, the problem is an over-production of the hormones. This is frequently caused by an ACTH-producing tumor, usually of the pituitary gland. The extra ACTH stimulates the adrenal glands to increase production of glucocorticoids, resulting in a number of symptoms, including: muscular weakness and wasting; a thinning of the skin, leading to easy bruising and stretch marks; excessive hair growth; and a humped, moon-faced appearance caused by an accumulation of fat on the face, trunk and back of the neck. High blood pressure, increased vulnerability to infection and, sometimes, the development of diabetes mark advanced stages of the disease. Cushing's syndrome is treated by determining and then removing the cause of the increased hormone production.

The sex hormones produced by the adrenal glands supplement those secreted by the ovaries and testes and, under normal circumstances, have little effect of their own. The exception might be the male sex hormones—androgens—produced by the adrenal glands in women. These androgens influence the growth of pubic and other body hair in women and also are instrumental in a woman's sex drive. Excessive production of these male hormones in a woman prompts development of male characteristics: excessive growth of facial and other body hair, a deepened voice, increased muscular development, enlarged clitoris and, perhaps, heightened sex drive.

The catecholamines, which are produced in the adrenal medulla as well as in the brain and sympathetic nervous system, are instrumental in the fight-or-flight response. The instant that danger is perceived, the body steps up its production of epinephrine and norepinephrine. A similar reaction takes place in response to low blood sugar, exposure to the cold, a shortage of oxygen, lowered blood pressure and other such circumstances.

These hormones have similar functions; both cause the heart to beat faster and more forcefully, increase alertness and break down fats to provide extra energy if it is needed. Norepinephrine raises blood pressure by constricting or narrowing blood vessels; epinephrine counters this somewhat by constricting some blood vessels while opening up, or dilating, vessels in the skeletal muscles and the liver. This permits the delivery of more blood to the muscles, thereby giving a person the extra strength that may be needed to escape from danger. Epinephrine also breaks down the glucose, stored as glycogen, in the liver, and the increased blood flow to this organ helps carry the glucose to other parts of the body.

THE PANCREAS

The pancreas is a long, narrow organ that extends across much of the upper abdomen. It is both an endocrine gland —with specialized cells that produce insulin and glucagon, hormones that are essential in metabolism and maintaining glucose balance—and an exocrine gland, manufacturing digestive enzymes that travel through pancreatic ducts to the small intestine to aid in digestion.

Insulin, glucagon and somatostatin are manufactured in the Islets of Langerhans, which are collections of specialized cells scattered throughout the pancreas. Insulin, which is produced in the islets' beta cells, is crucial to the body's ability to metabolize carbohydrates and to utilize glucose, or blood sugar—the body's principal fuel. After eating a meal, especially one rich in carbohydrates, blood sugar rises. This results in increased secretion of insulin, which enables the body to make use of the glucose. If the beta cells are unable to produce adequate insulin, diabetes results—a disease in which the body is unable to metabolize its glucose (see Chapter 10 on diabetes and hypoglycemia).

Glucagon, which is secreted by islet alpha cells, stimulates the liver to break down glycogen (stored blood sugar) and to return it to the bloodstream for use as fuel. When blood sugar falls, glucagon production rises, thus helping maintain a steady supply of glucose. Glucagon also enhances the conversion of protein to glucose. Still another substance instrumental in maintaining this hormonal balance is somatostatin, which is produced by the islet delta cells. It inhibits alpha and beta cell production, thereby suppressing insulin and glucagon secretion.

THE GONADS

The sex hormones are probably the ones that are the most familiar to the general public, but they also are greatly misunderstood. At puberty, hormones from the pituitary and hormonelike substances from the hypothalamus signal the reproductive organs—the testes in males and the ovaries in females—that it is time for them to develop and start functioning. The testes increase production of testosterone, which, with other male sex hormones, comprise the androgens; the ovaries begin to make more estrogen. In both boys and girls, the adrenal gland increases production of androgens, which stimulates the growth of body hair, among other functions. (The basics of sexual development are discussed in detail in Chapter 3.)

Men get their "maleness" from androgens; women, their femininity from estrogens. Sex hormones are often thought of as a major ruling force for both sexes, particularly women. While male sex hormones are secreted at a fairly steady rate, female hormones follow a cyclic pattern. This ebb and flow controls a woman's menstrual cycle and her fertility, and has been blamed for everything from spurts of elation and tremendous energy to depression and murderous rage. So many myths and misconceptions surround the role of sex hormones that it is hard to sort out facts from fallacies. Indeed, since this is the major goal of this book, we will present only a brief overview of the sex hormones here, with more detailed discussions in subsequent chapters. For both sexes, the production of reproductive hormones is controlled by a feedback system between the hypothalamus/pituitary axis and the gonads. In men, the pituitary hormone FSH regulates the production of sperm, while LH, also a pituitary hormone, controls secretion of testosterone. Testosterone and the other androgens are responsible for what we generally consider maleness: the growth of a beard, deepened voice, and the broad-shouldered, muscular development of a man's body. Androgens control our sexual desires; they also are thought to be responsible for certain behavior associated with maleness—aggressiveness, a greater willingness to fight, boisterousness and so on.

The female ovaries manufacture three hormones: estradiol, progesterone and relaxin. Estradiol is an estrogen, a general term that applies to "feminizing hormones." Estrogen helps promote breast development and is also responsible for the growth of the endometrium—the lining of the uterus—during the first phase of the menstrual cycle. Progesterone, in conjunction with estrogen, prepares the uterine lining for pregnancy during the second phase. Relaxin acts on the pelvic ligaments during labor, enabling the birth canal to widen so a baby can be born.

The secretion of all these hormones is controlled by a complex and extremely sensitive feedback system. In order for the ovaries to function, the other endocrine glands and organ systems must be working properly. Malnutrition, obesity, stress, illness, too much or too little body fat and a host of other factors can cause the ovaries to cease producing their hormones. The pituitary may be the body's master gland, but, for a woman, the ovary is also a very temperamental mistress; if the other glands are not up to par, the ovaries are likely to "shut down."

MISCELLANEOUS OTHER HORMONES

Hormones also are manufactured in a number of organs that are not generally considered a part of the endocrine system. For example, the gastrointestinal tract secretes gastrin, gastric inhibitory polypeptide (GIP) and other substances that stimulate the release of insulin and enhance its action when blood glucose is high. The heart produces a substance called atrial naturitic factor, which is thought to be instrumental in controlling blood pressure.

THE KIDNEYS

The kidney normally is not thought of as part of the endocrine system, but this organ is instrumental in the production of at least two important hormones. One of these hormones, renin, is important in maintaining blood pressure. The other, REF (renal erythropoietic factor), helps control the production of red blood cells in the bone marrow.

Although renin was first discovered several decades ago, its precise function is still poorly understood. It differs from most hormones in that it does not act directly on an organ or tissue, but, instead, on a protein called angiotensinogen, which is formed in the liver and released into the blood. When this protein comes in contact with renin, a substance called angiotensin I is formed. This, in turn, is converted to angiotensin II in the lungs. Angiotensin II constricts the small arteries and arterioles, thereby raising blood pressure.

This substance also influences the release of aldosterone and seems to control thirst—an important factor in ensuring that the body gets enough fluids. A number of researchers believe that hypertension, or high blood pressure, is somehow caused by an imbalance of the renin/angiotensin/aldosterone system, but it is not known how this works. For example, it is not known exactly what prompts the kidneys to release renin. Also, it appears that organs other than the kidneys also produce renin; high levels have been found in the uterus of pregnant women and in the blood of people whose kidneys have been removed.

The role of REF in red blood cell production also is poorly understood. It is known that a hormone called erythropoietin controls the bone marrow's production of red cells. In the past, researchers thought that the kidneys produced this hormone, but now it appears that the kidneys secrete REF, which, together with a substance produced by the liver, makes the erythropoietin in the bloodstream. The body produces more erythropoietin following a serious bleeding episode, when the number of red blood cells has been lowered. The hormone is also increased when a person goes to a high altitude and needs more red blood cells to get enough oxygen from the thinner air. As with renin, it seems that the kidneys are not the only source of erythropoietin; people who have had their kidneys removed continue to manufacture the hormone.

The lungs also perform endocrine functions. For example, the substance in the blood stream called angiotensin I is converted to angiotensin II as it passes through the lungs; angiotensin II then stimulates the secretion of aldosterone —the hormone that, along with the renin/angiotensin system, is instrumental in regulating blood pressure and the body's fluid balance. Also, in some pulmonary disorders, such as certain types of lung cancer, ACTH and other hormones are secreted that upset the body's hormonal balance.

HOW HORMONES WORK

Since only very minute amounts of hormones circulate in the blood, they require highly efficient mechanisms of action and extremely sensitive receptors. As a hormone travels through the blood, it seeks out receptor sites that are programmed to recognize and receive it. Protein hormones such as insulin are too large to enter a cell itself, so their receptor sites are located on or near target cells. After a protein hormone attaches itself to its receptor site, the receptor transmits a message to the area of the target cell that is programmed to respond to the hormone. This entails activating an enzyme called adenyl cyclase, which is in the cell membrane, to form a second messenger, or hormone "mediator," called cyclic AMP, which ultimately carries out the hormonal action.

Steroid hormones are small enough to cross the cellular membranes, so, instead of binding with a receptor site on the cell surface, they seek out a receptor within the cell itself. The hormone and receptor form a smaller molecule that enters the cell nucleus and goes directly to its encoded portion of DNA, which activates specific genes to form messenger RNA and carry out the hormone's intended function. RNA and DNA are the specific genetic information of each woman.

These various conversions and interactions with second messengers are complex processes that are not fully understood even by scientists who have spent their lives studying them. But the more that is learned about how hormones act and the messengers they employ, the more likely we are to be able to correct genetic errors that have profound effects on growth, development and other body processes.

PROSTAGLANDINS

Prostaglandins are substances formed from fatty acids that are produced throughout the body, and are instrumental in carrying out a number of hormone-mediated functions. Prostaglandins were first discovered in semen and seminal vesicles, and at first were thought to be produced in the prostate, hence the name prostaglandins. Researchers then discovered that similar substances were in the kidneys, uterus and numerous other organs.

Like cyclic AMP, prostaglandins have many different functions, depending upon which tissues produce them and the hormones that mediate their action. Some researchers believe that prostaglandins actually act as second messengers for hormones and that cyclic AMP is the third messenger.

In the uterus, prostaglandins stimulate muscle contractions and are thought to be instrumental in initiating labor. During menstruation, prostaglandins cause uterine contractions, and excessive prostaglandin production causes menstrual cramps.

Urinary prostaglandins are instrumental in carrying out the functions of aldosterone and vasopressin in maintaining the body's fluid balance and blood pressure. Other functions that are known to involve prostaglandins include blood clotting and clumping of platelets, the inflammation process, immune responses, intestinal motility and gastric secretion, metabolism, and nervous system function, among others. In fact, many scientists feel that almost every bodily process that involves hormones also involves prostaglandins.

Improved understanding of how prostaglandins work has made it possible to develop more specific treatments for many disorders. For example, the realization that prostaglandins are involved in menstrual cramps has led to the widespread use of antiprostaglandin agents to treat this disorder, which afflicts millions of women. Antiprostaglandin drugs also are important in the treatment of arthritis and other inflammatory disorders. Millions of people who are at high risk of a stroke or heart attack are now advised to take a single aspirin a day, which is enough to inhibit the prostaglandins that cause clumping of blood platelets and formation of clots that can block vital blood flow to the heart or brain.

Although most therapies involving prostaglandins entail blocking their action, there is at least one application that calls for promoting prostaglandin activity—namely, inducing labor. It is thought that prostaglandins, which are produced in increasing amounts by the placenta as the time of delivery approaches, somehow increases uterine sensitivity to the hormone oxytocin, and that this initiates normal labor. By injecting prostaglandins into the amniotic cavity or by inserting it into the cervix, uterine contractions can be induced. This is now the preferred method of performing a late abortion.

SUMMING UP

In this brief overview, we have described the endocrine system and its hormones, as well as a simplified account of how hormones are believed to work. The endocrine system is perhaps one of the body's most complex. It is involved in virtually every body process, and, when something goes awry with one of the endocrine glands, the results may be experienced in dozens of different ways. Fortunately, it is a finely tuned system that generally works so smoothly that most of us are barely aware of it.

Part II

The Role of Hormones in the Milestones of a Woman's Life

Chapter 2

The Early Growing Years

INFANCY AND CHILDHOOD ARE USUALLY THOUGHT OF AS THE growing years. Actually, physical growth begins with fertilization and continues to adulthood and beyond. Much of our growth is encoded at the time of conception, but there are numerous circumstances that may alter this intended growth pattern. The growth process does not stop upon reaching adulthood; many cells continue to replace or replicate themselves throughout life.

Growth is largely controlled by complex hormonal interactions with other body systems. Over the years, researchers have engaged in lively debates over whether our genes or our environment are most important in determining height, weight and other characteristics. Obviously, both are important—even if one's genes are programmed to produce a person who is six feet tall, illness, the use of certain drugs, or deficiencies of calcium, protein, and other nutrients may intervene and produce stunted growth. Still, it appears that many aspects of growth and development that we once considered largely environmental are, instead, genetic and determined at the moment of conception.

GROWTH BEFORE BIRTH

Typically, we measure growth and development from the time of birth, forgetting the tremendous amount of growing that takes place in the uterus. By the time a human baby is born, the fertilized egg has undergone forty-two successive cycles of cell division, and only five more would be required in order to reach full adult size. This very rapid growth continues in the first year of life; by the time the average baby is a year old, he or she more than doubles in weight and increases by fifty percent in height.

The first week after fertilization takes place is called the germinal phase, and is marked by cell development and division. Typically, fertilization takes place in the fallopian tube, and this two-cell embryo (made up of the sperm and the egg) almost immediately begins the process of cell division. By the time it reaches the uterus, the embryo is usually four cells; it implants itself in the uterine wall at the four- to eight-cell stage.

Throughout the embryonic period, which usually refers to the first ten weeks, the tissues begin to form what will eventually be the various organ systems. The neural tube, which is formed along the backbone, develops first, and the other organ systems bud off from it. The embryonic heart starts beating at about the fourth week; formation of the other organ systems rapidly follows. By the fifth and sixth weeks, the eyes, facial features and limbs form. Between weeks eight and ten, virtually all of the organ systems are formed, and many are functioning. (See Figure 4.)

During these first few weeks of pregnancy, the embryo is particularly vulnerable to X rays, chemicals or other substances that can affect organ development. Most congenital birth defects develop during these first few weeks of embryonic life, as opposed to chromosomal or hereditary defects, which are determined at the moment of conception. Frequently, a woman may not even know she is pregnant and take a drug or other substance that can result in birth de-

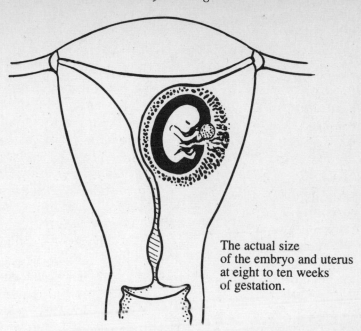

The actual size
of the embryo and uterus
at eight to ten weeks
of gestation.

fects. This is why it is so important for a woman to be attuned to her body, and, if there is any chance she may be
pregnant, to immediately start looking out for the best inter-
ests of her baby. Many substances that are relatively harmless later in pregnancy may have a profound effect on a
rapidly developing embryo.

After the tenth week of gestation, the fetus experiences
several marked growth spurts. (See Figures 5 and 6.) The
most pronounced of these occurs at about the twentieth
week. Almost overnight, the mother suddenly is very aware
that her baby is rapidly growing. The baby's movements become stronger and more frequent, and the woman finds she
can no longer fit into her regular wardrobe. During the
growth spurt that starts during the twentieth week, the fetus
is adding an inch a week to its height. If this rate of growth
were sustained throughout a forty-week pregnancy, the
baby would be more than four feet tall at birth!

It is virtually impossible to predict birth weight and size.
To a degree, a baby's size is determined by the size of the
mother and her uterus. Small women tend to have smaller

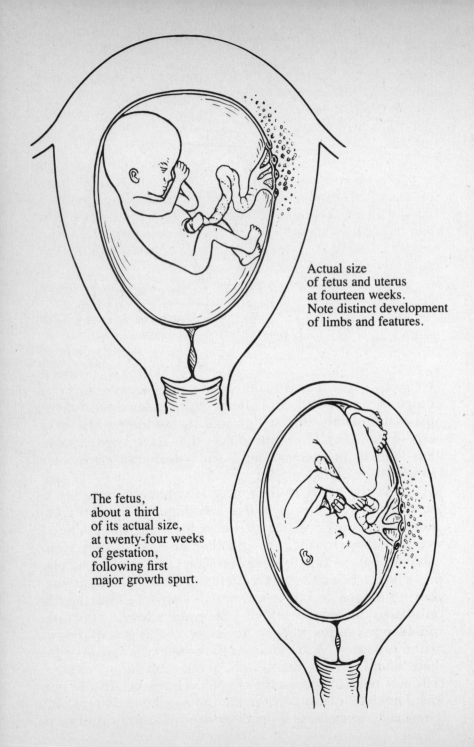

Actual size
of fetus and uterus
at fourteen weeks.
Note distinct development
of limbs and features.

The fetus,
about a third
of its actual size,
at twenty-four weeks
of gestation,
following first
major growth spurt.

babies, but there are numerous exceptions to this; it is not unheard of for a normally 100-pound woman who is barely five feet tall to have twins weighing six or seven pounds each. Similarly, a tall, large-boned woman may have a tiny full-term baby weighing less than five pounds.

Environmental factors also play a role in size. Babies born to women who live in the Andes Mountains of Peru, for example, are significantly smaller than those born in Lima, which is at sea level, where the air has more oxygen than in the high mountains. Heredity is also important; the mean birth weight of Cheyenne Indian babies is about eight pounds, five ounces, compared to a mean birth weight of five pounds, four ounces for babies born to the Luni tribe in New Guinea.

First babies tend to be a few ounces lighter than subsequent ones, and boys are usually heavier than girls. And, according to a study published by C. and M. Uusted in 1970 in *Lancet*, the presence of a male fetus in mixed twins appears to produce a larger baby girl than is seen in sets of girl twins. The age of the mother also may be a factor—teenagers and first-time mothers over the age of thirty-eight seem to have smaller than average babies.

Basically, there are two types of growth: an increase in the number of cells (hyperplasia) and an increase in cell size (hypertrophy). Growth during the early embryonic stage is mostly due to an increase in the number of cells, while later growth involves both an increase in the number of cells as well as cell size.

Tissue growth is further classified by the nature of cell populations. Some tissue is constantly renewing itself; examples include the skin, blood, intestinal lining and male germ cells. Such cells have a short lifespan. In contrast, static tissue, such as neurons and muscle cells, normally live as long as the organism. If these tissues are injured or destroyed, there is little or no regeneration, although the remaining cells may enlarge in an attempt to compensate for what was lost. The third category is referred to as "expanding tissue." These cells normally grow to their appropriate size and then stop, but regeneration is possible if the tissue is injured or destroyed. Examples include the endocrine glands, liver, kidney and lungs.

A number of hormones are instrumental in promoting growth. Before birth, the major growth hormones are insulin and human placental lactogen. Insulin is particularly important; babies born to women who have high blood-sugar levels start making large amounts of insulin on their own in response to the sugar which stimulates production of this hormone. These babies tend to grow very large—they usually weigh nine or more pounds at birth. (See Chapter 5 for a more detailed discussion.)

Following birth, human growth hormone (hGH), which is secreted by the pituitary, becomes the major hormone controlling growth. Its effect on growth is similar to that of insulin. A failure of the pituitary to produce adequate hGH results in dwarfism. Pituitary dwarfs have a normal body conformation, but are abnormally small.

The largest amounts of growth hormone are secreted during sleep. The fact that babies sleep so much promotes their rapid growth. (Adolescents, during their growth spurt, also sleep more than usual.) The ancient Chinese observed that children who did not sleep failed to grow; even today, mothers will tell their children that if they don't take their naps or go to bed early, they won't grow.

For proper growth to take place, the secretion of growth hormone must be balanced with calcium intake and metabolism. Calcium absorption is particularly high during the growing years, and it is vital that the diet contain adequate amounts of this essential mineral. Since milk, one of our best calcium sources, is the major food for infants, most babies get enough calcium to grow strong bones and teeth. But large amounts of calcium are needed throughout the growing years, so it is important that children continue to drink three or four glasses of milk a day and consume other foods that are high in calcium. Children who cannot tolerate milk may need supplements or a diet carefully balanced to provide adequate calcium.

Thyroid hormone also is essential for proper growth and development, especially following birth. Babies born to women with a thyroid deficiency are usually normal size, but are likely to be thyroid-deficient themselves. If this is not detected and treated in early infancy, the child will develop cretinism, a disorder marked by profound retardation and dwarfism, with a large head, thick limbs, pug nose, swollen eyelids, short neck and other deformities. Cretinism can be prevented by giving thyroxine to the mother, especially late in pregnancy when brain growth takes place, and then to the baby following birth. Development of thyroid deficiency later in childhood also results in arrested growth but not necessarily retardation; however, this can be reversed by giving thyroxine. In fact, correcting the thyroid deficiency results in a period of speeded, or "catch-up" growth.

The sex hormones estrogen and androgen also promote growth after birth. An excessive amount of these hormones in infancy and early childhood will result in a rapid growth spurt and may also initiate premature sexual development. Although children with high levels of these hormones will be larger than normal during their early years, if the sex hormones are not suppressed and sexual development takes place, growth will stop and the child will be abnormally short as an adult. (See Chapter 3.)

Some hormones stop growth. The most notable example is cortisol, which arrests skeletal growth by closing the bones' growth plates. Steroids also affect the growth of nonrenewing tissue, such as skeletal muscle. The effects tend to be permanent; unlike the catch-up growth spurt that follows correction of a thyroid deficiency, there is no comparable growth following removal of the excess cortisol. This explains why children who are given large amounts of steroids stop growing. Since steroids are commonly used to treat asthma, juvenile arthritis, or as part of the treatment for an organ transplant, the trade-offs in benefits versus the impact on growth must be carefully weighed.

In addition to hormones, there are a number of growth factors that influence specific organs or tissues. These growth factors are peptides—substances composed of amino acids—and are instrumental in both the growth of normal tissues and of tumors. Examples include nerve growth factor, which regulates development of the nervous system, or platelet-derived growth factor, which is important in healing cuts and other wounds, and which may play a role in the development of atherosclerosis—the buildup of fatty deposits in the coronary and other arteries. There also are a number of insulinlike growth factors, called somatomedins. The levels of somatomedins in the blood are hormonally controlled, and these growth factors are believed to control the action of the pituitary's growth hormone. Their precise role is not fully understood, but these growth factors are thought to be important in a number of diseases.

PATTERNS OF GROWTH

Everyone wonders whether a baby is going to be short or tall, fat or thin, fair or dark. Some of these characteristics can be surmised by looking at the parents, grandparents, siblings and other close relatives. If both parents and other family members are tall or short, it is likely that their off-spring will follow suit. But there are many exceptions, making it impossible to accurately predict future growth based on family history alone.

The pattern of growth is a more accurate predictor of adult size. There is little or no relationship between a baby's size at birth and adult size—many very small babies grow to be above-average-size adults and vice versa—but charting a child's growth pattern can give a fairly accurate picture of potential growth. Growth curves show normal patterns of both height and weight; for example, if a child is in the upper fifth percentile on the height curve at age two, it is a good indication that he or she will remain taller than average into adulthood, barring illness or other unforeseen circumstances.

Parents often become concerned that a child does not

seem to be growing. It is important to recognize that growth is not a steady process; there are periods of rapid growth followed by a few months or even years of slow growth. Any change in pattern or marked difference from the normal growth curves merits checking. For example, if a child has been progressing in keeping with the growth curve (see Figures 7 and 8), and then without apparent reason starts to deviate from the pattern, it may be a signal that something is wrong. The child may still fall within the normal range for the population as a whole, but may not be growing consistently with what is normal for him or her.

SHORT STATURE

About two million children in the United States are shorter than "normal," defined as two or more standard deviations below the mean for their age. Most of these children *are* normal; they are simply genetically programmed to be short. But in others, the short stature may have some other cause. And even in instances where we assume the shortness is genetic, poor nutrition or other factors may be the cause. For example, we once assumed that the short stature of the Japanese in relation to other Orientals was a genetic characteristic. But this has been disproved by the marked increase in stature among Japanese in the United States, and also among children born after World War II. It is now thought that the earlier short stature was caused by the lack of calcium in the Japanese diet or some other nutritional deficiency; when corrected, the Japanese grow to be as tall as other Orientals.

How can parents tell whether a child has a growth problem or is simply shorter than average? A look at the family history may provide important clues. Is short stature a common family characteristic? It may be useful to ask parents and grandparents about their children's rate of growth, and to review old baby books in which past generations recorded the height and weight at each birthday and various

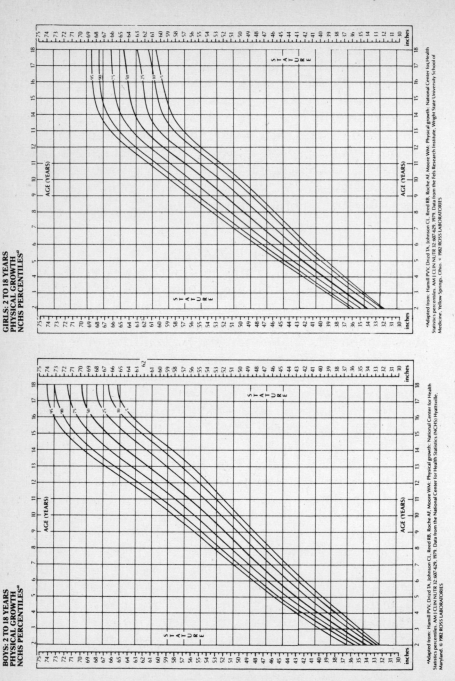

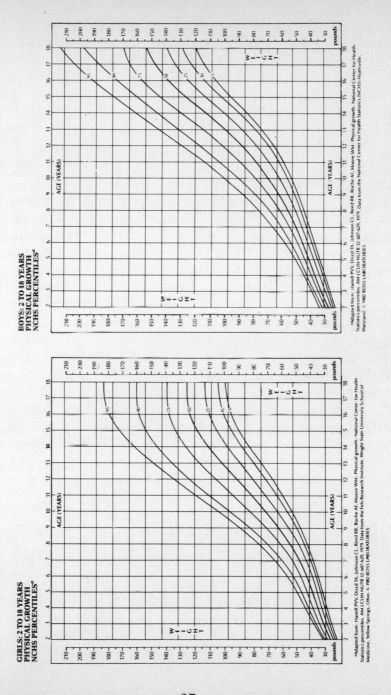

GIRLS: 2 TO 18 YEARS
PHYSICAL GROWTH
NCHS PERCENTILES[a]

[a]Adapted from : Hamill PVV, Drizd TA, Johnson CL, Reed RB, Roche AF, Moore WM: Physical growth: National Center for Health Statistics percentiles. AM J CLIN NUTR 32 607-629, 1979. Data from the Fels Research Institute, Wright State University School of Medicine, Yellow Springs, Ohio. © 1982 ROSS LABORATORIES

BOYS: 2 TO 18 YEARS
PHYSICAL GROWTH
NCHS PERCENTILES[a]

[a]Adapted from : Hamill PVV, Drizd TA, Johnson CL, Reed RB, Roche AF, Moore WM: Physical growth: National Center for Health Statistics percentiles. AM J CLIN NUTR 32 607-629, 1979. Data from the National Center for Health Statistics (NCHS) Hyattsville, Maryland. © 1982 ROSS LABORATORIES.

landmarks, such as the age at which a child started walking, talking and so on. These records may prove valuable in deciding whether a child is reflecting family history.

Another question to ask is, has there been a noticeable change in the growth pattern? If the child is progressing at a steady rate that matches a normal growth curve without any pronounced departures or signs of abnormalities, there probably is no cause for concern. But if there is an abrupt change in the curve that is not in keeping with the normal slope, further investigation may be in order.

As a rule of thumb, pediatricians begin to be concerned if a child falls two or more standard deviations below the norm for his or her age. Initially, the doctor will do a series of screening tests, which include gathering a detailed family history, conducting a physical examination, analyzing the growth pattern to date, performing blood and urine tests and taking X rays of the hand, wrist and skull to determine whether the bone age matches the actual age. If the child is a girl, a chromosome analysis also may be done to check for Turner's syndrome, a defect of the female sex chromosomes. Turner's girls are characteristically short, have short webbed necks and tend to be mentally retarded.

There are three general categories of failure to grow: environmental factors; hormonal abnormalities and other diseases; and inborn defects of the bones or other growing tissues. Within these categories, there are numerous specific causes for short stature, which are described below.

ENVIRONMENTAL FACTORS

Malnutrition

Worldwide, two-thirds of all children suffer from malnutrition, making this the leading environmental cause of failure to grow. A lack of sufficient calories and protein causes marasmus, a disease marked by the wasting and shrinking of internal organs. The nutritional deficiency is compounded by chronic diarrhea, caused by a flattening of the intestinal lining and a lack of digestive enzymes. In kwashiorkor, which is caused by severe lack of protein, the intake of calories may be high enough to maintain some body fat, but the protein deficiency causes a failure to grow normally. This disease is characterized by a large, distended abdomen.

Many people think of nutritional deficiencies as being a problem more in developing countries with large numbers of poverty-stricken people. While it is true that malnutrition is more common in Third World countries, it still occurs in the more developed world and should be considered as a possible cause of growth failure. Anorexia nervosa, a serious disease marked by voluntary starvation, is a relatively common cause of arrested growth among older children, especially adolescent girls.

Younger children sometimes stop eating out of fear of getting fat, but they do not engage in self-induced vomiting, laxative abuse, excessive exercise or other strategies anorexics use to limit weight gain. There also have been instances of growth failure caused by mothers' limiting their children's food to prevent their getting fat. Often, these mothers have a history of anorexia nervosa themselves, and their preoccupation with being thin and their distorted body image is concentrated on their children. Although these are relatively uncommon, they are among the factors a doctor should consider in trying to find the cause for possible nutritional deficiencies.

Other nutritional deficiencies that can cause a failure to grow include inadequate supplies of iron and zinc in the body. The deficiencies may stem from an inadequate diet, or from disorders that prevent their absorption.

Studies have found that babies who are denied human contact often fail to grow normally. Some of these children do not get enough to eat, but there are instances in which the babies have been adequately fed and still fail to thrive because of emotional neglect or abuse. This is sometimes referred to as psychosocial dwarfism. Typically, the children have a variety of emotional problems and sometimes bizarre eating habits.

HORMONAL ABNORMALITIES AND OTHER DISEASES

Pituitary Dwarfism

This term is used to describe a range of growth problems related to a lack of growth hormone. Causes include: genetic defects resulting in an abnormal pituitary gland; infections or injuries that damage the pituitary; or tumors of the hypothalamus or pituitary. Radiation treatments, such as those for a brain tumor, may damage the hypothalamus. Also, a rare inherited disorder (Laron dwarfism) makes some children resistant to growth hormone. This is seen mostly in people from the Middle East with a history of intermarriage.

After pituitary dysfunction has been diagnosed, many children can be effectively treated by administering growth hormone. In the past, this involved giving hormone extracted from human pituitary glands obtained during autopsies. Follow-up studies found that several youngsters treated with extracted growth hormone later died of cancerous tumors. It was as though large doses of growth hormone not only made the children grow, but also made certain cells in the body grow rampantly. Perhaps the use of synthetic human purified growth hormone in smaller, more natural doses may eliminate this problem.

Thyroid Deficiency

Arrested growth always accompanies a deficiency of thyroid hormone. Blood tests for thyroxine or thyroid-stimulating hormone can detect this deficiency in newborns, and always should be done. Failure to administer adequate thyroid hormone in the first few weeks of life can result in permanent retardation and other aspects of cretinism.

Older children also may develop thyroid deficiency,

often from Hashimoto's disease—an auto-immune disorder that damages the thyroid gland—or a failure of the thyroid to grow properly. Often these children do not have symptoms characteristic of an underactive thyroid, and the condition frequently goes undiagnosed for several years. After a proper diagnosis is made and the children are given adequate hormone replacement, they usually enjoy a catch-up growth spurt.

Excessive Steroids

As noted earlier, excessive cortisol causes arrested growth which is not reversed by removing the cause of the hormonal imbalance. Sometimes the excessive steroids are produced by cortisol-secreting tumors. More commonly, they result from excessive production of ACTH, which stimulates production of steroids, or from steroid drugs, which are used to treat a number of inflammatory disorders, asthma and other diseases. The growth problems can be minimized by giving the steroid drugs on an intermittent basis.

Malabsorption Syndromes

Although failure to grow accompanies malabsorption syndromes, it usually is not the major factor that prompts parents to see a doctor. Apathy, loss of appetite, recurrent diarrhea, unusual stools and other symptoms usually are more apparent than the failure to grow. There are instances, however, in which the other symptoms may be mild or absent, and arrested growth is the worrisome sign. Two of the most common malabsorption syndromes are lactose intolerance—caused by a lack of the enzyme lactase, which is needed to digest lactose, or milk sugar—and celiac disease, an intolerance to gluten, a protein in wheat and rye flours.

Lactose intolerance is characterized by diarrhea, cramps, abdominal gas and rumblings, and, in children, weight loss and failure to grow. Treatment consists of avoiding milk and products containing lactose, or milk sugar.

Lactose intolerance is most common among blacks and Orientals, and the disorder usually worsens with age. Babies who are lactose intolerant can be fed a soy formula or other milk-free foods.

In addition to failure to grow, symptoms of celiac disease include abdominal bloating, anemia and the passage of foul-smelling, fatty stools that float to the top of the toilet water. If left to progress, the disease causes a flattening of the fingerlike villi that line the intestinal walls and which are instrumental in absorption of nutrients from the digestive tract. Treatment consists of avoiding foods that contain gluten.

Crohn's Disease and Other Inflammatory Bowel Disorders

Children with inflammatory bowel disorders may experience several years of retarded growth before suffering symptoms of the intestinal disorder. Failure to eat an adequate diet is a major factor in the failure to grow. Others include: use of steroids and other drugs that interfere with growth to treat the disease; malabsorption; and anemia caused by intestinal bleeding.

Diabetes

Before the discovery of insulin, failure to grow was a common characteristic of children with diabetes who survived for any length of time. Even now, diabetic children often experience below-average growth. Much of this is attributed to poor control of the diabetes; children whose blood sugars are kept in the normal range, or who use an insulin pump that delivers a steady supply of insulin, often experience a catch-up growth spurt once the diabetes is brought into control.

Mental Retardation

Frequently, children who are mentally retarded or who have other disorders of the central nervous system are abnormally short. This may be caused by eating disorders accompanying the retardation, or, in some uncommon instances, a lack of growth hormone. Otherwise, the cause for failure to grow among retarded children is unknown.

Kidney Disease

Chronic kidney disease contributes to a number of factors that can affect growth, including reduced intake of protein and calories, depletion of calcium and potassium in body chemistry, hormonal imbalances and use of steroids in treatment.

Heart Disease

Many children born with congenital heart defects also have retarded growth. This may be caused by inadequate oxygen, but factors such as impaired blood flow also can contribute to the failure to grow.

Other Miscellaneous Disorders

A number of other illnesses, such as rickets, metabolic diseases and cancer, interfere with growth. In most of these diseases, other symptoms overshadow the retarded growth, although in some, a loss of weight or arrested growth may be the first obvious sign of a problem.

TALL STATURE

Being taller than average is just as common as short stature, but people usually are not as concerned by tallness as they are by being short. There are two reasons for this: Fewer disorders are associated with tall stature, and there is less social stigma attached to tallness. If the excessive growth is associated with premature sexual development or abnormalities in body proportions, the cause should be promptly diagnosed and treated to avoid future problems. Disorders associated with excessive tallness include:

Pituitary Gigantism

This is usually caused by a tumor that secretes growth hormone. It is a rare disorder characterized by a very rapid growth spurt and a change in features similar to those that occur in acromegaly—namely, an overgrown lower jaw, a thickening of the hands and feet and an overgrowth of soft tissue. If the tumor presses upon the pituitary, other hormonal disorders may appear. Treatment entails removing the tumor and, at the same time, trying to preserve normal pituitary function. This involves complex and delicate surgery, and parents should make sure the surgeon is experienced in this type of operation.

INBORN ERRORS

Beckwith-Wiedemann Syndrome

Babies with Beckwith-Wiedemann syndrome, another growth disorder that is present at birth, tend to be very large, with excessive body fat. They have very large tongues and often have an umbilical hernia. The excessive growth is attributed to overproduction of insulin. Typically, the babies are born with low blood sugar (hypoglycemia) and high insulin, although the excessive insulin secretion usually disappears during infancy. Nisidioblastoma is similar to Beckwith-Wiedemann syndrome, but the cause of its overproduction of insulin is a pancreatic tumor. The treatment is removal of the tumor.

Premature Puberty

Early onset of puberty is the most common cause of excessive growth in infants and young children. Typically, the unusual growth spurt is accompanied by signs of sexual maturity—the growth of pubic hair, development of breasts in girls and enlargement of the penis and testes in boys. Steps should be taken to halt premature puberty because, if it is allowed to progress to maturity, all further growth will stop. So, even though the child may be taller than his or her peers at onset of early puberty, this will be relatively short-lived and the youngster will end up with short adult stature. (See Chapter 3.)

SUMMING UP

The large majority of children follow an orderly pattern of growth from birth until puberty. A relatively small number —about four million in all—are evenly divided between those shorter or taller than average. Often, these youngsters are simply genetically programmed to be either short or tall, but there are instances in which a growth disorder is causing the abnormal stature. Environmental factors, such as malnutrition or neglect, may result in retarded growth; hormonal imbalance and a variety of diseases can also cause growth disorders.

Chapter 3

Adolescence and Sexual Development

ADOLESCENCE ENCOMPASSES THAT TURBULENT TIME BEtween childhood and adulthood when everything seems to be in a state of flux and conflict. It is often referred to as one of the most difficult times of life for parent and child alike—years that are emotionally charged as the youngster strives to obtain greater independence, come to terms with sexuality and resolve the many psychological conflicts that are an inevitable part of growing up.

During the adolescent years, a youngster goes through puberty—the life stage marked by a tremendous growth spurt and sexual development and maturity. This growth and development are hormonally controlled and are examples of the exquisitely fine-tuned interdependence of the various endocrine glands. Despite the psychological turbulence of adolescence, puberty itself normally follows in orderly progression over a period of five to eight years. In girls, the first noticeable sign is a "budding" of the breasts, and, at about the same time, an increase in the rate of growth. During childhood, most youngsters grow an average of two to three inches a year, but during the puberty growth spurt, height increases an average of twenty-five percent and weight almost doubles, all in the space of two or three years. Early infancy is the only comparable period of such rapid growth.

The ages at which these changes occur vary from girl to girl. Quite often, breast growth is apparent before any appreciable change in height, and may begin at any time between the ages of eight and thirteen or fourteen. Pubic hair usually begins to grow a year or so later, although in some girls, these two developments are noticed at about the same time. Armpit hair develops somewhat later; its growth usually peaks about a year after the beginning of breast development and continues at a slower rate until ovulation and menstruation are established.

Menarche, the onset of menstruation, is the hallmark of puberty, even though other signs have already appeared. In Western societies, the mean age of menarche is now about 12½ years, but any time between the ages of eight and sixteen is considered normal. The age of menarche has been decreasing by about eight months per generation in this century, but appears to be stabilizing. Numerous theories have been advanced to explain why girls develop earlier today than in the past, with most experts agreeing that improved nutrition is probably a key factor. Studies have found that menarche begins when a girl reaches about 105 pounds, or attains what researchers call a "critical body mass." Two British researchers, Drs. Tanner and Frisch, who have studied the sexual development of several hundred schoolgirls, found that 105 pounds was the key weight. Not everyone agrees with this critical body mass theory, nor is it known why a certain weight is important. Some experts think that the hormonal effects of an increase in body fat is important, but this has not been proved. It is known, however, that very thin girls who have very little body fat—for example, ballet students or long-distance runners—have a delayed menarche.

Contrary to popular belief, regular ovulation does not always coincide with menarche; in fact, it often takes one to two years for regular ovulation to become established. This explains why many adolescents have irregular, sometimes very heavy periods; their bodies are producing enough hormones to cause a proliferation and shedding of the uterine lining, but they are not yet producing enough FSH to always cause an egg to ripen and be released.

The onset and regularity of ovulation are quite unpredictable. Some adolescents who become sexually active at an early age may have unprotected intercourse for months or even years without becoming pregnant, and mistakenly assume that they have no need to worry. Others start to ovulate regularly with the onset of menarche, and may become pregnant at a very early age. Thus, any sexually active adolescent who does not want to become pregnant should practice contraception, because there is always a chance that she may be ovulating.

HORMONAL CONTROLS OF PUBERTY

The fetus has high levels of FSH, LH and LHRH (luteinizing-hormone-releasing hormone), especially during the first half of gestation. As the time of birth approaches, the fetus develops a negative sex steroid feedback system, and is insensitive to pituitary stimulation of sex hormone. During the first two years of life, this feedback system matures and becomes highly sensitive to sex steroids. As a result, the hypothalamus has a very low "set point" for sex hormones throughout childhood. For example, before menarche, the ovaries secrete small amounts of estrogen; small amounts of adrenal hormones also are converted to estrogen. The hypothalamus senses these tiny amounts of estrogen, and signals the ovaries to continue producing them so there is no rise in the other steroids, which would take place if the estrogen level was to fall. As puberty approaches, this hormone point gradually rises, and secretion of LHRH rises. This leads to increased production of the gonadotropins FSH and LH, and the gonads respond by producing more sex hormones—estrogen in girls and testosterone in boys.

As the feedback system changes, the level of gonadotropins rise gradually—a phenomenon that occurs at an earlier age in girls than in boys. Exactly what prompts the changes in the hypothalamus is unknown, although it appears that neural signals may play an important role. The hormonal changes also are closely related to the sleep-wake cycle; pulses of LH, and, to a lesser degree, FSH, are secreted during sleep, with smaller amounts released during the day.

It is not known precisely what triggers these hormonal changes; or why the hypothalamus develops a different set point that promotes the production of sex hormones. Parents usually notice that children approaching adolescence seem to sleep more than before. A child who was always up at dawn and protested going to bed or resisted naps may suddenly want to sleep half the day or take a nap when coming home from school. Interestingly, both the gonadotropins and the growth hormones are released in their largest amounts during sleep; parents who are often impatient with their sleepy adolescents—one mother refers to it as the "torpor stage"—are more understanding when they realize the sleep is needed for growth and development.

During this stage of development, the child's appetite seems to "perk up" and often becomes quite voracious. This may be more noticeable in boys than girls, but adolescents of both sexes usually consume much more food as they enter puberty than even a few months earlier. The extra food is needed to provide the tremendous amount of energy for the growth spurt, and, for girls, to achieve the weight and proportion of body fat needed to signal the onset of menarche. Researchers still do not understand all of the interrelated factors that are responsible for the changes which take place during puberty, but there is little doubt that the hypothalamus acts as the control center. The sleep-wake and appetite centers all are situated in the hypothalamus, which also constantly receives signals from other parts of the brain and the central nervous system. With the approach of puberty, the hypothalamus becomes more sensitive to rising levels of gonadotropin and steroid hormones, and a positive feedback system matures which prompts the ovaries and adrenal glands to start producing larger amounts of sex hormones (see Figure 9.). In this positive feedback system, a high level of estrogen stimulates a surge in LH secretion, which in turn promotes ovulation.

Throughout puberty, different hormones influence development of secondary sex characteristics. In girls, estrogens account for breast development, changes in sweat glands to produce body odor, changes in the vagina and its secretions and enlargement of the external genitals. Andro-

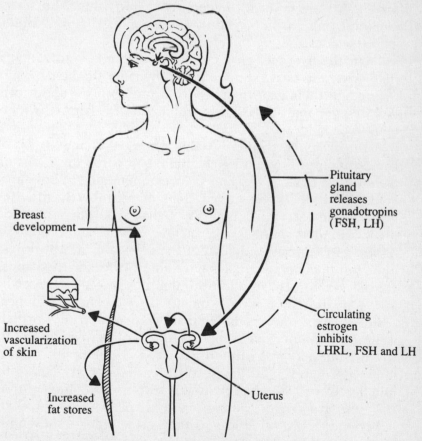

Breast development

Increased vascularization of skin

Increased fat stores

Pituitary gland releases gonadotropins (FSH, LH)

Circulating estrogen inhibits LHRL, FSH and LH

Uterus

How Hormones Initiate Puberty

With the onset of puberty, the pituitary hormones stimulate the ovaries to increase production of the female sex hormones, which in turn stimulate development of secondary sex characteristics.

gens, which are secreted in small amounts by the ovaries and adrenal glands, control the growth of pubic and axillary hair.

The hormones responsible for the tremendous adolescent growth spurt are in some ways independent of the gonadotropins; youngsters who fail to develop sexually may still experience a growth spurt and vice versa. But in other respects, the two are interdependent. For example, maximum growth in an adolescent girl takes place before menarche; growth slows with menarche, and when she starts ovulating and achieves adult levels of estrogen, further growth ceases.

On the average, girls enter puberty at a younger age than boys, and boys, who are generally taller than girls when they begin their growth spurt, continue to grow about two years longer than girls. This combination explains why men tend to be taller than women.

During puberty, there is also a marked change in body composition of boys and girls. Before puberty, the ratios of lean muscle mass, bones and fat are about equal in boys and girls. But with the hormonal changes of puberty, girls develop more fat and a typically female contour—broader hips, rounded buttocks, a slender waist and rounded breasts. In contrast, adolescent boys develop more muscle mass (on the average, males have about twice as many muscle cells as women; in addition, the muscle cells themselves are larger in men than in women) as well as heavier bones. Males also have less body fat than women. A trim, normal-weight woman may have about a fourth of her weight in fat, whereas fat may make up only twelve to fifteen percent of a man's normal weight. These differences in body composition account for the fact that men tend to have more physical strength than women and explain why women experience more bone loss as they grow older—they have less bone mass to start with. (See Chapter 6.)

PSYCHOLOGICAL CHANGES

The physical changes of puberty are accompanied by varied and often unexplained or disturbing emotional upheavals. Parents often are puzzled and upset by a child's temperament and unpredictable mood swings. A normally friendly, loving child may be affectionate and agreeable one moment and irritable, irrational and totally impossible the next—bursting with enthusiasm and energy, then suddenly, for no apparent reason, becoming grumpy, exhausted and withdrawn. Peers and peer influence become terribly important: Any parent who has experienced a child's adolescence (or remembers their own) knows all too well the exasperated refrain, "Everyone else does it," or, "All the other kids do it."

When a parent tries to find out what is behind the bad-tempered outburst or mood swings, the adolescent is at a loss to explain what is going on. "I don't know why I feel this way," is an honest evaluation, even though many parents find it a difficult one to accept: "You must know why you feel so angry—can't you tell me about it?" The honest answer is likely to be "no."

Mothers who experience symptoms associated with premenstrual syndrome, especially the psychological components, can perhaps best empathize with what an adolescent is experiencing. The surges in certain hormones can produce mood swings and emotional upheavals.

In addition, adolescence is a time of emerging independence, of testing one's wings, so to speak. At this stage of life, a young person is under tremendous pressure on all sides. There is parental pressure to do well in school and to succeed, often beyond the success of the parents themselves. "I am working so hard so you can go to a good college and make more of your life than I did" is an admonition that is passed from generation to generation. There is peer pressure to conform, to accept a dare, meet a challenge. Early adolescence is the time of life when youngsters start experimenting with alcohol, drugs, tobacco and other harmful substances.

Perhaps most of all, there are the internal pressures to come to terms with one's own self, including sexuality. Understandably, many parents are reluctant or embarrassed to discuss sex, especially sexual practices, with their children. Many fear that such discussions imply permission to become sexually active, but, regardless of whether parents talk about it or not, chances are that most adolescents do engage in sex while still in their teens. Surveys have found that up to eighty percent of boys and seventy percent of girls have had sex while in their teens. The dilemma is not so much whether a youngster will become sexually active, but instead, when this does occur, how to ensure that there are no unwanted consequences, such as pregnancy or a sexually transmitted disease. About sixty percent of sexually active teenage girls to do not practice contraception regularly, and forty percent get pregnant before their twentieth birthday.

Despite the increased openness about sex, most teenagers are sadly lacking in knowledge about even the most basic facts. For example, large numbers of adolescent girls become pregnant because they think conception occurs only during menstruation, or that they can't conceive the first time they have sex. Obviously, parents cannot make decisions regarding sexual matters for their children, but they can make sure that their youngsters have the support and information they need to make wise choices. There is nothing wrong with a parent letting a teenager know his or her views, even though the child may think they are hopelessly old-fashioned. Honesty and respect are important to children.

There is no one approach to dealing with the many emotional aspects of adolescence that works for all families. Obviously, parents want their children to achieve a healthy independence and to avoid the pitfalls of drugs, sexual promiscuity and other problems. It is important for parents to sort out what is important—for example, drug or alcohol use—and to resist the temptation to make an issue of annoying, yet relatively trivial, factors, such as haircuts or style of dress. No one ever died of a punk haircut, but each year, thousands of youngsters are killed because of drunk driving. Even though it is sometimes difficult for parents and adolescents to calmly discuss an issue, it is vital that lines of communication be kept open. Respect and love for one another go a long way toward overcoming the difficulties of the moment. On the brighter side, adolescence is a temporary state that certainly has both joys and difficulties and, no matter what, it eventually ends.

DELAYED PUBERTY

Delayed puberty, or failure to mature sexually, is a relatively rare occurrence. Although there is no specific age at which puberty begins, most experts agree that a girl of thirteen or a boy of fourteen who shows no sign of sexual development (breast budding in girls, testicular and penile growth in boys) should be evaluated by a doctor. It is estimated that only one out of every 160 otherwise normal youngsters of both sexes reach these ages without signs of puberty.

Some of these children turn out to be "late bloomers" who eventually enter puberty without any treatment. These youngsters have no obvious abnormalities, such as unde scended testicles, or illnesses that may explain the failure to develop. Clues that may indicate a simple delay in growth and puberty include short stature and a family history of late sexual development, such as a mother who did not start menstruating until her late teens, or a father who did not enter puberty until he was fourteen or older. Also, bone studies may often find that the youngster's bone age, or development, is lagging behind his or her chronological age; for example, the bone age may be what one would normally see in a child several years younger. When the bone age reaches twelve to fourteen years for a boy or eleven to thirteen for a girl, puberty usually begins. These youngsters often grow into shorter-than-average adults, but their sexual development is normal, despite the delay.

Sometimes hormone treatments with an artificial form of LHRH may be administered. This prompts the gradual rise in LH that is normally seen just before puberty, and, within a year, most youngsters will begin to show sexual development.

Not uncommonly, this type of delayed puberty causes self-consciousness and other psychological problems. Children worry that they are shorter than their peers and that their friends all are developing when they are not. Both boys and girls in this circumstance may resist participating in sports, and will try to avoid situations where their lack of sexual development is apparent. In such instances, the onset of puberty may be hastened by administering sex hormones —a three-month course of oral estrogen for girls or three months of periodic testosterone injections for boys. When done under proper medical supervision, hormonal treatment is safe and can prevent potentially serious emotional problems.

DISORDERS CAUSING DELAYED PUBERTY

There are a number of disorders that can upset hormonal function and lead to delayed puberty and failure to mature sexually. These include tumors, congenital defects, pituitary or thyroid disorders, malnutrition (including anorexia nervosa), serious diseases and a variety of rare syndromes. There also are instances in which a child appears to enter normal puberty, but then does not reach full sexual development. In general, a girl who does not menstruate within five years of entering puberty, or a boy whose secondary sexual characteristics are still immature 4.5 years following onset of puberty, should be seen by a doctor to determine if there is a problem. Following are brief descriptions of possible organic causes for delayed puberty.

TUMORS

Tumors involving the central nervous system are among the more common causes of delayed puberty. These usually are located in the part of the brain occupied by the pituitary gland and hypothalamus. Tumors in these areas may interfere with the secretion of the hormones essential to start puberty—LHRH from the hypothalamus and gonadotropins from the pituitary. These tumors also may interfere with the production of growth hormone. Typically, parents will note that a child has grown normally, but then seemed to stop. Other symptoms may include headaches, visual disturbances, and a weakness in the arms or legs. Diabetes insipidus, a disorder marked by thirst, dehydration and excessive production of urine, also may be caused by a pituitary tumor that interferes with the production of vasopressin, the antidiuretic hormone that helps maintain the body's fluid balance.

Some tumors disrupt hormonal balance by secreting hormones on their own. For example, there is a type of tumor that produces prolactin. These tumors rarely occur during childhood, but are sometimes seen in older teenagers. A girl may have experienced a normal puberty and started menstruating, only to have her periods stop for no apparent reason. Laboratory studies will show high levels of prolactin, the hormone that stimulates the breasts to make milk, and, in fact, both boys and girls may actually begin to produce milk.

If a tumor is suspected as the cause for the delayed or interrupted puberty, a CT (computerized tomography) brain scan usually will confirm the diagnosis. Treatment depends upon the type of tumor that is present. Some can be successfully treated by surgery; others may be treated with radiation therapy or a combination of radiation and surgery.

OTHER PITUITARY DISORDERS

There are a number of relatively rare disorders in which the pituitary fails to produce one or more of its hormones. In Kallmann syndrome, for example, the pituitary does not secrete the hormones that stimulate the production and release of gonadotropins. Boys with this disorder may have undescended testicles and lack normal male sex characteristics; girls do not develop breasts or other female characteristics. There also may be associated congenital defects, such as cleft lip, cleft palate, epilepsy and an impaired sense of smell.

In pituitary dwarfism, the gland does not secrete growth hormone, and the child is abnormally short. Sexual development may eventually take place if the pituitary produces the necessary gonadotropins. Some growth usually can be achieved by treatment with growth hormone, but this should be done before the bones close, preventing further growth.

DEVELOPMENTAL DEFECTS

Several forms of mental retardation and other developmental defects are associated with abnormal puberty. They include the Prader-Willi syndrome, which is characterized by massive obesity, short stature and other defects in addition to the retardation; and the Laurence-Moon-Biedl syndrome, also characterized by obesity, retardation and retinitis pigmentosa, an eye disorder.

A number of hormonal deficiencies can be caused by malformations of the head and midline portion of the brain, which affect the pituitary and hypothalamus. In addition to causing growth and developmental disorders, these malformations also may affect the optic nerve, resulting in visual problems or even blindness.

GONADAL DISORDERS

A variety of chromosomal and congenital disorders can result in delayed or abnormal puberty. Sometimes babies are born lacking the proper reproductive organs; for example, a girl may lack ovaries or a boy may not have testes. Or the external genitalia may not match the internal reproductive organs. In some rare instances, a child may have female genitalia but lack the proper female chromosomes.

Klinefelter's syndrome is the most common of the male gonadal abnormalities. Men with this disorder will have small, hard testes and impaired sperm production. They may have a eunuchoid appearance—small penis, developed breasts, little or no body hair—and suffer from mental retardation or serious psychological problems.

In girls, Turner's syndrome is the most common gonadal malformation. It is characterized by short stature, failure to mature sexually and, depending upon the chromosomal pattern, a variety of birth defects.

THYROID DISORDERS

An underactive thyroid (hypothyroidism), resulting in a deficiency of thyroid hormones, may cause delayed puberty or, in a woman who already has gone through menarche, a cessation of periods. The problem may be the thyroid gland itself or the pituitary, which secretes a thyroid-stimulating hormone that in turn prompts the thyroid to produce its hormones. Treatment with the appropriate thyroid hormones will usually solve the problem.

Conversely, severe hypothyroidism may cause premature puberty. In an effort to get the thyroid to produce its hormones, the pituitary will release large amounts of thyrotropin-releasing factor. The mechanism is not understood, but this appears to stimulate the secretion of gonadotropins and prolactin, leading to an early onset of puberty and production of breast milk. Treatment with thyroid hormone resolves these problems.

MALNUTRITION

Anorexia nervosa is one of the more common causes of delayed or interrupted puberty among girls in this country. It is a puzzling, often life-threatening disorder in which the person becomes so obsessed with body image and thinness that she resorts to self-starvation. Sometimes the problem is masked by preoccupation with physical activity, such as running or ballet dancing.

Although anorexia nervosa occurs in both sexes, it is by far the most common in adolescent girls or young adult women. Why the person suddenly embarks on self-starvation is unknown. Some experts have theorized that an abnormality of the hypothalamus, which houses the appetite center, may be a factor. But it is more likely a combination of factors. Most victims of anorexia nervosa are bright young women who are driven to succeed and to be in control. They usually are from middle- or upper-class families, with high standards and expectations. The eating problem usually begins with the onset of puberty; some researchers have suggested it may be related to a youngster's fear of menstruation and assuming adult responsibilities.

Frequently, the parents are not aware of the eating problem until it reaches an advanced stage. The youngster may appear to eat normally, but will secretly force herself to vomit or will use laxatives to rid herself of the food. Sometimes the problem becomes apparent if the girl has started to menstruate and then stops or menstruates only infrequently. This is due to the loss of weight, which signals the body to stop producing the hormones that stimulate the ovaries. In a sense, it is a protective mechanism; the body senses that it is being starved and it takes action to conserve as much energy as possible. All metabolism slows down, and lean body tissue is converted into energy. This can lead to serious muscle wasting, including loss of heart muscle.

Even though she may look emaciated, like a concentration camp victim, the girl will continue to maintain that she is too fat. If left untreated, a large percentage of these young women will eventually succumb to starvation. Hospitalization and forced feeding are temporary measures that can lower the death rate, but relapses are common. A combination of individual psychotherapy, family therapy and group treatment with other anorexics has been the most useful approach. Even so, eating problems often persist and require long-term treatment.

Of course, not all malnutrition is voluntary. There are many parts of the world in which poverty and famine are ever-present threats. Fortunately, this is rare in this country, but there are isolated examples of extreme parental neglect in which a youngster may fail to develop normally.

PRECOCIOUS PUBERTY

The premature development of adult sexual characteristics is just as disturbing as delayed puberty. About six in every thousand otherwise normal, healthy children will enter puberty prematurely—a phenomenon referred to as precocious puberty. This is defined as signs of puberty before the age of nine years in boys and eight years in girls. Newborn babies often have tiny breasts and enlarged genitalia due to the high levels of sex hormones in the mother during pregnancy and fetal development. But these soon disappear, and the baby's breasts and genitalia take on the appearance of those of a normal infant. A child's body retains this so-called sexual infantilism until puberty.

In some unusual instances, the child may have inherited a tendency for early maturation. This is referred to as constitutional precocious puberty, and usually occurs in children with a family history of early development. These children tend to fall at the youngest limits of the natural development curve, at eight or nine years of age in boys and at seven or eight in girls.

More commonly, early puberty is not constitutional, but

instead can be traced to any of a number of identifiable causes. The most common of these are tumors that affect the hypothalamus. In fact, the possibility of a brain tumor always should be investigated when premature puberty occurs, especially in a baby or very young child.

Sometimes the tumor interferes with the normal feedback system that keeps the hormones in balance. This may lead to a premature rise in the gonadotropins, and produce an early onset of puberty. Alternatively, the tumors may produce hormones themselves. Radiation therapy is useful in reducing these tumors; surgery often is difficult or impossible because of their location in the brain.

Other brain injuries or disorders also can lead to precocious puberty. These include encephalitis (an inflammation of the brain); a brain abscess; infections; head injuries; and brain cysts.

Other Miscellaneous Causes

Several disorders affecting the central nervous system have been associated with precocious puberty. Two of these, McCune-Albright syndrome and von Recklinghausen's disease, are characterized by brownish "café-au-lait" spots on the body. Children with von Recklinghausen's (also referred to as neurofibromatosis) also have overgrowth of the sheaths encasing the nerves and other fibrous tissue; seizures, visual defects and mental retardation are other common characteristics. In these children, puberty may be either premature or delayed.

The use of steroid drugs during infancy or early childhood sometimes leads to precocious puberty by stimulating an overgrowth of the adrenal glands and overproduction of adrenal hormones. There also have been reports of children who have inadvertently absorbed or consumed androgens or estrogens who went on to develop signs of puberty. For example, some cosmetics and creams contain estrogens. The amounts are insufficient to produce symptoms in an adult, but if a young child accidentally consumes these products, she may get enough estrogen to stimulate her own ovaries to increase their hormone production. Boys who receive hCG, a gonad-stimulation preparation, for undescended testes may start producing testosterone and, consequently, experience an early puberty.

Sometimes puberty is incomplete. A little girl, for example, may develop breasts and perhaps pubic hair, but the changes will either regress or stop without start of menstruation. This is most commonly caused by increased estrogen production, usually from a small cyst on the ovary. More rarely, the estrogen may be from some other hormone-producing tumor.

A condition called premature thelarche is occasionally seen in girls up to the ages of three or four years. It is characterized by breast enlargement that persists for several months and then regresses. This may be caused by ovarian cysts or an unexplained rise in follicle-stimulating hormone.

In rare instances, a child may develop a hormone-producing tumor that produces characteristics of the opposite sex, namely, feminization in a boy or virilization in a girl. These are very unusual, and generally signal a very serious disorder.

Not uncommonly, however, boys approaching puberty will experience breast development. This is caused by an excessive amount of estrogen, and usually resolves itself as puberty progresses. However, a boy may be very self-conscious about breast development and become the brunt of considerable teasing from his peers. Surgery to reduce the breast mass may be considered in these circumstances.

Treatment of Precocious Puberty

Treatment of precocious puberty depends upon the cause. Understandably, parent and child alike can become very concerned about the various consequences of premature puberty. The idea of a little girl having periods while still in nursery school or a young boy growing a beard or showing other signs of premature puberty is disturbing. And while children who experience premature puberty tend to be taller than their peers, they are likely to end up as abnormally short adults because once their puberty is complete, they will stop growing.

The condition can cause serious psychological problems for the child, for while the youngster may have adult sexual characteristics, his or her social and intellectual development will not be similarly accelerated.

Usually, drugs can be prescribed to reduce the levels of hormones that are producing the sexual development. In the United States, the most commonly used agent is a progesterone compound, which reduces testicular growth and other symptoms in boys, and suppresses menstruation and breast development in girls.

SUMMING UP

Puberty is a difficult time for both children and their parents, and it is all the more difficult when it is delayed or premature. Fortunately, the large majority of youngsters experience a normal physical transition from childhood to adulthood. The emotional problems of puberty often are much more difficult to deal with than the physical changes. An open mind, mutual respect, understanding and a sense of humor get most families through adolescence with minimal scars.

Chapter 4

The Menstrual Cycle

THROUGH THE AGES, MENSTRUATION HAS BEEN VIEWED with a mixture of awe and distaste—an attitude that continues to plague women throughout the world. Although we consider ourselves enlightened and knowledgeable about bodily functions, it is surprising how many age-old misconceptions about menstruation are still with us.

In primitive societies, magical properties were often ascribed to menstruation. These early humans recognized that blood was vital to life, and for a woman to bleed without any lasting effect was, to them, awesome. In many cultures, menstrual blood and, by extension, menstruating women were considered unclean. During menstruation, women often were isolated from other members of society—banished to huts apart from the rest of the village where they could not contaminate others or exercise their magic. Little wonder that such beliefs gave rise to an assortment of superstitions and taboos concerning menstruation. In these early societies, people truly believed that a menstruating woman could ruin crops, make milk cows go dry, sour milk or wine, cause floods and other natural disasters and summon demons to possess a person's mind.

An elaborate set of religious taboos and customs, still

practiced by some faiths, evolved governing sexual relations, menstruation and childbirth. Those of greatest interest to Western society are outlined in the Bible. Under the laws of Moses, a menstruating woman was unclean, as was everything she touched. Sex was strictly forbidden during, and for a week after, menstruation. Indeed, no man was to come in contact with a menstruating woman or anything that she had touched, even the chair she sat upon. Thus, the sexes were kept separated in public places, lest a man unwittingly come in contact with an "unclean" woman.

Of course, in this enlightened age, such restrictions strike us as unreasonable and even highly discriminatory. Still, if one carefully analyzes these ancient laws in light of current knowledge of conception, it becomes clear that the taboos on menstruation go beyond fear of contamination. In biblical times, a woman's primary function was to produce as many children—preferably males—as possible. Biblical law decreed that a menstruating woman be separated from her husband and society for seven days, or for the entire time of her bleeding: "But if she be cleansed of her issue, then she shall number to herself seven days, and after that she shall be clean."(Lev. 15:28.)

On the eighth day, she was to go to the tabernacle with offerings, and then she could return to her husband. In other words, on the eighth day after the cessation of menstruation, she could resume sexual relations. Somehow, the ancients had timed this to coincide with the beginning of a woman's most fertile period, just before ovulation. Since the couple had abstained for two weeks, the chances that intercourse would take place during the fertile period were high. In addition, since the man had abstained for two weeks, his sperm would be mature and more likely to produce a pregnancy than if he had been having frequent intercourse and was releasing immature sperm.

The ancients also may unwittingly have maximized the chances of conceiving a boy. Folklore holds that conception early in the fertile period is more likely to produce a boy than later, and there may be some foundation for this. The male determines the sex of a baby, since his sperm carry both male sex characteristics (Y sperm) and female characteristics (X sperm). (Women's eggs carry only female characteristics, in an XX configuration.) Y sperm are somewhat smaller and lighter than the X ones, because they have less chromosomal material. They are thought to be able to swim faster than the X sperm and are more likely to reach the egg first. This has not been proved scientifically, but even the ancient Chinese observed that the best way to produce a male child was to abstain for a period of time and then try for pregnancy at a woman's midcycle.

Although we have learned much about menstruation since the days of Moses, it is astounding how many myths still persist. For example, menstruation is still popularly referred to as "being sick." This is understandable because bleeding is associated with illness or injury. The traditional view that menstrual blood is unclean is reflected in our use of the term "sanitary" for napkins and other menstrual products. In reality, menstrual blood is sterile. It is also odorless until it is exposed to air. Thus the myth that menstruating women are in any way "unclean" is contrary to both fact and common sense.

However, many, if not most, people still think that women are somehow "sick," or at least more delicate and vulnerable, during menstruation, and that menstruating women should refrain from vigorous exercise and heavy work. "Old wives" still advise against having a hair permanent during menstruation because "hair doesn't curl then."

Attitudes toward menstruation are clearly exemplified in the euphemisms applied to it: "the curse," "that time of the month," "getting sick," "falling off the roof," among many others. It's little wonder that, even in this enlightened era, so many women are embarrassed or reluctant to talk about what is, in reality, one of our most natural functions.

Although all healthy women menstruate during their reproductive years, our perceptions of and experiences with menstruation vary widely. Some women do feel unwell during menstruation, suffering from cramps, headaches and other symptoms. Others experience no untoward physical effects, but find they may be irritable, nervous and emotionally out-of-kilter at specific times during their menstrual cycles. For some, such effects may be sporadic, with some months passing without even a twinge of discomfort, while others are truly miserable. Still other women experience neither physical nor psychological effects and are puzzled or unbelieving when they encounter women who do.

Regularity is another major area of difference: Some women menstruate every twenty-seven to thirty days; others are very erratic, with two or three periods close together and then a couple of months until the next one. Some women menstruate for two or three days, others for five or six. The flow may range from scanty to heavy. In short, although menstruation is a natural phenomenon shared by all women, it is also a highly individualistic function that is different for each of us. Since so many women are reluctant to talk about menstruation, even to their doctors, they often worry needlessly that they are different or abnormal because their menstrual patterns do not conform to what they mistakenly believe is the norm.

HORMONAL CONTROLS

In the simplest terms, menstruation is the periodic shedding of a portion of tissue that lines the uterus. During the early part of each menstrual cycle, this lining—the endometrium—grows, becoming thicker and enriched with blood vessels in preparation to receive a fertilized egg and establish a pregnancy. If conception does not occur, the lining stops growing and the superficial two-thirds of the endometrium breaks down and is shed through the vagina. About half to three-fourths of the menstrual fluid is actually blood; the rest is made up of shed cells, mucus and bits of endometrial membrane. There is more calcium in menstrual fluid than regular blood.

The uterus produces an enzyme that destroys some of the clotting factors normally found in blood, explaining why menstrual blood does not clot. (What seem to be clots are more likely to be clumps of cells and other material shed from the uterus lining. If the flow is very heavy, some clots may form in the vagina after the blood has left the uterus.) During an average period, only four to six tablespoons of blood are shed (the amount varies from woman to woman), but the volume seems greater because it contains other fluids and material, so women think they are losing considerably more.

A woman's menstrual cycle is one of the best examples of the complex interrelationship of various hormones. Many people assume that only the sex hormones are involved in regulating the menstrual cycle; in reality, however, the entire endocrine system, and often other organ systems as well, must be functioning properly to ensure normal cycles. For example, thyroid disorders often cause menstrual irregularity or a complete cessation of periods. Stress, extremes in weight, certain drugs, infection and other illnesses are but a few of the many factors that can upset a woman's reproductive cycle. This extreme sensitivity of the reproductive cycle is a protective measure intended to produce a healthy baby, something that may be impossible if other body systems are malfunctioning.

Both positive and negative feedback systems come into play in regulating the menstrual cycle. These are illustrated in Figure 10 and work something like this for a twenty-eight-day cycle:

Days 1–5: The Menstrual Phase

During this phase, while menstruation is taking place, estrogen and progesterone are at low levels, which signals the hypothalamus and pituitary to begin secreting their stimulating hormones, LH and FSH. These two hormones prompt the ovaries to begin a new reproductive cycle; as its name implies, follicle-stimulating hormone (FSH), stimulates the development of a follicle within the ovary, setting in motion the maturation of an egg to be released upon ovulation. LH stimulates the ovaries to produce estrogen.

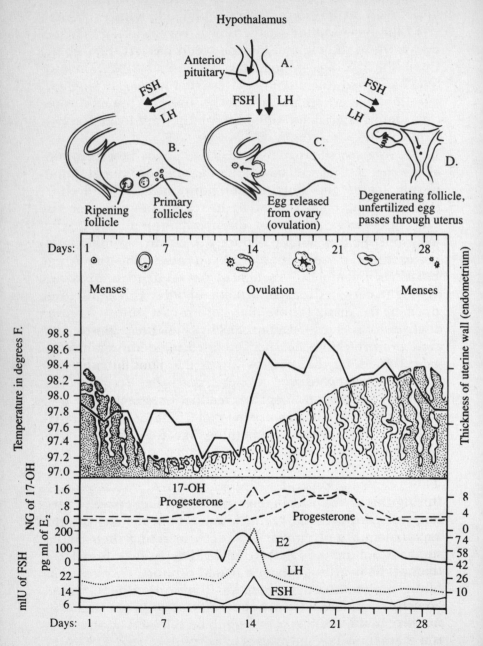

The Menstrual Cycle

Days 6–12: The Proliferative/Follicular Phase

LH levels continue to rise, as do those of estrogen. The rising estrogen produces a negative feedback effect on the pituitary, signaling it to cut back on the production of FSH. The rising estrogen also prompts the pituitary to secrete LH.

Day 12–13: The Proliferative Phase

Estrogen production surges, causing a corresponding increase in LH. Estrogen then falls, and there is a corresponding rise in FSH.

Day 14: Ovulation

Within thirty-six hours of the LH surge, the follicle releases its mature egg and ovulation takes place. The egg is embraced by the fingerlike fimbriae of the fallopian tubes, and begins making its way toward the uterus. This is the time during the cycle that fertilization can take place if a sperm unites with the egg. Following ovulation, the ruptured follicle that has produced the matured egg undergoes a process called luteinization and becomes the corpus luteum—the structure that produces progesterone, the hormone that prepares the uterus lining to establish a pregnancy.

Days 15–27: The Luteal Phase

During this second half of the cycle, progesterone continues to rise and FSH drops to its lowest level during the cycle. There is also a sharp drop in LH following ovulation, and this hormone also falls to its lowest level. The rising progesterone, which peaks at about the twenty-second day if fertilization does not take place, produces marked changes in the superficial layer of the endometrium, which doubles in thickness during this phase. The glands of the endometrium fill up with fats and glycogen to provide vital nutrition for an embryo should fertilization take place. If pregnancy does not take place, the corpus luteum begins to shrink and there is a marked fall-off in progesterone production. The endometrium begins to break down and loosen. On about the twenty-seventh day of the cycle, estrogen, progesterone, FSH and LH all are at their lowest levels.

Day 28
Menstruation begins, starting the cycle anew.

What we have just described, in simplified terms, is the hypothetical ideal. No woman has a precise twenty-eight-day cycle month after month. The mean menstrual cycle is twenty-five to thirty days, but some women have twenty-day cycles and others, forty days. All are within the normal range. But no matter what the length of the cycle, ovulation takes place about fourteen days before menstruation; thus, a woman with a twenty-day cycle will ovulate on about the seventh day, while one with a forty-day cycle will ovulate on about day twenty-six. Many women make the mistake of assuming that ovulation takes place midway between periods, but this is not the case. The proliferative phase may vary in length, but the luteal phase is consistent at about fourteen days.

Some women who have regular cycles of about twenty-eight days mistakenly think they are irregular because they forget that their menstrual cycles are following a lunar calendar, and not our normal twelve-month calendar. For example, a woman may have her period during the first week of January, and expect to have the next in the first week of February. If her cycles are twenty-eight days, her period is likely to start at the end of January rather than the first week in February, and during the course of the year, she will have thirteen periods instead of twelve. If a woman does not know the average length of her cycles, she should keep track on a calendar.

PROBLEMS RELATED TO MENSTRUATION

Premenstrual Syndrome

The hormonal changes during the menstrual cycle prompt a number of often subtle physical changes affecting almost every organ system in the body, but how these hormonal shifts affect the way a woman feels and behaves remains a subject of controversy and debate. At one time, it was commonly believed that women experienced periods of temporary insanity associated with their menstrual cycle.

Since estrogen increases salt and water retention, many women experience bloating, particularly of the abdomen, ankles, feet and fingers. Some women find their rings are suddenly too small; others report their feet seem to change size (if they buy shoes during their premenstrual phase, they may be too loose later; conversely, shoes purchased in the first half of the cycle may suddenly seem too tight). Aching joints, muscle stiffness and feelings of heaviness all are common. Acne, especially during the high-estrogen portion of the cycle, also is common.

Breasts swell during the high-estrogen phase of the cycle; many women find they need two sizes of bras— a smaller size for the first part of their menstrual cycle and a larger one for the latter half. Women with benign cystic disease may be particularly aware of this phenomenon because the cysts accumulate fluid and swell—a process that can be quite painful. As the endometrium thickens, there may be cramping, especially on the first couple of days of menstruation. This is related to increased progesterone; the higher the levels of this hormone, the thicker the endometrium and the more likely that there will be cramping.

The gastrointestinal system also may be affected. High levels of steroid hormones may result in intestinal cramping and diarrhea; conversely, some women experience constipation in the premenstrual phase, or constipation alternating with diarrhea. The tiny muscles that control the circumference of blood vessels also are sensitive to high levels of steroids. Many women are susceptible to migraine or vascular headaches in the premenstrual phase; these are caused by an expansion of the arteries in the head, followed by a contraction of the vessels. Some women complain that their varicose veins swell and ache just before menstration; some also notice episodes of rapid heartbeats.

Many women experience mood swings—one minute they may feel cheerful and optimistic and then, suddenly, for no apparent reason, they are irritable and depressed. Feelings of restlessness, difficulty in sleeping and fatigue all are common. Women who keep careful diaries of premenstrual symptoms often find they are more likely to have disputes with spouses or children during the latter part of their menstrual cycles. Studies have found that premenstrual women are more likely to have accidents.

Food cravings, especially for sweets or salty foods, may occur. Some women feel ravenously hungry, others may lose their appetite. Increased thirst is common. Many women find their tolerance for the effects of alcohol is lowered when they are premenstrual. All of these changes (see Table 1) are normal and experienced in varying degrees by most women. For some, symptoms are so subtle they are barely noticed. Most women are aware that they are undergoing physical changes, but the symptoms are manageable. But some women undergo extreme, almost incapacitating changes—a phenomenon commonly referred to as premenstrual tension or syndrome, or PMS for short. Until recently, PMS symptoms were regarded as psychological. In the early 1950s, Dr. Katharina Dalton, a British gynecologist, published results of her studies on the menstrual cycle, detailing symptoms associated with the premenstrual phase. Although premenstrual tension or syndrome had been described some twenty years earlier by an American physician, it was Dr. Dalton who brought PMS to widespread public attention.

Table 1. COMMON SYMPTOMS OF PREMENSTRUAL SYNDROME

General

Altered sex drive
Bloating or swelling, especially of the abdomen, feet and ankles
Breast swelling and pain
Dizziness
Fatigue
Increased hunger or food cravings, especially for salt or sweets
Insomnia
Headaches, often vascular or migraine
Muscular or joint pain
Tendency to hypoglycemia (low blood sugar)
Palpitations
Restlessness
Ringing in the ears
Swollen or aching varicose veins
Thirst
Urinary frequency
Weight gain

Gastrointestinal

Bowel cramping
Constipation
Diarrhea
Nausea
Vomiting

Psychological

Anxiety
Crying spells
Depression
Irritability
Mood swings

Undoubtedly, women have been aware of PMS through the ages, but perhaps never associated the symptoms with their menstrual cycles. In more recent years, a growing number of doctors have become more sympathetic to women with PMS. Although there is still no specific treatment for PMS, a number of PMS clinics have opened and strategies have been developed for relieving specific symptoms. For example, women who experience excessive bloating may be advised to limit salt intake, eat high-potassium foods and drink plenty of fluids—all strategies that help minimize excessive salt and water retention. In extreme cases, a mild diuretic, or water pill, may be prescribed. However, women should be cautioned against treating themselves with water pills since their overuse can upset the body's fluid and chemical balance and lead to serious metabolic problems.

Most women find that a common-sense approach goes a long way toward easing premenstrual discomfort. If breasts are swollen and tender, avoid breast stimulation and wear a larger-size bra that gives adequate support. If waistbands are too tight and uncomfortable, have a few outfits that are a size larger, or wear looser, more comfortable styles. If alcohol tolerance is lowered, avoid alcoholic beverages at this time. Try to schedule important business meetings or extra work at other times. Make sure you get enough rest and consume a healthful, balanced diet.

Mood swings, sudden feelings of depression or irritability may be harder to deal with. Recognizing that these feelings are part of your normal cycle helps; learning how to anticipate and avoid potentially upsetting situations is another coping technique. Still other strategies include deep-breathing exercises, an aerobic workout, meditation or other activities that help counter stress. Avoid excessive caffeine consumption, which can add to feelings of nervousness or jumpiness.

Some of the physical symptoms, such as vascular headaches, often are preventable. In recent years, it has been established that beta-adrenergic blocking drugs—medications that are often prescribed to treat angina, high blood pressure and other cardiovascular problems—also can prevent migraine headaches. A low dose of a beta blocker such as propranolol (sold under the brand name Inderal), may be prescribed during the premenstrual phase.

Hormonal treatments for PMS remain controversial. Dr. Dalton postulated that PMS is caused by a progesterone deficiency and has long advocated the use of this hormone to treat severe PMS symptoms. Some women seem to achieve relief with progesterone, but many do not. Also, many women with severe PMS have normal progesterone levels, which tends to discount hormone deficiency as a cause.

Researchers also have studied the use of drugs to suppress prolactin in treating PMS. Studies have found that some women have high prolactin levels during the latter part of their menstrual cycles; however, this is not a universal finding and a large percentage of women given bromocryptine (Parlodel) to suppress prolactin either experienced excessive side effects or obtained no relief. Some doctors still recommend it for women with severe fibrocystic disease who suffer breast swelling and pain, since it specifically eases these symptoms.

A number of dietary approaches have been tried, with varying results. Supplements of vitamins B_6, A and E all have been studied. Large doses of vitamin E appear to relieve fibrocystic breast symptoms for some women, but a woman should check with her doctor before taking any vitamin or mineral in excess of the Recommended Dietary Allowances (RDAs). There is no convincing evidence that vitamins B_6 or A are particularly beneficial. In addition, large doses of vitamin A, a fat-soluble vitamin that is stored in the body, should not be taken because they can lead to potentially life-threatening vitamin A toxicity.

Some researchers have attributed certain PMS symptoms to metabolic factors. This theory is based on observations in the 1940s and 1950s that carbohydrate metabolism is altered before and during menstruation, with an increased tendency toward hypoglycemia. Later studies have found an increase in insulin receptors during the latter half of the menstrual cycle, which may account for the lowered blood sugar. Based on these observations, some PMS symptoms have been attributed to hypoglycemia, in particular, fatigue, nervousness, sweating, lightheadedness and increased hunger, particularly for sweets. Some doctors recommend a diet high in complex carbohydrates in the premenstrual phase on the theory that this will help counter the possible hypoglycemia. There is little or no evidence, however, that this helps. If the symptoms were truly caused by low blood sugar, they would be relieved by eating. This is not the case. Still, a balanced, nutritious diet that is high in complex carbohydrates, moderate in protein and low in fats, salt and simple sugars is in the interest of all-around good health.

As might be expected, the debate over possible psychological causes of PMS continues to rage in both medical circles and among women themselves. "It's all in your head" is an oft-repeated refrain that is sure to raise the ire of any woman who feels miserable and knows that her symptoms are not imaginary. Many people overlook the fact that psychogenic pain is just as real as organic pain—it simply has a different source. In addition, little is known about the role of the brain in numerous bodily functions. The brain plays a vital role in hormonal feedback systems, and it is difficult to isolate all of the factors that influence hormonal production.

The noted endocrinologist and writer, Dr. Estelle Ramey, points out that through the ages, women have been conditioned to believe that menstruation sets them apart from men, that they are supposed to feel miserable. It is therefore sometimes difficult to sort out whether certain symptoms are exaggerated by our expectations; if we are firmly convinced that we are going to feel good or bad, chances are increased that our expectations will be fulfilled. But this is far different from implying that the symptoms of PMS are imaginary or nonexistent. We know that as different hormone levels rise or fall, a number of specific changes take place. Whether these changes are subtle and barely noticed or extreme and even incapacitating depends upon many factors, some of which may be psychological as well as organic.

Menstrual Cramps

Menstrual cramps, or dysmenorrhea, is another common problem associated with menstruation, but, happily, recent advances in its treatment now provide relief for millions of women.

There are two types of menstrual pain. In about five to ten percent of women, an organic cause can be diagnosed, such as endometriosis, fibroids or other tumors, or an abnormal narrowing of the cervix. In such instances, the painful menstruation is referred to as secondary dysmenorrhea, and usually, treating the underlying cause will resolve the problem. For the vast majority of women, however, no organic cause can be found; this is referred to as primary dysmenorrhea.

For centuries, women who suffer from menstrual cramps have resorted to a variety of treatments—heating pads, painkillers, bed rest, exercise, a variety of herbal potions and other folk remedies—most of them largely ineffective. In addition, many doctors have maintained that the pain is largely psychological and Valium and other tranquilizers have been a favored treatment.

Since women have so long been told that their menstrual cramps are due to emotional problems, many have accepted this and suffered in silence rather than face the scorn or skepticism of employers, colleagues, even spouses. Fortunately, this has become unnecessary with the discovery that a class of drugs—the nonsteroidal anti-inflammatory drugs (NSAIDs), used to treat arthritis—are effective in preventing or relieving menstrual cramps for up to ninety percent of women who suffer from dysmenorrhea.

These drugs block the production or action of prostaglandins, hormonelike substances that are produced in many body tissues and which seem to have numerous functions. Researchers have found that menstrual blood contains high levels of prostaglandin; it is also known that prostaglandins are instrumental in producing uterine contractions.

Exactly what role they play in causing menstrual cramps is unknown, however. Some researchers theorize that a high level of prostaglandin causes excessive contractions of uterine muscles. These contractions may clamp the blood vessels that bring oxygen to the muscle, resulting in pain due to lack of oxygen. This may explain why many women cease to experience dysmenorrhea following childbirth. During pregnancy, the number of blood vessels supplying the uterus increases and some of this expanded vascularization remains after childbirth. Thus, even though the uterine muscle still may contract during menstruation, there is enough circulation to keep it from being starved for oxygen, thereby preventing ischemic pain. Still, this does not explain why some women who never had cramps before childbirth experience them after it, or why pregnancy seems to have little effect one way or the other.

While researchers continue to seek an explanation for dysmenorrhea, most women who suffer from it can obtain welcome relief from taking NSAIDs. Aspirin is a mild NSAID, and for many women, it is sufficient. If not, a stronger drug may be recommended. These include ibuprofen, which comes in a mild nonprescription dosage marketed under the brand names of Advil or Nuprin, or in a stronger prescription dosage marketed as Motrin or Rufen. Other NSAIDs include diflunisal (Dolobid), fenoprofen (Nalfon), idomethacin (Indocin), meclofenamate sodium (Meclomen), mefenamic acid (Ponstel), naproxen (Anaprox), sulindac (Clinoril) and tolmetin sodium (Tolectin). The drugs recommended most often for dysmenorrhea are ibuprofen, fenoprofen, mefenamic acid or naproxen. Although the NSAIDs are similar to each other, they are not identical. Often, a woman may find she gets no relief with one drug, but does when switched to another. Therefore, she should not give up and assume that NSAIDs will not help her unless she has given two or three a trial.

As with all drugs, NSAIDs have potential side effects, and should not be used by some people, especially those who are hypersensitive to aspirin or other drugs in this category. In general, NSAIDs have less potential of causing gastrointestinal bleeding and irritation than large amounts of aspirin, but they, too, may have these effects. Other potential side effects include nausea, heartburn, stomach ulcers, bloody or tarry stools (indicating intestinal bleeding), rash, kidney irritation, sedation, ringing in the ears and mood changes. These side effects are relatively rare, especially when taken in the low dosages recommended for dysmenorrhea. But if they occur, you should stop taking the drug and contact your doctor.

The most effective approach in using NSAIDs to treat dysmenorrhea is a preventive one. This means the drug should be taken at the first sign of a period instead of waiting until the cramps strike full-force. Some doctors recommend that the drug be taken a day or two before menstruation. On the average, only three to six pills are required per cycle—a dosage low enough to prevent the side effects that are more common in arthritis patients who may take NSAIDs several times a day over prolonged periods.

Dysmenorrhea usually occurs only among women who are ovulating. This explains why some young women experience no dysmenorrhea when they first start having periods, but begin to suffer severe cramps several months, or even a couple of years, later. (It often takes up to two years for ovulation to become established.)

Also, women who take birth control pills usually find they no longer have menstrual cramps, even though they may periodically bleed. This is because the pill works by suppressing ovulation; women may continue to bleed periodically, but this is not true menstruation. In fact, until the discovery that NSAIDs relieved dysmenorrhea, oral contraceptives often were prescribed as a treatment for cramps. For women who elect this means of birth control, it remains a happy solution to painful menstruation.

Dysfunctional Bleeding

Technically, any vaginal bleeding that occurs in the absence of ovulation is termed dysfunctional uterine bleeding. The bleeding may coincide with and be very similar to normal menstrual periods. More often, however, the bleeding is irregular and may be heavier than in normal menstruation. Causes include tumors, both benign fibroids or cancer, and hormonal imbalances in which ovulation does not take place —an occurrence referred to as anovulatory cycles.

Anovulatory cycles occur most often in young women who are just beginning menstruation and in older women who are approaching menopause. This is what happens: Estrogen stimulates the endometrium to grow in the typical proliferative phase of the menstrual cycle. But, if ovulation does not occur, no corpus luteum forms and, without its progesterone, the endometrium never enters its second secretory stage. Instead, it continues to grow, and when estrogen levels fall, the endometrium is shed. Such periods tend to be irregular, often with only a few days between them, and heavier than normal. Many young girls thus may menstruate every two or three weeks and experience very heavy bleeding; the same is true of older women who are entering menopause. These episodes of frequent, heavy bleeding are referred to as menometrorrhagia. Since excessive blood may be lost, it is important to get extra iron to prevent anemia. The diet should include iron-rich foods (see Table 2); if this is not enough to maintain adequate iron stores, a supplement may be recommended.

Table 2. HOW MUCH IRON YOU NEED

Group	Mg. Iron Per Day
Infants	10
Preschool children	18
Adolescents	18
Adult Men	10
Adult Women	18
Pregnant Women	18 +

SOURCES OF IRON

Food	Serving Size	Iron (mg.)
Apricots (dried)	8 halves	2.5
Avocado (Calif.)	½ med.	1.3
Beef, roast	3 oz.	6.1
Beet greens	1 cup (cooked)	2.8
Blood sausage	2 oz.	1.0
Calves' liver	3 ½ oz.	14.2
Chicken	3 oz.	1.5
Chicken livers	3 oz.	7.0
Clams or oysters	3 oz.	5.0
Collard greens	1 cup (cooked)	1.7
Corn grits	¼ cup (cooked)	1.4
Egg	1 med.	1.1
Farina	1 cup (cooked)	2.0
Kidney beans	½ cup (cooked)	2.8
Lima beans	½ cup (cooked)	3.5
Liverwurst	3 oz.	4.5
Molasses (black-strap)	1 tbsp.	3.2
Mustard greens	1 cup (cooked)	2.5
Oatmeal	1 cup (cooked)	1.7
Orange (Valencia)	1 med.	1.0
Pork chop	3 ½ oz.	4.5
Pumpkin seeds	3 oz.	7.1
Raisins	½ cup	2.5
Rice (enriched)	1 cup (cooked)	1.6
Sardines	3 ½ oz.	5.2
Shrimp	3 oz.	2.5
Soybean curd (tofu)	3 ½ oz.	1.9
Spinach	1 cup (cooked)	0.8
Sunflower seeds	3 oz.	7.1
Veal cutlet	3 ½ oz.	3.0
Walnuts	¼ cup	1.1

An older woman who experiences irregular, heavy periods should see her doctor to rule out the possibility of cancer or a benign tumor. Chances are, her dysfunctional bleeding is simply heralding the onset of menopause, but since the risk of uterine and other reproductive cancers rises with age, it does not pay to take chances. By keeping a basal temperature chart, a woman can confirm that she is not ovulating. If she is not, the cause for her bleeding should be determined. This may involve doing an endometrial biopsy or perhaps a D&C.

Hormones can be used to prevent or stop the hemorrhaging associated with menometrorrhagia; by taking progestin, a synthetic progesterone, the endometrium can be "forced" into a secretory phase, resulting in a more normal shedding. Estrogen and progestin can be given in sequence to mimic what happens during a normal cycle, which should put an end to the abnormal heavy bleeding if it is related to failure to ovulate. (See Chapter 6 for a more detailed discussion of hormone replacement.) But before embarking on hormone therapy, it is important to rule out a possibly serious cause of the dysfunctional bleeding.

Failure to Menstruate

Although we usually think of menstrual difficulties in terms of cramps, PMS or abnormal bleeding, there are some women for whom the problem is failure to menstruate at all—a condition called amenorrhea. Sometimes this occurs in a young woman who simply never starts to menstruate— a situation referred to as primary amenorrhea. More often, however, we are confronted with secondary amenorrhea, which occurs in women who have menstruated at one time, but for some reason, have stopped having periods.

Primary Amenorrhea

Very often, an adolescent girl—and her mother—become concerned when she has not started having periods after many of her friends have. Usually, it is simply a matter of time. As noted in Chapter 3, some girls start to menstruate as early as age ten or eleven, while others do not begin until they are fifteen or sixteen. The average age is about twelve to thirteen, but anything between ten and fifteen or sixteen is perfectly normal.

Table 3. AMENORRHEA

Causes of Primary Amenorrhea
Lack of sufficient body fat caused by nutritional deficiency, weight loss, anorexia nervosa, athletic training, disease
Hormonal disorders, including tumors of the hypothalamus and pituitary
Congenital abnormalities, including lack of ovaries or uterus
Chromosomal abnormalities
Completely intact hymen
Thyroid disease
Hormone-producing tumors or cancers
Diseases affecting the central nervous system
Diabetes, infection, other chronic diseases

Causes of Secondary Amenorrhea
Pregnancy
Menopause
Breast feeding
Stress
Post-pill amenorrhea
Weight loss
Athletic training
Obesity
Hormone-producing tumors or cancers
Thyroid disease
Hormonal imbalances
Hysterectomy
Destruction of endometrium by radiation or excessive curettage
Diabetes or other chronic diseases
Drug or alcohol addiction
Adrenal disorders
Pituitary tumor or insufficiency
Ovarian cysts or tumors
Radiation
Side effect of cancer chemotherapy and other drugs
Infection

The causes of primary amenorrhea are listed in Table 3. If an adolescent girl is otherwise healthy, most experts advise delaying an elaborate workup to determine a cause of primary amenorrhea until she is sixteen. Such a workup, which may require elaborate hormonal and chromosomal studies, costs up to several thousand dollars. And before embarking on any workup, a doctor also will want to know at what ages the girl's mother, aunts, sisters and other close relatives started menstruating. Although there has been a tendency for girls to start menstruating earlier than in previous generations—thanks largely to improved nutritional standards—a woman who started to menstruate when she was fifteen or sixteen is likely to have daughters who mature at about the same age.

Many girls experience delayed menstruation because they lack adequate body fat. Young ballerinas and other youngsters who undergo vigorous athletic training that prevents their building up body fat very often have delayed menarche. Similarly, girls who are anorexic or seriously underweight because of illness or other factors, may fail to menstruate. The causes and treatment of primary amenorrhea are discussed in greater detail in Chapter 3.

Secondary Amenorrhea

As might be expected, the two most common causes of cessation of menstruation are pregnancy and menopause. Although it seems obvious that a woman of reproductive age immediately should consider pregnancy as a possibility for failure to menstruate, it is surprising how many are stunned when this turns out to be the cause. "I've been having sex for years without using birth control and since I never got pregnant, I just assumed I couldn't" is an oft-heard refrain. Or, "I only had sex once—I didn't think I could get pregnant from just that...." If there is even the remotest possibility that a woman may be pregnant, she should see her doctor as soon as possible. Alternatively, there are a number of highly accurate home pregnancy tests now on the market. But even if a woman uses one of these tests to confirm that she is pregnant, she still should plan to see a doctor, since an early examination and prenatal care are essential elements in having a healthy pregnancy and producing a healthy baby.

Following childbirth, women who nurse usually do not menstruate for several months because of the high levels of prolactin, which suppresses ovulation. Even though a nursing mother may not be ovulating, however, it is not safe to assume that no contraception is needed during this time. Ovulation may return at any time, and very often a nursing woman assumes that her lack of menstruation is due to the fact that she is breast-feeding, only to find that she is, instead, pregnant again.

Some women enter menopause without being aware of it until they stop menstruating. If this happens at an early age, they may not associate the amenorrhea with menopause. (For a more detailed discussion of menopause, see Chapter 6.)

Other causes of secondary amenorrhea are outlined in Table 3. In general, these fall into three categories: organic or anatomic abnormalities; psychological and environmental causes; and hormonal imbalances. Women often are surprised to learn just how many factors affect menstruation. Although many women menstruate regularly every four weeks, there are others whose bodies are very sensitive to any change. This sensitivity is often reflected in their menstrual cycles, and is why the female reproductive system is often described as extraordinarily temperamental—everything has to be just right in order for it to function. Consequently, causes of secondary amenorrhea often are hard to track down, especially those of psychological or environmental origin.

For example, it is well known that many women stop menstruating during times of stress. College finals, starting a new job, a death of a loved one, or getting married or divorced are but a few examples of stressful events that have been implicated in menstrual irregularities. The list could go on and on. Both an excessive fear of pregnancy or deep desire to conceive have been found to cause secondary amenorrhea. A traumatic event, such as rape or a natural disaster, also may disrupt menstruation.

Amenorrhea related to stress usually is not serious unless the woman is desperate to have a baby. It is often difficult to will yourself to "relax"; if stress is thought to be the cause of failure to menstruate, professional counseling may be advised. There also are many techniques for coping with stress; what works for one woman may not necessarily help another. Exercise, yoga, meditation, self-hypnosis and biofeedback training are but a few stress management techniques that can be tried.

Life-style also can be instrumental in secondary amenorrhea. Perhaps one of the best examples can be found among the increasing number of women marathon runners and other athletes, as well as the traditional example of pencil-thin ballerinas. Rigorous physical training is usually accompanied by a marked reduction in body fat. Normally, about twenty-five to thirty-five percent of a woman's ideal weight is from fatty tissue. When a woman's body fat falls much below this, the hypothalamus perceives her in much the same manner as she was before puberty and it simply stops producing the hormones needed for normal menstrual cycles. A similar thing may happen when a woman goes on a crash diet and loses a large amount of weight.

More serious is secondary amenorrhea due to anorexia nervosa, a puzzling, distressingly common disease in which young women literally starve themselves. The failure to menstruate in itself is not medically serious, but the self-starvation can be life-threatening unless it is recognized and treated. The most common victims of anorexia nervosa are young women—usually teenagers. Typically, they are highly intelligent, motivated young women who develop a morbid preoccupation with being thin. They can starve themselves to the point where they are little more than emaciated skeletons and still perceive of themselves as being too fat. Tragically, it is a disease that is difficult to cure and carries a high death rate. Often, one of the first symptoms of anorexia nervosa is a cessation of menstruation. When this occurs in a young woman who suddenly seems to be losing excessive weight, it is a clear signal to seek medical help as soon as possible.

Interestingly, very obese women also may fail to menstruate. This time the answer lies in the excessive body fat, which converts adrenal hormones to estrogen. If the estrogen levels are high enough, ovulation will be suppressed in much the same manner as it is when a woman takes birth control pills.

Of course, some causes of secondary amenorrhea are obvious; hysterectomy is a prime example. But, surprising as it may sound, there are some women who have undergone a hysterectomy without realizing that the operation would forever end their menstruation. Fortunately, in this era of increased knowledge about our bodies and medical procedures, such lack of knowledge is becoming increasingly rare.

Not so obvious is a blocked cervix or vagina due to an abnormal hymen or scar tissue from an infection or injury. In such instances, menstruation is taking place, but the flow is blocked and is eventually reabsorbed. Normal periods can be established by surgically opening the cervix or vagina.

A variety of endocrine disorders also can lead to secondary amenorrhea, again demonstrating the finely tuned interaction of hormonal feedback systems. These include various ovarian diseases, such as polycystic disease—a disorder in which cysts form on the ovaries—or ovarian tumors. Thyroid disorders, pituitary tumors (or other disorders marked by pituitary failure) and certain cancers that produce hormones are still other examples. (For more detailed discussions dealing with the specific glands, see Chapters 7–14.)

Often drugs and other medical treatments result in amenorrhea. The most common example is the use of oral contraceptives.

There are several different types of pills with differing mechanisms of action. "Combination" pills contain both synthetic estrogen and progestin to maintain a constant level of sex hormones, suppressing ovulation. Typically, a woman takes these pills for twenty-one days, then either takes no pill or a "blank" placebo for seven days. The withdrawal of the hormones during the seven days off the pill usually, but not always, results in a shedding of the endometrium. These pseudo-periods are usually lighter and shorter than normal menstruation. Very often, women on the pill cease bleeding entirely.

In contrast, the mini-pills which contain only progestin usually do not suppress ovulation. They prevent pregnancy by making the cervical mucus thicker and more hostile to sperm, and by altering the endometrium to prevent implantation of a fertilized egg.

Most experts agree that today's oral contraceptives, which contain much lower doses of estrogen than the original "Pill," are safe when used by women who have no contraindications, such as tobacco use, a history of certain types of cancer, high blood pressure and other cardiovascular disorders. But many women find that when they cease taking the pill, ovulation and menstruation do not return as quickly as expected. Most women resume ovulation and menstruation within three or four months, but for up to five percent, normal ovarian function may not return for six months or more. This usually is not a problem unless the woman is anxious to become pregnant. The problem usually can be overcome by administering hormones to, in effect, "wake up" the ovaries and prompt them to again start producing the hormones needed to ripen and release mature eggs.

Post-pill amenorrhea does not appear to be related to how long a woman uses oral contraceptives, since it occurs both among women who have used the pill for only a short time as well as those who have been on it for years. Instead, the risk of post-pill amenorrhea seems to be greatest among women who are very thin, who have had irregular periods in the past, or who started to menstruate late. Some doctors advise very thin young women who have a history of menstrual irregularities to use other methods of contraception if they plan to eventually have children. It should be noted, however, that permanent infertility as a result of oral contraceptive use is rare.

Oral contraceptives are not the only drugs that may interfere with menstruation. Secondary amenorrhea also may be caused by psychotropic drugs and some of the powerful cancer chemotherapy agents. Radiation therapy also can damage the ovaries if they are exposed to its beams. Often, when a young girl is undergoing radiation therapy for cancer, the ovaries will be moved surgically out of the field of treatment and then shielded so they will not be exposed to any of the powerful X rays. Following completion of the treatment, the ovaries can be returned to their proper place. Obviously, unnecessary X-ray examinations should be avoided, and the reproductive organs of both men and women should be protected with lead shields, even during such routine low-dose procedures as dental X rays.

Heavy cigarette use, which suppresses estrogen, may be a factor in some instances of amenorrhea, especially among women who are very thin. Other possible causes include nutritional deficiencies—especially in calories—or heavy alcohol use. Since there are so many possible causes of secondary amenorrhea, considerable detective work is often needed to track down the cause. As a first step, a woman should keep a careful diary and also review both her own medical history and that of her mother, grandmother, aunts and sisters—all of which may provide important clues.

Endometriosis

Endometriosis is the abnormal growth in other parts of the abdomen of tissue that normally lines the uterus. At one time, it was thought to be a rare condition; today, we know that it is quite common and is a major cause of infertility, menstrual pain, abnormal bleeding, painful intercourse and other symptoms.

The cause of endometriosis is unknown. One theory holds that the cells that give rise to it are formed during the embryonic stage and remain undifferentiated until they are stimulated by the female sex hormones. Other researchers theorize that some of the menstrual blood escapes into the fallopian tubes and is expelled into the pelvic cavity. They suggest that the blood may be forced backward by uterine contractions or even by intercourse during menstruation. Since menstrual blood contains clumps of endometrial cells, it would follow that these might then implant themselves at various locations and develop into clumps of endometrial tissue.

Regardless of the cause, these external implants function as if they were actually lining the uterus. (See Figure 11.) Each month, they go through the same proliferative cycle in response to changing hormone levels that we see in the endometrium itself. If conception does not take place, these implants will bleed in much the same manner as the shedding of endometrial tissue inside the uterus. But there is a major difference—the displaced endometrial implants

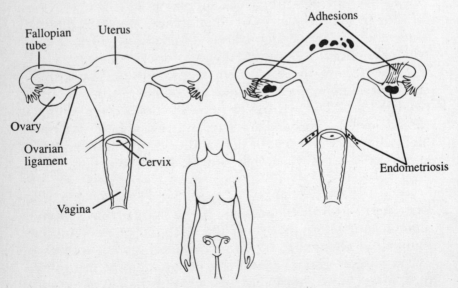

What Happens in Endometriosis

Even very small clumps of endometriosis on an ovary can cause infertility. Similarly, adhesions caused by endometriosis can twist reproductive organs into abnormal shapes and prevent conception.

have no mechanism for elimination from the body, so they heal and go through the same process over and over again. Eventually, scarring and adhesions form around the reproductive organs. Sometimes the uterus is twisted out of shape and adhesions may prevent eggs released from the ovaries from reaching the fallopian tubes. Sometimes the endometrial masses grow quite large or form dark brown blood-filled cysts on the ovaries.

Many women have endometriosis without experiencing any symptoms, while others may experience abnormal bleeding, menstrual pain, infertility and pain during intercourse or bowel movements and urination. Sometimes the pain of endometriosis is mistaken for ordinary menstrual cramps, but there are differences. The pain often begins even before menstruation starts and continues longer than most menstrual cramps. Taking antiprostaglandin drugs usually does not produce sufficient relief. Most women with endometriosis find that the abdominal pain gets worse as they get older. Often they do not experience any symptoms until they are in their early twenties because it may take several years for the implants to develop to the point where they cause problems.

Tenderness may develop in specific areas of the abdomen. Some women find that a particular sexual position may be painful or that pressing on a certain spot will produce pain. Masses near the rectum or bladder may cause constipation or pain during urination or bowel movements. Sometimes the pain and other symptoms are similar to those caused by pelvic inflammatory disease, a potentially serious infection of the internal reproductive organs. The symptoms are not necessarily related to the size of the masses; sometimes very tiny implants can cause symptoms just as severe as those the size of an egg or larger.

Many women with endometriosis have difficulty getting pregnant, especially as they grow older. The increased trend for women to have fewer children and to delay motherhood until they are in their thirties, by which time endometriosis may be well established, has led to our increased awareness of the disorder. Also, researchers who have studied endometriosis note that most women today experience many more menstrual periods than their counterparts in the past. We start to menstruate at an earlier age and the onset of menopause is later. In the days when women started having babies at an early age and commonly had six or more children, endometriosis did not have as much opportunity to become established as it does now when a woman may delay her first pregnancy until she is past thirty and then have only one or two children (endometriosis recedes almost to the point of disappearance during pregnancy because the implants do not go through the repeated cycles of growth, bleeding and regrowth).

Treatment of endometriosis involves manipulating the female sex hormones to mimic what happens during pregnancy or menopause—the two instances in which the condition disappears. One strategy involves taking birth control pills on a continuous basis, rather than the usual twenty-one-day cycle, which will suppress menstruation. Alternatively, drugs derived from progesterone (Provera, Norlutin or Norlutate) may be given daily in increasing doses for two or three months and then continued at a relatively high level for six to nine months. This also stops ovulation and the periodic shedding of the endometrium, although some women experience breakthrough bleeding. A false menopause can be created by taking Danocrine, a drug derived from a synthetic male sex hormone, which will stop ovulation. The drug is usually taken for six to nine months. During that time, a woman may experience hot flashes and other symptoms of menopause.

All of these strategies may produce varying degrees of side effects. Women on the progesterone regimen, for example, may experience bloating, breast tenderness, depression and other symptoms associated with pregnancy. In addition to menopauselike symptoms, Danocrine can cause a deepening of the voice, reduction in breast size, increased growth of facial and body hair, growth of the clitoris and other signs of masculinization related to taking male hormones. As might be expected, many women are alarmed by these side effects, and, for some, they may be intolerable. The realization that the effects are temporary and will disappear once the drug is stopped may make them more tolerable. Switching to one of the other strategies may produce the desired results with more tolerable side effects.

Sometimes the implants can be surgically removed, but they often reappear since it is difficult to eliminate all of the misplaced cells. A combination of surgery and drug therapy seems to work well for some women, especially if the endometriosis has caused adhesions, ovarian cysts or other structural abnormalities that are interfering with fertility.

SUMMING UP

In discussing menstruation and menstrual problems, it is important to remember that although virtually all women menstruate, the experience can vary widely from woman to woman. Cultural attitudes, anatomy, inherited characteristics, personal attitudes, environment, stress, life-style and overall health are among the myriad factors that affect menstruation. Fortunately, menstrual problems are no longer shrugged off as imaginary or a burden that women must bear in silence. We now know the cause of, and how to treat, many of these problems; the use of antiprostaglandin drugs to relieve menstrual cramps is a notable example. Other problems, such as premenstrual syndrome, still defies clear treatment, but our increased understanding of factors causing PMS makes it easier for women to cope and provides strategies for treatment of many of the symptoms.

Chapter 5

Pregnancy and Childbirth

Pregnancy is certainly a major milestone in any woman's life, and perhaps more so today than ever before because of the many choices and options available to her. Through the ages, childbearing has been considered the primary life's role for a woman. As we saw in the discussion of menstruation, many of the cultural or religious taboos and laws regarding sexual practices evolved to maximize a woman's childbearing potential. Even in the early part of this century, American women were expected to have many more children than they are today—a situation that still prevails in all but China and the more advanced industrialized countries of the Western world.

Still, for the first time in human history, women can have control over their reproductive lives—deciding if and when they want to have a baby. They also have a greater choice of contraceptive methods. This new freedom has not been without a price, however. A growing number of women who delay having their children until they have established their careers are finding they have waited too long, or that the delay has made it more difficult for them to conceive. Disorders such as endometriosis and fibrocystic breast disease are increasingly common, in large part because modern women are experiencing fewer pregnancies and many more menstrual cycles with the attendant hormonal fluctuations throughout their reproductive years. More than ever, it is important that a woman understand the intricate workings of her reproductive system so that she can make wise decisions regarding contraception and conception.

SELECTING A CONTRACEPTIVE

In this day and age, there is no need for an unplanned pregnancy, unless it is by personal choice. Yet studies have found that about three million sexually active American women who want to avoid pregnancy do not use any method of birth control. A third of these cite fear of side effects as the reason. According to Planned Parenthood, most of the 1.6 million abortions that are performed in this country each year could be avoided if women used one of the safe and highly effective means of birth control that are now widely available.

Of course, there are religious and cultural restrictions that may proscribe contraception for some women, but this is a matter of personal choice; these women know that their protection against pregnancy is to have sex only at times when they are sure they are not fertile. In any instance, before engaging in sexual activity, a couple should consider the possibility of pregnancy and plan accordingly.

Ideally, birth control is something both partners should partake in. In practice, however, birth control is most often considered the woman's responsibility. When selecting a method of birth control, most of us are more concerned with avoiding pregnancy than with planning for eventual conception. Both are very important, but neglecting the possibility of a desired future pregnancy can be a big mistake, as many women who used intrauterine devices (IUDs) are now learning. There are also a growing number of couples who are now seeking reversal of an earlier sterilization, either a vasectomy for the man or a tubal ligation for the woman, because their situation has changed and they now want to have a baby. Thus, the first consideration in selecting a method of contraception is a realistic determination of what effect it may have on a future pregnancy. Only couples who have had all the children they want and are absolutely certain that they will never want to have more should consider sterilization or even a birth-control method that has a high probability of interfering with a future pregnancy.

REVERSIBLE CONTRACEPTIVES

Hormonal Birth Control Methods

Oral contraceptives, popularly referred to as birth control pills, or simply, the pill, are the leading reversible birth control method now used by American women, and our major form of hormonal birth control. (The other is an IUD that releases small amounts of progesterone directly into the uterus.) A recent study by the National Center for Health Statistics found that twenty-nine percent of American couples that practice birth control rely upon the pill. This is slightly less than the thirty-three percent who use sterilization.

Next to sterilization, the pill is also the most effective of all birth control methods. It has now been available for more than twenty years, and earlier concerns about its long-term safety have, for the most part, been disproved. There are some women who should not use the pill, but for the majority who can, it appears to be both safe and effective. In addition, as more has been learned about the pill and its effects, and as different types of pills have been formulated, doctors are now able to prescribe a form that both matches a woman's natural chemistry and also meets her individual needs.

There are two types of oral contraceptives—the combination pill, which contains synthetic forms of estrogen and progesterone (progestogen), and the mini-pill, which contains only progestogen. The combination pill works by interfering with a woman's normal hormone fluctuations, thereby preventing the egg from maturing and being released for fertilization. The mini-pill does not necessarily prevent the egg from maturing, but it alters the cervical mucus and uterine lining in such a way as to create an inhospitable environment for the sperm, egg or embryo.

Combination pills now come in a variety of strengths and formulations, as well as in different types of packaging. Some come in twenty-one-pill packs, with a pill to be taken daily for twenty-one days, then nothing for seven days, with a new cycle beginning on the twenty-ninth day. Others come packaged with twenty-one active pills and seven blanks or placebos; the effect is the same as the twenty-one-pill packs, but some women find it easier to keep track of when to take a pill if there is one for every day of the cycle. Mini-pills are taken daily. Women who are inclined to forget to take a pill now and then should stick with a combination type; missing an occasional pill and then taking two the next day usually will not result in pregnancy, but missing a mini-pill might.

In all, two different types of synthetic estrogens and five types of progestogen are used in today's pills. Since the effects of hormones can vary widely from woman to woman, more than one type of pill may have to be tried before finding one that provides contraception with a minimum of problems. For example, some women experience uncomfortable bloating, breast tenderness and swelling, nausea and weight gain while on the pill. These are effects associated with estrogen; a low-estrogen formulation, a progestogen-only mini-pill, or one of the new triphasic versions designed to more closely mimic a woman's own hormonal balance may be better.

Women who are troubled with acne may be helped by a pill with slightly more estrogen or one with a different type of progestogen. However, several months may be needed to determine whether a higher estrogen pill will help; sometimes acne may actually worsen for a month or two after going on a certain type of pill, and then clear up.

Pill-related headaches may be caused by too much estrogen, especially if they occur only during the weeks on an active pill. The development of migraine headaches is a sign that the pill should be discontinued and another method of birth control used. Breakthrough bleeding is most common with the mini-pill or a low-estrogen formulation. Bleeding that occurs early in the cycle usually can be cleared up by adding a bit more estrogen; late-cycle bleeding may be stopped by more progestogen.

Women on the pill usually find that their periods are much lighter and free of cramps. Since ovulation stops while on the combination pill, women who suffer from premenstrual syndrome and/or endometriosis also may experience relief from their symptoms. In fact, it is not unusual for menstruation to stop completely while one is on the pill. Many women worry that this is a sign that something is wrong, and some doctors will prescribe extra hormones once a year or so to bring on a period. But others feel that this is not necessary; in fact, they feel that not having a period actually may be beneficial.

Many women who go off the pill expect that their periods will return in a short time; in fact, it may take up to six months or longer for this to happen if a combination pill has been used. Normally, the pituitary senses when circulating estrogen falls below a certain level and releases the hormones that stimulate the ovaries to secrete estrogen. But, while one is on the pill, there is a consistently high level of circulating estrogen, similar to that during pregnancy, so that the pituitary's feedback system between it and the ovaries shuts down, often taking several months to "wake up" and start secreting the LH and FSH again. This is referred to as post-pill amenorrhea; it usually is resolved with time, but the waiting can be very troubling for a woman, especially if she is eager to conceive. Post-pill amenorrhea is more common in women in their thirties; if ovulation does not resume within six months and a woman does not want to take a chance on waiting longer, clomiphene (Clomid), a fertility drug that stimulates the pituitary to produce FSH and LH, may be prescribed.

There are several factors that should be considered in deciding whether to use the pill. A very young woman should make sure that her ovaries are fully functional and that she is ovulating regularly before going on the pill. After the age of thirty or so, it usually takes longer for the ovaries to resume functioning after going off the pill. Thus, the pill may not be the best choice of contraception for a very young woman who has recently started menstruating, or for a woman in her thirties who thinks that she may want to have a baby soon. As a woman grows older, she does not ovulate as regularly as she did when she was younger, and her chances of pregnancy diminish. She still needs to practice birth control until menopause is firmly established and there is no chance that she is ovulating, but a woman over the age of forty may be advised to use some other form of birth control, as the risk of side effects from the pill may begin to outweigh the benefits derived. Still, it should be noted that the risks of pregnancy for most women are greater than the small risks associated with the pill.

Although most women can use the pill safely, there are some who cannot. Early fears that long-term use of the pill may increase the risk of cancer have not been borne out, but some pill users have an increased risk of stroke and heart disease, especially if they smoke. Women who smoke, particularly those over the age of thirty-five, are strongly advised to stop smoking; if they cannot, they should use some other form of birth control. The pill also is contraindicated for women who have blood-clotting disorders, such as thrombophlebitis; cancer of the breast, uterus, cervix, ovaries or other reproductive organs; heart disease; liver disorders; gallbladder disease; diabetes; high blood pressure; migraine headaches; or mental depression. The development of visual changes, leg pains that may indicate phlebitis, high blood pressure and other symptoms are among the indications that the pill should be discontinued and a doctor consulted.

The IUD

Intrauterine devices, or IUDs, have been used in various forms for centuries, but modern versions have had a troubled existence. In the last few years, most manufacturers of IUDs have removed them from the market in this country, largely because of the large number of lawsuits brought by women who have suffered their ill effects. As of this writing, the only IUD that is still available is the Progestasert, a plastic T-shaped device that releases small amounts of progestogen directly into the uterus. This device is not as likely to cause the heavy bleeding experienced by many women using conventional IUDs.

It is not known exactly how an IUD acts to prevent pregnancy, but it is generally assumed that it alters the environment of the uterus in such a way that it prevents implantation of the embryo. Although many IUD wearers have not experienced problems with the devices, enough have to indicate that it should not be used by a woman who may want to eventually have a baby. Even though the IUD is a highly effective contraceptive, one to six out of every hundred users do become pregnant. About half of these pregnancies end in miscarriage; if the IUD is removed, the rate of miscarriage drops to twenty-five percent. But there are instances in which the IUD cannot be safely removed; women who continue these pregnancies have a higher risk of infection, premature delivery and stillbirth.

Many IUD pregnancies occur in the fallopian tubes. These are called tubal or ectopic pregnancies. If detected early enough, the tube sometimes can be saved, but often such pregnancies go undetected until the embryo is large enough to cause the tube to rupture, a serious, even life-threatening event. A tubal pregnancy markedly decreases the chance of a successful future pregnancy. Often, the affected tube is so damaged that it can no longer carry an egg from the ovary to the uterus. If the remaining tube is also damaged, then normal conception may become impossible. The problem is compounded by the fact that the IUD increases the risk of pelvic inflammatory disease (PID), a serious infection of the reproductive organs that often damages the fallopian tubes, uterus and even the ovaries. There has been a marked increase of PID in recent years, especially among women with multiple sex partners who may be exposed to a number of sexually transmitted infections, including gonorrhea and Chlamydia—two leading causes of PID.

Barrier Contraceptives

These include the diaphragm, condom, cervical cap, contraceptive sponge and contraceptive foam. They are the safest of all contraceptives, and highly effective if used properly and faithfully. Many couples find them inconvenient, messy and unromantic; still, they may be the best method of birth control in a number of circumstances. Women who cannot use the pill or who have sex infrequently may find a barrier contraceptive best meets their needs. These contraceptives also protect against certain sexually transmitted diseases. A condom, for example, may prevent a disease-causing organism from being transmitted to a woman; a diaphragm and spermicide also may offer some protection. Indeed, the marked increase in sexually transmitted diseases, along with doubts, however unjustified, about the safety of the pill, has led to a marked increase in barrier contraceptives.

The Rhythm Method

Also referred to as natural family planning, the rhythm method of birth control is based on the premise that sexual relations be avoided during a woman's fertile period of the menstrual cycle, or that birth control be practiced during this time. In theory, this should work, but in practice, it can be difficult and demands that a woman be very aware of her body and the different phases of her menstrual cycle. It also requires considerable self-discipline. Natural family planning has the highest failure rate of all birth control methods, but couples who are sufficiently motivated and knowledgeable can enjoy a reasonable degree of success.

There are several ways to determine when ovulation takes place. The simplest, but most unreliable, is the calendar method. In theory, this should be a simple matter of counting days. A woman ovulates fourteen days before the onset of menstruation. Sperm can live up to four days and an egg lives for a day or two. Thus, to be absolutely safe, intercourse should be avoided during the period from about a week before ovulation until three days afterwards. The problem with this is that no woman has regular twenty-eight-day cycles month after month.

To get a rough idea of safe versus unsafe days, a woman should keep track of her menstrual cycles for a year. She then should subtract eighteen from the shortest cycle (the fourteen days before ovulation plus four days for the average life span of sperm) and eleven from the longest (fourteen days from ovulation until menstruation, less a day for the life span of an egg and two more for safety). The results are the first and last unsafe days of a woman's cycle, counting the first day of menstruation as day one. A specific example would work like this: The longest cycle is thirty-one days, the shortest is twenty-four. Thus, thirty-one minus eleven equals twenty and twenty-four minus eighteen equals six. This woman, then, should avoid intercourse or use a contraceptive from days six through twenty of her menstrual cycle.

A second method of determining approximately when ovulation takes place involves keeping a daily basal temperature chart. The basal temperature is the lowest body temperature, which is measured immediately upon awakening in the morning, before getting out of bed. When a woman's levels of estrogen and progesterone are low during the first phase of the menstrual cycle, the basal temperature is also low—usually about 97 to 97.5 degrees F. Toward the end of the first phase of the cycle, there is a slight dip in estrogen

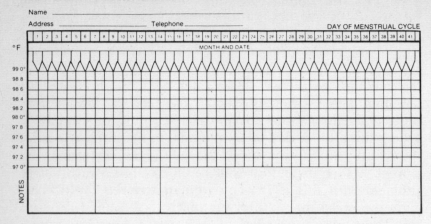

BBT CHART BASAL BODY TEMPERATURE

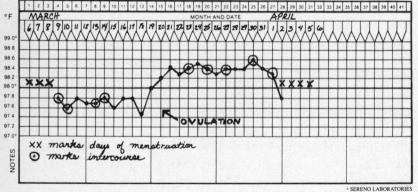

Sample Chart

ᶜ SERENO LABORATORIES
280 POND STREET
RANDOLPH, MA 02368

(see Figure 12), which signals the pituitary to step up hormone production. This dip is accompanied by a corresponding drop in basal temperature. A woman keeping a temperature chart, for example, may record 97.3 degrees F for several days, then 96.9 and then 98, 98, 99.

The dip followed by the rise indicates ovulation, and safe days begin about three days after that. This method is useful for determining the days that are safe after ovulation, but is not helpful in determining when a couple should stop having intercourse before ovulation takes place. To overcome this, the couple should assume that the unsafe period begins about six days after day one of menstruation, assuming that the woman's shortest menstrual cycle is twenty-four or twenty-five days.

There also are physical signs that a woman can observe that tell her when she ovulates. The most reliable of these is observation of cervical mucus, which changes in consistency during the course of the menstrual cycle. Typically, the mucus is sparse just after menstruation, becoming thicker until just before ovulation, when it becomes thin. Some women also experience what is called mittelschmerz—pain which may range from a mild twinge or two to severe cramping—at the time of ovulation. The pain is caused by bleeding when the mature egg breaks out of its follicle. Many women do not notice any pain, and those who do may experience it only sporadically, so this is not a reliable indicator of ovulation. But by following a combination of these indicators—keeping a calendar of menstrual cycles and a daily basal temperature chart, and observing cervical mucus and other physical signs—a woman can become more attuned to her body and better determine her "safe" days.

To make natural family planning easier and more reliable, at-home tests are being developed to further help a woman time ovulation. One that is already available uses monoclonal antibodies to detect the surge in luteinizing hormone that occurs just before ovulation. When the LH starts to rise, ovulation will take place within twenty-four to forty-eight hours. Beginning a week or so after menstruation, a woman uses a chemically treated dip-stick to test her first morning urine. The stick is treated to change color when there is a sufficient amount of LH in the urine. When this occurs, a woman knows that ovulation is about to take place. However, these tests are more useful for a woman who wants to achieve pregnancy than for one who is seeking to avoid it because she may have had intercourse a day or two before the tests show a rise in LH, and have viable sperm still present to fertilize the egg when she does ovulate.

Another at-home test which is not yet generally available involves using chemically treated paper to test the cervical mucus. Further information about all aspects of the rhythm method of birth control can be obtained from the National Family Planning Federation of America, Inc., Suite A, 1221 Massachusetts Avenue, N.W. Washington, D.C. 20005.

The Morning-After Pill and Other Postcoital Methods

The morning-after pill is actually a large dose of DES, or diethylstilbestrol, a synthetic estrogen. If given within a day or two of unprotected intercourse, the DES alters the uterine lining and thereby prevents implantation of a fertilized egg should conception take place. Although this strategy is appropriate under certain circumstances, such as rape, incest, a broken condom or other such unexpected incidents, it should not be relied upon as a regular method of contraception. DES can cause unpleasant side effects, such as nausea and vomiting, breast tenderness, menstrual irregularities and other problems. It also has been implicated in reproductive abnormalities among daughters of women who were given DES to prevent a threatened miscarriage—a practice that was halted in the early 1970s after reports of a rare type of vaginal cancer among DES daughters. Recent research also has linked DES to an increased risk of breast cancer among women who took it years ago.

Another postcoital method of contraception that has been used in the past entails insertion of an IUD shortly after the unprotected intercourse. This also prevents the implantation of a fertilized egg in the uterine wall. However, recent decisions by IUD manufacturers to halt distribution of the devices have altered the availability of this strategy; previously, the IUD containing copper was used, but this is no longer available.

PLANNING A PREGNANCY

Many people make the mistake of assuming that all there is to planning a pregnancy is to stop using birth control and let nature take its course. To be sure, this may be all that is needed to achieve conception, but planning parenthood should involve more than simply achieving pregnancy.

Obviously, one of the major objectives should be to produce as healthy a baby as possible with a minimum of risk to the mother. So, before pregnancy is attempted, a couple should make sure that they are doing everything they can to get their baby off to a healthy start. This should begin with the woman getting a complete check-up to make sure that there are no health problems that may endanger her or the baby. The woman should tell her doctor she is planning a pregnancy, and the check-up should include a careful family medical history of both the man and woman. A family history of inherited disorders, such as cystic fibrosis, hemophilia, sickle-cell disease, diabetes, etc., should be noted; in some cases a couple may want to undergo genetic counseling before attempting a pregnancy. The National Genetics Foundation, a nonprofit information clearinghouse, offers a unique computerized service that helps couples determine whether they may need genetic counseling. For $20 per person, the foundation will supply a fourteen-page questionnaire to obtain medical histories for three generations. The completed questionnaires are analyzed by a computer and the printout alerts a person of both the risk factors that may face the baby as well as problems the individuals themselves may develop. (For more information, contact the National Genetics Foundation, Inc., 555 West 57th Street, New York, N.Y. 10019, (212) 586-5800.)

In recent years, we have become increasingly aware of the danger to the developing fetus of a variety of substances consumed by the mother. Although we have long known the importance of factors such as good maternal nutrition, it was not until the tragic Thalidomide-induced birth defects of twenty-five years ago that we realized just how profound an effect certain substances could have on an unborn child. Today, we know that almost anything the mother consumes can affect the baby. Cigarette smoking, for example, results in an increased risk of low birthweight babies, miscarriages, stillbirths, crib death, and perhaps even learning problems later in life. Alcohol consumption, especially heavy drinking in the early part of pregnancy, can result in fetal alcohol syndrome, a constellation of birth defects that include small head size, facial deformities, mental retardation, heart defects, poor coordination, crossed eyes and other problems.

Illicit drugs, especially cocaine and heroin, are known to be harmful to the developing fetus. Mothers who use these drugs risk having babies that are born addicted. Women who use cocaine have an increased risk of miscarriages, birth complications and babies with developmental disorders. Doctors caution that the same hazards of cigarette smoking apply to marijuana use.

The prospective father also should stop using illicit drugs before pregnancy is attempted. For example, studies have found that marijuana decreases sperm production. It is not known whether illicit drugs can cause birth defects by altering the sperm, but some studies have found that men who work with certain chemicals and toxic substances father children with a higher-than-normal incidence of congenital problems.

Medications, including nonprescription drugs such as aspirin and cold pills, also should be avoided during pregnancy, or used only after checking with a doctor. Sometimes the mother needs to use medication to control a health problem such as epilepsy, but she may require a different type of drug during pregnancy to minimize the risk of birth defects. Hormones, including those in birth control pills, also can increase certain birth defects. A woman should not use birth control pills or other hormones if there is any chance she may be pregnant.

Unnecessary X-ray examinations should be avoided during pregnancy. According to the American College of Radiology, there is no increased risk to the fetus if the total exposure during pregnancy is no more than five rads. If a woman thinks there is a possibility she may be pregnant, she should let the doctor know this before being X-rayed, and also ask how high a dosage of radiation she is being exposed to. The amount of X rays in a dental examination, for example, probably is not harmful, especially if the mother is covered with a lead apron. Still, many doctors advise their would-be mothers to have these examinations before attempting pregnancy just to be on the safe side. In addition, routine dental work such as cleaning and scaling of teeth, should be done before pregnancy because these procedures release a number of bacteria into the bloodstream. Normally, these are harmless to the woman, but they may pose a danger to the fetus.

Some environmental chemicals also are hazardous to the fetus. Benzene, for example, increases the risk of cleft palate and growth disorders. There are some chemicals that pose a risk if either the prospective father or mother is exposed to them. Vinyl chloride, used in the manufacture of plastics, and certain insecticides are notable examples. If either the man or woman works with chemicals, the list should be given to the obstetrician to check. More information about chemicals, drugs or other substances that may cause birth defects can be obtained from the March of Dimes/ Birth Defects Foundation, 1275 Mamaroneck Avenue, White Plains, N.Y. 10605, (914) 428-7100.

There are several tests a woman should undergo before attempting pregnancy. These include a rubella antibody titer to make sure that she is immune to German measles, a disease that can cause serious birth defects. If the test shows a lack of immunity, the woman should be vaccinated, and then not attempt pregnancy for three months. In any event, she should not be vaccinated if there is any chance she already may be pregnant, since the vaccine itself may cause rubella in the fetus. Other prepregnancy tests include a Chlamydia culture; a blood test to rule out anemia; and a test for toxoplasmosis, a disease that can be contracted from contaminated cat feces or raw meat. Toxoplasmosis usually is not serious for an adult, but it can cause eye abnormalities and other birth defects. There is no harm in petting a cat, but during pregnancy, a woman should let someone else change a cat's litter box.

ACHIEVING PREGNANCY

After a couple has made sure that they have followed the general health precautions outlined in the preceding section and that "all systems are go," the next step is relatively simple; namely, stop practicing birth control, relax and enjoy frequent love-making. If a woman is using the pill, she should go off it about three months before attempting a pregnancy just to make sure that the extra hormones are cleared out of her body. If she has used an IUD, she should have it removed and wait about two cycles before attempting pregnancy; this will give the uterine lining time to recover.

On the average, a couple using no birth control and having sex frequently, for example, every other day, especially during the woman's midcycle when she is apt to ovulate, will achieve a pregnancy within six months. Some couples may succeed in the first month; others may need eight or nine. Generally, doctors are not concerned about a possible fertility problem until a full year of attempting pregnancy has elapsed without success.

Many times, couples become overly anxious when nothing happens month after month. They frequently make the mistake of assuming they have a fertility problem, when it is most likely a matter of timing—their sexual intercourse simply is not coinciding with a woman's most fertile days. The new at-home ovulation test kits may be particularly helpful for couples in this situation. A basal temperature chart is useful in that it tells a woman when she is ovulating (some women may have periodic bleeding as if they were menstruating normally, but in fact, may not be ovulating), but it is not always helpful in telling a couple that "this is the day." Often, couples wait for the rise in temperature that signals ovulation has taken place, but this may already be too late. Instead, they should concentrate on the small dip in temperature that immediately precedes the rise—a subtlety that is easy to miss.

If careful observation of temperatures, changes in body mucus and other clues do not help, the ovulation test may provide the needed information. As noted earlier, this test involves inserting a chemically treated dip-stick into a sample of the first urine passed in the morning. The stick will change color when the surge in LH takes place. This is the hormone that prompts the ovarian follicle to release its ripened egg; ovulation takes place within forty-eight hours of the LH surge. A couple can use the ovulation test to determine the exact day when they should have intercourse. Figure 12 shows the hormonal changes that take place at different stages of the menstrual cycle, along with the pattern of basal temperature.)

If pregnancy still is not achieved, even though these tests indicate that a woman is ovulating normally and the couple has properly timed intercourse, the couple still should not jump to the hasty conclusion that there is an infertility problem. The failure to conceive may simply be a matter of poor technique—something that many doctors fail to discuss, but still, a major reason why many couples have difficulty. For example, a woman may get up immediately after having intercourse to go to the bathroom or take a shower. Such actions will not necessarily prevent pregnancy—indeed, one of the old wives' birth control methods involves getting up and running around the bed three times —but they do increase the chance of losing some of the semen and thereby lessen the chance of conception. It is better to relax for an hour or so before moving around.

CAUSES OF INFERTILITY

Infertility among American couples has more than doubled in the past decade; it is estimated that nearly ten million

Americans, or about one out of every five couples, are unable to achieve pregnancy despite trying for a year or more. There are many reasons for this alarming increase in infertility: the rise in sexually transmitted diseases; the trend of postponing parenthood, thereby missing a woman's most fertile years of eighteen to twenty-eight; the use of an IUD; and other reasons that are not entirely clear.

Contrary to popular belief, fertility problems are about equally divided between men and women—about forty percent for each, with the remaining twenty percent resting with both partners. Doctors advise most couples to wait for at least six, and preferably twelve, months before seeking the help of a fertility specialist. Before seeing a doctor, couples can try the approaches outlined earlier in this chapter; for example, doing at-home tests and/or keeping a temperature chart to make sure that a woman is ovulating and that intercourse is properly timed. If a couple is fairly certain that a woman is not ovulating, it may be wise to see a fertility expert without further delay. Remember, however, it may take six months or longer for normal menstruation and ovulation to resume after going off the pill; if a woman has been taking oral contraceptives, a specialist will likely recommend waiting a while longer to see if ovulation resumes on its own.

The most common causes of infertility are listed in Table 4. The leading cause of infertility among women is the failure to ovulate. Some of these women ovulate irregularly; others do not ovulate at all. In either instance, the problem usually is hormonal. Since the normally ovulating woman has a low level of circulating estrogen in the first part of her menstrual cycle, this lack of estrogen signals the hypothalamus to secrete its gonadotropin-releasing hormone, which in turn stimulates the pituitary to release its follicle-stimulating and luteinizing hormones. This surge in FSH and LH stirs the ovaries into action; a follicle that contains a ripening egg matures and erupts, releasing the egg. After the egg is released, its follicle is transformed into a hormone-producing structure, called a corpus luteum (yellow body), which secretes the progesterone that is needed in

Table 4. POSSIBLE CAUSES OF INFERTILITY

Female	Male
General	
Overweight	Overweight
Underweight	Underweight
Anemia	Excessive alcohol use
Hostile mucus	Excessive smoking
Turner's syndrome	Klinefelter's syndrome
Developmental	
Uterine malformations	Undescended testicles
Undeveloped ovaries	Varicocele
Incompetent cervix	Underdeveloped testicles
	Poor sperm count
	Defective sperm
	Impotence
	Ejaculatory disorders
Hormonal	
Pituitary failure	Pituitary failure
Thyroid disease	Thyroid disease
Ovarian failure	Adrenal disorders
Adrenal disorders	
Genital Disease	
Infection (PID, Chlamydia, gonorrhea, cervicitis, etc.)	Infection (gonorrhea, other sexually transmitted diseases)
Tubal scarring, other abnormalities	Injury to testes
Endometriosis	Hydrocele
Cervical polyps	Orchitis
Uterine fibroids	Prostatitis
Endometriosis	
Both Sexes	
Marital maladjustment	
Poor timing of intercourse	
Immunological incompatibility	
Genetic disorders	

Adapted from *Why Can't We Have a Baby* by Albert Decker, M.D., and Suzanne Loebl, Dial Press, 1978.

order for a fertilized egg to implant itself in the uterine lining, thus establishing a pregnancy.

At a number of points, something can go awry in this delicately balanced hormonal system, resulting in infertility. Not uncommonly, the problem may be related to weight loss or weight gain, both of which can alter the hormonal balance. For example, a woman who wants to get pregnant may reason that she would like to lose a few pounds first because she has heard the old wives' tale that it may be hard to shed unwanted weight after having a baby. If her weight already is near the "set point" that the hypothalamus has established for proper ovulation, simply losing a few pounds may be enough for the system to "shut down." Conversely, gaining excessive weight may raise the level of estrogen to the point where it acts like a birth control pill.

Any disruption in the finely tuned hormonal feedback systems can result in failure to ovulate. For example, the pituitary may fail to produce the LH and FSH that stimulate the ovaries to produce a mature egg. Hormones from the adrenal glands or thyroid may interfere with the message system. The ovaries themselves may be incapable of responding to the signals from the pituitary. The ratio of FSH to LH may be slightly off, thereby preventing the ovaries from producing an egg.

Some women develop polycystic ovaries, a condition known as Stein-Leventhal syndrome. Typically, this disorder causes an imbalance in hormones: low FSH, high estrogen, erratic surges of LH, low progesterone and elevated male hormones. During a normal menstrual cycle, these various hormones go through cycles of rises and falls, but in polycystic disease, they tend to remain constant throughout the cycle. A follicle swells but fails to release an egg, so it becomes a cyst. The cells around the cyst pump out weak male hormones, which the body converts into estrogen. The feedback system in the brain senses the high level of estrogen, assumes that the ovaries are functioning properly, and that a ripe egg is ready to be released. The pituitary cuts back the secretion of FSH and sends out the LH, which normally would cause the ripened egg to break away from the follicle. But there is no mature egg, so the follicle forms a cyst. The process is repeated, and cycle after cycle, the problem gets worse. The high level of estrogen prevents the uterus from shedding and this buildup of the endometrium increases the risk of uterine cancer. A woman with polycystic ovaries may experience a number of other symptoms, principally abnormal growth of hair on the face and body and other signs of virilization from the male hormones.

Sometimes the hormonal imbalance is caused by excessive prolactin, the hormone that stimulates milk production. A number of factors, including stress and certain drugs, particularly antidepressants, hallucinogens, alcohol and painkillers can cause elevated prolactin. So can brain tumors and an underactive thyroid.

Still another hormonal imbalance may occur during the latter part of the menstrual cycle (the luteal phase). Normal ovulation may take place, but then a hormonal imbalance may prevent proper implantation. For instance, the pituitary may not send out enough LH, or the egg follicle may not be able to respond to the LH.

Most of these hormonal problems can be corrected, but before this can be achieved, the nature of the problem must be identified. This usually requires careful hormone studies by a specialist, generally an endocrinologist experienced in diagnosing and treating fertility problems. If the problem turns out to be polycystic ovaries, post-pill failure to ovulate, or other defects related to a lack of FSH and LH, clomiphene (Clomid) may be prescribed. About thirty percent of women who are infertile because of a failure to ovulate, and who have ovaries capable of producing eggs, can be helped by clomiphene.

This drug works by blocking the estrogen receptors in the hypothalamus, which tricks the brain into signaling the pituitary to stimulate estrogen production by secreting FSH. This will stimulate the ovaries to ripen an egg, which produces even more estrogen. But the hypothalamus still does not sense this increase in estrogen until the drug is stopped; suddenly, the brain detects the high levels of estrogen and responds by signaling the pituitary to send out a surge of LH. This causes the egg to break free of the follicle, thereby completing ovulation. If the LH surge does not take place, a factor that can be determined by the urine test for ovulation, a woman can take human chorionic gonadatropin (hCG), a pregnancy hormone that is chemically similar to LH and which can "trick" the ovaries into releasing the ripened egg.

Frequently, several cycles of clomiphene may be needed to achieve pregnancy. Sometimes, however, one or two courses of the drug will "shock" the endocrine system into resuming ovulation on its own. In all, about three-fourths of women who do not ovulate, but who have otherwise normal reproductive systems, are able to achieve pregnancy using clomiphene. About one out of fifty will have twins, compared to the normal twinning rate of one out of a hundred. This is because the extra stimulation of the ovaries prompts them to produce more than one egg; therefore, the increased number of twins will be fraternal rather than identical. Normally, one out of two hundred pregnancies results in identical twins; this number is not changed by the use of clomiphene or other fertility drugs.

Failure to ovulate due to excessive prolactin is treated by a drug, bromocryptine, which suppresses production of prolactin. Sometimes a woman will need to take this drug for several months before the prolactin falls enough for her to get pregnant. Once pregnancy occurs, bromocryptine should be stopped immediately, since the drug has been associated with birth defects.

Hormonal problems that occur during the later, or luteal, phase of the cycle are relatively easy to correct. If LH is low, hCG may be given. Low levels of progesterone may mean that the corpus luteum has died and is not producing the hormone. This can be corrected by treatment with vaginal suppositories containing progesterone, which is absorbed by the endometrium and prepares it to receive the fertilized egg. Low levels of FSH and estrogen may indicate that there is a defect in the hormone receptor sites on the corpus luteum, a problem that may be corrected with chlomiphene.

Sometimes these various measures fail to stimulate ovulation; in such instances, a woman may be a candidate for a more powerful fertility drug, Pergonal, which is a combination of LH and FSH obtained from the urine of menopausal women. Following menopause, these two hormones rise markedly in an attempt to stimulate the ovaries back into action, a fact discovered by an Italian biologist, Donini Serano, who also hit upon the idea of collecting urine from older nuns to make the drug. (The rise in hormones is reflected by increased excretion in the urine.) The Serano Pharmaceutical Company, which continues to produce Pergonal, still collects urine from Italian convents and older women from the Italian villages.

Unlike clomiphene, which acts on the hypothalamus to produce its results, Pergonal acts directly on the ovaries, making it a risky drug. The dosage must be carefully monitored to make sure the ovaries are not overstimulated. This can cause the release of too many eggs, or, in extreme cases, the rupture of an ovary. A woman takes Pergonal for five to ten days during the cycle. While on the drug, she must be checked daily to make sure that the ovaries are not being overstimulated. This can be determined by measuring the estrogen levels or by using ultrasound to view the ovaries and see how many eggs are ripening. When ultrasound shows that one or two eggs are mature enough to be released, the woman is given hCG to complete the ovulation.

Pergonal is the fertility drug that sometimes results in the birth of triplets, quadruplets, and, in rare instances, quintuplets and more. While such births generate considerable interest in the media, they should be avoided if at all possible because of the tremendous risk to both the mother and babies. If a doctor sees that too many eggs are maturing, the drug should be stopped and the woman advised not to attempt a pregnancy on this cycle. Alternatively, if too many embryos are implanted, it is advisable to interrupt the pregnancy and try again in another cycle.

MECHANICAL CAUSES OF INFERTILITY

Although hormonal factors are the leading cause of female infertility, there also are a number of mechanical obstructions and problems that can cause infertility. In recent years, there has been a marked increase in some of these problems, particularly those related to endometriosis and blocked or damaged fallopian tubes.

Endometriosis

As noted in Chapter 4, endometriosis is a common disorder in which some of the endometrial cells that normally line the uterus escape into the pelvic cavity and form clusters of endometrial tissue. These clusters may become attached to the uterus, ovaries, tubes, colon and other abdominal structures. Even though these clusters are outside the uterus, they still respond to hormonal stimulus as if they were in their normal place. During each menstrual cycle, the endometrial implants grow and become engorged with blood, similar to the normal endometrium. If conception does not take place, the normal endometrium is shed in the menstrual flow; in endometriosis, the tissue also bleeds, but there is no place for it to go. Scar tissue forms and in the next cycle, it again grows and bleeds. Eventually, the implants may form adhesions or distort the reproductive organs. Even a very tiny bit of endometriosis on an ovary or fallopian tube can cause fertility problems. Many women with endometriosis also experience severe menstrual pain that, unlike ordinary cramps, is not relieved by antiprostaglandin drugs.

In recent years, there has been a marked increase in endometriosis, which is now a major cause of infertility. The cause of endometriosis is unknown, but the increase is attributed to the fact that women today are having fewer babies and at a later age than in the past. During pregnancy, the endometriosis tissue is not subjected to the cyclic stimulation, and the implants shrink and disappear. In the past, a woman might start having babies in her late teens and spend much of her reproductive life either pregnant or nursing. She also started menstruating at a later age and entered menopause earlier than she does today. Thus, she did not have as many menstrual cycles during her reproductive years as women do today. Experts think that these changes account for at least part of the increase in endometriosis.

Endometriosis can sometimes be diagnosed through characteristic symptoms and response to drugs that temporarily halt ovulation. It usually takes six months of drug therapy to clear up the endometriosis enough to restore fertility. Sometimes, if the implants are large or if they have caused scarring and distortion of the reproductive organs, surgery also will be needed. (For a more detailed discussion, see Chapter 4.)

Tubal Abnormalities

Fertilization usually takes place in the fallopian tube as the egg passes through it on its way to the uterus. Scarred or blocked fallopian tubes are another major cause of infertility, and again, one that is increasing. Pelvic inflammatory disease, which can be caused by gonorrhea, Chlamydia or other pelvic infections, as well as IUD use, is a leading cause of scarred and damaged fallopian tubes. Ectopic or tubal pregnancy can damage or destroy a tube and result in infertility. Of course, voluntary sterilization in which the tubes have been divided or tied, also results in infertility.

Increasingly, skilled microsurgeons using lasers or conventional surgical techniques are able to repair damaged fallopian tubes, and about half of the women whose tubes are successfully repaired are able to achieve pregnancy. Those whose tubes cannot be repaired, or who remain infertile even after surgery, may be candidates for in vitro fertilization, or so-called test-tube fertilization. This involves removing one or more ripened eggs from a woman's ovary, fertilizing it in a test tube with the husband's sperm, and then returning it to the woman's uterus where, it is hoped, it will establish a pregnancy. Although great strides have been made in in vitro fertilization since the technique was first developed a few years ago, the failure rate is still very high, and the entire procedure is very expensive.

Other Miscellaneous Causes of Female Infertility

As indicated in Table 4, there are many other possible causes of infertility, including "hostile" cervical mucus that prevents the sperm from reaching the egg; the development of antibodies that attack the sperm; infection or other diseases, including diabetes when blood sugar control is inadequate; and stress, among others.

Even after an extensive fertility workup, there are a significant number of couples for whom a cause cannot be identified. Not infrequently, a couple will despair of having a baby, only to find that years later, the woman discovers she is pregnant. Most of us know of couples who have had this happen after adopting a baby. Others, after years of futile trying, give up, only to later find that, at long last, they are going to be parents as they enter middle age. Usually, there is no explanation for the turn of events, and, in many instances, parenthood may come as something of a shock after having given up hope.

CAUSES OF MALE INFERTILITY

Not as much is known about infertility in men as in women, nor are there as many treatments for men. This is changing, however, as research into the causes of male infertility increases and microsurgical repair of structural defects becomes more common.

Among men, a low sperm count is the most common cause of fertility problems. Very few men—probably less than two percent—are completely sterile. Instead, their semen contains too few sperm, or the sperm are in some way defective. A number of factors can interfere with sperm production, including alcohol or tobacco use, drugs, radiation, exposure to certain chemicals and infection.

About ten percent of male fertility problems occur in the sperm transport system: One of the passageways becomes blocked or is structurally defective. Microsurgery can sometimes correct these problems. Hypospadias, a structural defect in which the man's penis has its opening on the underside, preventing him from depositing the sperm deeply enough in the vagina, also can cause fertility problems. This can be remedied by surgical correction or using artificial insemination to achieve pregnancy.

Sperm are very sensitive to heat; the testes are situated outside the body because it is cooler for them there than being located internally. Any infection, inflammation or other condition that produces even a slight rise in scrotal temperature can hinder sperm production. Varicocele, a varicose vein in the testes, is one of the most common problems in this area. The swollen vein produces heat; it also may block a passageway. About thirty percent of infertile men have a varicocele; when this is treated, either by surgical removal or tying it off, the sperm counts improve in seventy percent of the men, and half go on to achieve successful impregnation.

As in women, a man's ability to make sperm and reproduce depends upon a finely tuned hormonal feedback system. Although hormonal causes of infertility are not as common in men as in women, they are a possibility that should be investigated if there are no other apparent causes. Sometimes the same fertility drugs that are used to treat ovulation problems in women will be given to men to stimulate their endocrine systems to produce male hormones. Recently, success has been reported in giving the LH-stimulating hormone LHRH (luteinizing-hormone-releasing hormone) in a pulsatile manner from a pump worn on the belt.

THE PREGNANT BODY

Let's assume that all goes well and conception takes place. A woman who is really attuned to her body often can tell that she is pregnant before doing any testing or seeing a doctor. For example, a woman who has been keeping a monthly temperature chart knows that there is the rise at the time of ovulation, and then a fall at the time her period starts. This fall corresponds to the drop in estrogen and progesterone just before menstruation. The increased blood flow plus the natural property of progesterone to increase body temperature account for the rise in basal temperature; the hormone levels remain high throughout pregnancy. Thus, basal temperature also remains high. So a woman who charts her basal temperature daily will immediately see that there is no drop that ordinarily heralds the onset of menstruation; instead, there may even be a slight continued rise. If her period is a day or two overdue and there is no fall in basal temperature, a woman can be pretty sure it is time for her to buy the pregnancy test kit to confirm what she already strongly suspects—that she is, indeed, pregnant.

The test kit contains a chemically treated dip-stick or slide, depending upon the brand used. As in the ovulation test kit, the stick or slide is used on the first morning urine. It senses the presence of hCG, the pregnancy hormone that is produced by the placenta. The newer at-home pregnancy kits are easy to use and can detect a pregnancy within two or three days of a missed period. A positive result practically always confirms that a woman is pregnant. In some women, however, the hormonal changes may not be as marked, so a negative result does not always rule out the chance of pregnancy; a test a few days later may be positive. At this point, a woman should make an appointment with her obstetrician to let him or her in on the news and to begin her prenatal medical care, which will continue throughout the pregnancy.

Almost from the moment of conception, a woman will notice subtle changes in her body. Her breasts will be even more swollen and tender than usual, starting in what would normally be her immediate premenstrual week. This is caused by the continued rise in estrogen and progesterone. As these two hormones continue to rise, a woman may experience nausea and even vomiting, the characteristic symptoms of morning sickness. This does not happen until about the sixth week of pregnancy, however, when the estrogen and progesterone plateau. Earlier or more pronounced morning sickness may indicate a multiple birth; a pregnancy with twins, for example, produces twice as much estrogen, progesterone and hCG as when there is a single fetus, and mothers of twins often recall that their first indication that there was more than one fetus was early, more severe morning sickness. (It should be noted that although it is called morning sickness, the feelings of queasiness may occur at any time during the day.)

Typically, the morning sickness continues until the tenth or eleventh week, and then subsides as the body adjusts to the high hormone levels. Although many women feel terrible during this phase, they can take comfort in the fact that it is a sign their hormones are there and working to maintain the pregnancy. For most women, morning sickness is more of an annoyance than a serious problem. Even though they do not feel like eating at certain times, they still consume enough to gain weight and provide adequate nutrition for the fetus. About one in ten women, however, may experience morning sickness severe enough to interfere with nutrition, and if the vomiting is so severe that they simply cannot hold down any food, they may require hospitalization and artificial feeding. This is very unusual, however; most women can control the nausea by eating small, frequent meals of bland foods—fruits, soda crackers, starchy foods, for example—and by avoiding foods that are strong-smelling or that provoke the nausea.

As stressed throughout this book, no two women are

exactly alike; it follows, therefore, that no two pregnancies are exactly alike, even though all women will share certain aspects. Some breeze through with virtually no discomfort, experiencing feelings of euphoria and glowing good health, while others may feel awkward, swollen and uncomfortable, almost from the moment of conception. Some women who have a very easy first pregnancy are surprised to find they have a more difficult time with a later pregnancy; the opposite also is true. Most women, however, take the changes in their bodies in stride and, if they know what to expect and the reasons why they are experiencing the various changes that accompany pregnancy, they find it is an exciting nine-month adventure with a wonderful, healthy baby as a reward at the end.

HORMONAL ADAPTION OF PREGNANCY

During the course of pregnancy, a number of hormonal changes take place that not only ensure the normal growth and development of the fetus, but also produce many of the physical and emotional changes associated with being pregnant.

The thyroid gland enlarges somewhat and increases production of thyroxine. This raises the body's metabolic rate to provide the energy needed for the developing fetus and the chemical changes taking place in the mother's body. This also explains why thyroid disease often appears during pregnancy among women susceptible to it. The parathyroid glands also increase production of their hormones to ensure proper calcium balance. The adrenal glands produce more hormones; increased aldosterone, for example, helps counter the sodium loss that would normally occur with such high levels of progesterone and increased cortisol helps ensure that energy levels are sustained.

The placenta is literally a hormone factory, turning out large quantities of estrogen, progesterone, hCG, ACTH and special pregnancy hormones such as human placental lactogen, which help ensure that the fetus is properly nourished. Some of these hormones are normally produced by other glands, such as the pituitary or the ovaries, which go into a sort of resting phase during pregnancy.

During pregnancy, the body achieves a hormonal balance that is unique to this period of life. The levels of some hormones are several times those of nonpregnant women, yet these very high amounts do not exert the same effect that would occur in a nonpregnant person. For example, a pregnant woman needs very high levels of estrogen to support the pregnancy, increase the blood volume, prepare the breasts and perform other functions. But this high level of estrogen results in a marked increase in angiotensin II, which is instrumental in increasing blood pressure. For unexplained reasons, a pregnant woman can tolerate a very high level of angiotensin II without experiencing a rise in blood pressure; in fact, most pregnant women have low blood pressure. But when a woman's body fails to develop this resistance to angiotensin II, she becomes more susceptible to hypertension and its serious consequences, such as toxemia. Toxemia, or eclampsia, is only seen in pregnancy and is a serious complex of problems which includes high blood pressure, swelling or edema, kidney damage, protein loss and a tendency toward seizures.

STAGES OF PREGNANCY

Traditionally, pregnancy is divided into three trimesters: the first goes through the twelfth week, the second from weeks thirteen through twenty-seven, and the third from weeks twenty-eight through forty, which is full-term. Major events, changes and precautions of each are discussed below:

First Trimester

In the first trimester, the uterus enlarges to three times its normal size to prepare for fetal growth in the last two trimesters. The breasts also grow larger and the amount of circulating blood doubles, both to provide for the growing fetus, and also, to prepare for the normal blood loss that occurs with childbirth.

About twelve percent of all pregnancies end in a miscarriage, or spontaneous abortion, and most of these occur in the first trimester, usually between the sixth and tenth weeks. Ectopic or tubal pregnancies, in which the embryo grows in the fallopian tube rather than in the uterus, also become apparent during the first trimester. Warning signs include lower abdominal crampy, menstrual-like pain, which may be quite severe, and vaginal spotting. Blood tests will show a rise in hCG, indicating a pregnancy; a pelvic examination, along with an ultrasonic examination of the lower abdomen, will confirm a tubal pregnancy. The treatment is surgical removal of the misplaced embryo, ideally before the tube has ruptured.

By the end of the first trimester, the fetus, although it weighs only fourteen grams (about half an ounce) and is about 7.5 centimeters (about three inches) in length, has a distinctly human shape and the various organ systems are formed. The fetus's sex can be distinguished, as can its ears, nose, mouth, eyes and other features.

The Second Trimester

Most women recall the second trimester as being the best of their pregnancy. The morning sickness ends and most women feel healthy, even euphoric. Although the fetus is now growing rapidly and most women need to start wearing looser clothes, the pregnancy is not advanced enough to make a woman feel awkward. At about the twentieth week, the woman will become conscious of the baby's movements —an exciting feeling that makes the baby seem even more real. By the end of the second trimester, the fetus will be about fourteen inches long and weight two pounds. The movements may be so active that they will waken the women at night.

The Third Trimester

The final three months of pregnancy are marked mostly by fetal growth. Fetal kicking and other movements are more pronounced and frequent; sometimes a woman will be conscious of the baby's hiccuping. As the pregnancy progresses, the woman will feel more awkward. Breathing may seem more difficult, and many women experience increasing heartburn and other discomforts described below. Breasts also become heavier and fuller as term approaches. By the end of this trimester, the baby will weigh about seven pounds and will be eighteen to twenty inches long.

BODY CHANGES

Pregnancy and the accompanying hormonal changes affect almost every part of the body. Some of the more obvious changes that most women experience include:

Skin Changes

The increased level of placental hormones affect the skin's pigmentation. The pregnancy hormone is similar to the hormone that signals the skin to produce more melanin, the pigment cells that give skin its color. Women who normally tan instead of burn when exposed to the sun find that they tan even faster and deeper than before. Fair-skinned women are often even less tolerant of sun, and will burn with only minimal exposure. Moles and freckles become darker, and the areola surrounding the nipples also becomes larger and darker. Most women also develop a dark line (linea negra) from the navel extending down the abdomen to the pubic hair; this disappears within a few months after delivery.

Some women develop the so-called "mask of pregnancy"—dark, butterfly-shaped blotches on the face. (This also may occur when taking an oral contraceptive which is high in estrogen.) This also disappears after delivery, but can be disturbing to a woman during pregnancy. Avoiding exposure to the sun can minimize the problem; makeup usually can be used to disguise the blotchiness.

Many women also develop stretch marks on their breasts, abdomens and thighs during pregnancy. As their name implies, these reddish marks are caused by a stretching of the skin, and some women have a genetic susceptibility to developing stretch marks with any weight gain. There is little that can be done to prevent stretch marks; they usually fade considerably after delivery. Creams and other products promoted as preventives do little more than lubricate and soothe the skin.

Teeth and Gums

Pregnant women notice that their gums are softer and bleed more easily during pregnancy. This change is due to the increased levels of progesterone, which expands the blood supply and makes the tissue softer and spongier. Good dental hygiene is particularly important during pregnancy, but the old wives' tale that a woman loses a tooth for every pregnancy is unfounded. Massage and proper care will help maintain the gum tissue; after childbirth, the swelling and bleeding will subside.

Hair

Most pregnant women notice that their hair is thicker and grows faster during pregnancy; then, large amounts fall out within a few months after delivery. All hair goes through three distinct phases: a growth stage, which lasts for about three years; a resting phase of two to three months; and a shedding phase. The hormone changes of pregnancy cause a larger than usual number of hairs to go into the growing phase, and after delivery, the sharp drop in these hormones forces the hairs into the resting and shedding phases. It is not unusual for a woman to lose up to half of her hair after a baby is born. (Interestingly, the same thing happens to the baby. Most babies are born with a lot of heavy, dark hair, which falls out shortly after birth and is replaced by fine baby hair.) Even when the mother's hair is being shed in large amounts, new hairs are growing in the shafts and within a few months, most women will again have a full head of hair. During the shedding period, a shorter, fluffier hair style will make the thinning less apparent. Avoiding permanents, hair dyes, excessive blow drying and other practices that damage hair also helps.

Vaginitis

During pregnancy, many women are more susceptible to vaginitis than usual. There are several reasons for this. The hormone changes of pregnancy change the acidity of the vagina, making it more conducive to yeast and bacterial overgrowth. The increased body temperature also promotes vaginitis, as does the increased weight and more closed-in environment of the lower body as pregnancy progresses.

Bowel and Urinary Changes

Many women claim that their entire waste-disposal mechanism goes awry during pregnancy, and to a degree, they are right. The hormonal changes relax the smooth muscles, including those of the intestines, and this can lead to diarrhea, constipation or a combination of the two. The increased pressure of the expanding uterus affects both the urinary bladder and colon. During pregnancy, women find they need to urinate more frequently, and some may have problems with involuntary loss of small amounts of urine. This is caused by the bladder being pushed out of its normal position, and also by the muscle relaxation that accompanies the hormone changes. The pregnant woman also has an increased blood volume and a change in fluid balance, which often results in fluid retention and swelling.

Swollen Hands and Feet

Toward the end of pregnancy, most women experience mild edema, or swelling of the hands and feet. This is caused by the increased fluid retention due to the expanded blood supply, pressure of the expanding uterus, and a tendency for blood to "pool," or collect, in the lower part of the body.

It is not a cause for worry unless the swelling is accompanied by headaches, high blood pressure and other symptoms, in which case the doctor should be called immediately. Diuretics (water pills) should be avoided unless specifically recommended by a doctor. Instead, one should try cutting down on salt, sitting with the feet resting on a stool and lying down with legs up a couple of times a day. Tight, knee-high socks should be avoided. Wearing a larger size shoe also eases foot discomfort—a rather obvious solution, but one that a surprising number of women overlook.

Allergy and Sinus Congestion

Many women find that their hay fever and other allergies are worse during pregnancy, and that they also are more susceptible to sinus congestion, postnasal drip and sinus headaches. The hormonal changes of pregnancy cause a swelling of the nasal tissues; this, combined with the increased venous pressure, results in increased production of nasal secretions. Saline nose drops may help, as may a cold-water vaporizer that moistens room air. Increased headaches, especially tension headaches related to the back discomfort that is common during the latter part of pregnancy, also may be troubling. Massage and relaxation exercises often help. Acetaminophen may be acceptable as a pain reliever; it is not as likely to cause bleeding problems as aspirin. All medications, including nonprescription drugs, should be checked with a doctor before use.

Varicose Veins and Hemorrhoids

Many pregnant women are troubled by varicose veins and hemorrhoids (which are varicosed veins in the anus). These are caused by the increased abdominal weight and pressure, the larger blood volume of pregnancy and the effect of progesterone, which relaxes the muscle wall in the veins. They usually disappear after childbirth, and can be minimized by common-sense measures during pregnancy. Resting with the legs elevated, wearing elastic stockings, avoiding prolonged periods of standing or sitting with the legs in the same position, and exercise all can relieve or minimize varicose veins in the legs. Hemorrhoids can be relieved by increasing the amount of fiber, or roughage, in the diet, which helps prevent constipation, and avoiding straining during a bowel movement.

Leg Cramps

Many pregnant women experience leg cramps, especially at night, as the pregnancy advances. These are caused by fluxes in the body's electrolyte balance. Specifically, atoms in sodium, calcium and potassium are responsible; the cramps occur when fluxes of these atoms are increased. Blood levels of the substances do not necessarily reflect their activity in the leg muscles; thus, increasing the oral intake of calcium, as is sometimes suggested, may not ease the cramping. A better approach is to do stretching exercises to relax the leg muscles and make them less prone to cramping.

Feelings of Euphoria

For most women, pregnancy is a happy time, and many experience exhilarating feelings of euphoria. These feelings are due both to the anticipation of having a baby and to the increase in steroid hormones. The euphoria all too often turns to depression, or post-partum blues, following the baby's birth. This, too, has a hormonal basis; the sharp drop in estrogen after delivery can cause feelings of depression that are understandably bewildering to the new mother and those around her. Fortunately, the depression is usually temporary (see section on post-partum depression).

Fatigue and Insomnia

Many women experience bursts of energy at different times during pregnancy, interspersed with marked feelings of fatigue, often compounded by insomnia, especially toward the end. There are numerous explanations for these feelings. During the fetal growth spurts and near the end of pregnancy, a woman uses a tremendous amount of energy simply providing for the fast-growing baby. She needs to rest more often, and an afternoon nap may well become necessary simply to get a woman through until an early bedtime. At the same time, many pregnant women are troubled by insomnia. It may be difficult for them to find a comfortable sleeping position, and they no sooner fall asleep than they are wakened by the need to go to the bathroom or by a leg cramp or the baby suddenly kicking and turning. Some women find it helpful to take a walk before going to bed or to do relaxation exercises. Sleeping with extra pillows may make breathing easier. In any event, sleeping pills should be avoided, since these are among the drugs that can cause birth defects.

As term approaches and the baby "drops," most women find they can again breathe normally because the fetus is no longer pressing against the lungs. At this time, many women also experience a renewed burst of energy, especially just before the onset of labor. Accounts of labor beginning while undertaking tasks unthinkable a few weeks earlier—scrubbing the kitchen floor or retiling a bathroom, for example—are common.

Heartburn

Indigestion is another common complaint during pregnancy. During the early stages, it may be related to morning sickness; later, it may be caused by increased abdominal pressure on the stomach, which results in a backup of gases and gastric juices into the esophagus. The problem practically always disappears a day or two after delivery. Eating frequent, small meals and avoiding foods that cause gassiness and acid secretion usually help. Typical foods which aggravate heartburn are coffee, tea, orange juice and piquant spices. A doctor's advice should be sought before taking antacids, and sodium bicarbonate, which increases fluid retention and can cause a rise in blood pressure, should be avoided.

WHAT THE DOCTOR LOOKS FOR
DURING PREGNANCY

Regular medical check-ups are essential during the course of pregnancy. A woman should know what the doctor is checking for and why, and be aware of any warning signs herself that may signal a developing problem. Some of these are obvious, such as vaginal spotting or bleeding, which may signal a miscarriage, or premature contractions, which indicate the onset of early labor. Others are more subtle and need to be checked for by the doctor. These include:

Abnormal Weight Gain

A pregnant woman soon learns that she is weighed every time she visits the doctor's office. Often, she mistakenly thinks the doctor is checking up on whether she has been overeating; in reality, however, he or she is looking for signs of abnormal fluid retention, which may be a sign of developing toxemia. On the other hand, if a woman does not gain weight as she is supposed to, there may be something wrong with the pregnancy.

Blood Pressure

This is measured during every medical visit, and if it is on the high side, a woman may be instructed to measure her own blood pressure periodically at home. Again, rising blood pressure may be a warning sign of toxemia, and needs to be carefully watched because of the dangers it can cause both mother and baby.

It is normal for blood pressure to drop by the second trimester. This drop may be a nuisance to the mother as it can cause dizziness when standing too long, but when the drop does not occur, it is a subtle sign of a blood pressure problem. Normal pressure during pregnancy is less than 120/80 mm. Hg. As more women are becoming pregnant at a later age, elevation of blood pressure has become more common, because high blood pressure is more common as aging occurs. A pregnant woman over the age of thirty-five probably should have her blood pressure checked every two weeks until her third trimester, and weekly thereafter. This frequent surveillance program is best performed by the woman at home with her own blood pressure monitor, thereby avoiding trips to the doctor just for pressure checks. She should be instructed to call her doctor if her pressure is greater than 120/80.

Elevated Blood Sugar and Sugar in the Urine

These are warning signs of gestational diabetes, the leading cause of stillbirths and early neonatal deaths in this country. It is vital that gestational diabetes be detected early in pregnancy, and steps taken to normalize the mother's blood sugar. (This disorder is discussed in detail in the following section on Complications of Pregnancy.)

Fetal Heartbeat and Development

The baby's heartbeat is checked on every visit. The doctor also will do periodic pelvic examinations to check that the baby is growing normally and that the ovaries are smooth and free of cysts. Sometimes, a large cyst develops in the ovaries during pregnancy that can upset the desired hormonal balance.

Other tests that may be performed during pregnancy include:

Sonography

This examination uses sound waves picked up by a microphone to map internal structures. It is useful in determining whether the baby is developing normally and whether there is more than one fetus. Sonography also may be done as the woman approaches her due date to make sure that her pelvic structure is wide enough for a vaginal delivery. Sonography does not expose the baby to radiation and is considered safe, although the long-term effects of sound waves are unknown.

Amniocentesis

This test involves withdrawing a small amount of the amniotic fluid surrounding the fetus and analyzing it for signs of genetic or chromosomal defects. It is done most frequently in older (over age thirty-five) women who have an increased risk of having a baby with Down's syndrome, a chromosomal abnormality that can be detected by amniocentesis. The fluid can also be used to detect Tay Sachs disease and certain other hereditary disorders, but these analyses are not done unless there is reason to believe that the baby may be at risk for them. A newer, still experimental test involves suctioning out a sample of cells shed by the fetus very early in pregnancy and analyzing them for defects. This test, called chorionic villus sampling, carries a somewhat higher risk of causing a miscarriage than amniocentesis, but has the advantage of detecting possible problems earlier in a pregnancy when an elective abortion is easier to do.

COMPLICATIONS OF PREGNANCY

Most women experience an uncomplicated, albeit exciting and eventful, pregnancy followed by normal delivery. But now and then, complications do develop. Increasingly, these can be spotted early and successfully treated. There are, however, inevitable pregnancy losses, often due to gross abnormalities in the fetus. In this sense, a miscarriage is a blessing in disguise, but still a painful experience for the couple. Some of the more common complications of pregnancy include:

Gestational Diabetes

This disorder occurs in two to four percent of all pregnancies in this country, making it our most common medical complication of pregnancy. In many countries, it is even more common; in Mexico, for example, gestational diabetes occurs in more than ten percent of all pregnancies.

As its name implies, gestational diabetes is high blood

sugar that occurs during pregnancy, and then disappears as soon as the baby is born. It is a result of a genetic predisposition to diabetes and the stress of pregnancy.

Even under normal circumstances, pregnancy demands increased insulin production. The increased metabolic needs of pregnancy require extra insulin. The placental hormones estrogen, progesterone and human placental lactogen all are somewhat anti-insulin in nature, and increased insulin is needed to overcome this negative action. In addition, cortisol rises during pregnancy, and this hormone also exerts a marked effect on glucose metabolism by increasing the conversion of glycogen stored in the liver to glucose. Women who are genetically predisposed to diabetes may not be able to handle all these extra demands, and will develop gestational diabetes, usually without any warning or symptoms. The onset is usually during the second trimester. Since the mother's blood sugar levels usually are not high enough to produce the characteristic symptoms of diabetes —excessive thirst and urination, hunger and weight loss—it can go undetected unless the doctor tests for it.

Failure to detect and treat gestational diabetes can lead to very serious problems for the baby. The mother's abnormally high blood sugar is also circulated to the fetus, causing it to produce insulin prematurely and to store the extra sugar as fat. As a result of this constant overnutrition, these babies are abnormally large at birth—often weighing nine or more pounds.

Because of the extra insulin in its blood, the baby often cannot stabilize its own blood glucose levels after birth, and, in many instances, these infants suffer from sudden life-threatening drops in their blood glucose. Gestational diabetes is the major cause of stillbirths in this country. It is also a leading cause of death or serious illness of the baby in the neonatal period. Women who develop gestational diabetes also frequently have later problems; about half will go on to eventually develop Type II diabetes as they age. (See Chapter 10.)

To protect against the fetal hazards of gestational diabetes, all pregnant women should be tested at some point between the twenty-fourth and twenty-eighth weeks of pregnancy. In the past, testing usually was limited to a urine analysis for sugar, but we now know that this is not sufficient to detect gestational diabetes in most instances. Instead of a urine test to screen for diabetes, at this time the woman will be asked to take a sugar drink, and have a blood test one hour after the drink. If her blood sugar reading is higher than 140, she must have a series of hourly blood tests after a second drink on a subsequent day. If two or more of these tests on the second test day are above normal, a diagnosis of gestational diabetes is established. Blood sugar readings on the second test day should be less than:

105—before the sugar drink
195—one hour after the drink
160—two hours after the drink
140—three hours after the drink

If gestational diabetes is diagnosed, the woman should first be put on a special diet to normalize her blood sugar. If diet therapy alone is not sufficient to normalize blood sugar, she will have to take insulin. Several injections of insulin each day are required and the woman must learn how to match her insulin dosage to her food intake and exercise. To ensure that she maintains a normal blood sugar level at all times, she also should be taught a simple home test to measure her own blood glucose. (For more details on how to control blood glucose, see Chapter 10.)

Women who have had gestational diabetes in one pregnancy are likely to develop it in subsequent pregnancies. Not infrequently, undiagnosed gestational diabetes is responsible for a poor obstetrical history—habitual miscarriages; stillbirths; toxemia; large, sick babies; or recurrent urinary tract infections. A woman at high risk of diabetes—i.e., with a family history of the disease, obesity, gestational diabetes in a previous pregnancy, poor pregnancy outcomes, or birthweights more than nine pounds—should be tested for gestational diabetes several times during pregnancy.

Hypertension

High blood pressure is an age-old complication of pregnancy, but one that is more easily detected and controlled today than in the past. If a woman has high blood pressure before pregnancy, she should talk to her doctor about the medication she is taking and the special risks she may encounter in trying to have a baby. Increasingly, women with hypertension are having normal pregnancies, but the babies are apt to be smaller than usual because the blood supply to the fetus is somewhat less than normal. Complications such as a partially detached placenta (placental abruption), and toxemia, a potentially life-threatening disorder for both the mother and fetus, are more common among women with hypertension.

Dizziness and Fainting

Many pregnant women experience dizziness or faint feelings, especially during the third trimester. This is caused by a pooling of blood in the legs, and also by lowered blood pressure. Women should avoid getting out of bed too quickly, or standing up abruptly after bending over or sitting down.

Urinary Tract Infections

Women who are prone to cystitis or kidney infections are especially susceptible to them during pregnancy. The expanding uterus puts extra pressure on the urinary bladder, and may impede the flow of urine. Sometimes a developing urinary infection may go unnoticed because pregnant women experience an increased need to urinate. But any burning, blood in the urine or other signs of infection should be checked promptly by a doctor, and treated with the appropriate antibiotic. Some antibiotics, such as tetracycline and sulfa drugs, should not be taken during pregnancy, but there are safe alternatives. Letting the infection go untreated poses a threat to both mother and baby.

Herpes

Some women have the mistaken idea that herpes inevitably means problems for the baby, or at least, that she must have the baby by cesarean section. This is not the case, although a woman with genital herpes does need to exercise certain precautions. A cesarean is necessary only if she shows signs of an active herpes virus near the time of delivery. The doctor should check her frequently during the last month of pregnancy, and if there is an active flare-up, then vaginal delivery is too risky for the baby and a cesarean should be performed. Otherwise, women with herpes can experience normal vaginal deliveries.

Placenta Previa

In this disorder, the placenta is implanted low in the uterus and covers part or all of the cervical opening. As pregnancy progresses and the cervix begins to thin out and dilate, the placental attachment to the uterus is disturbed and bleeding may occur. In some women, this is mild and the pregnancy proceeds without undue problems. In others, however, the bleeding may be profuse and require hospitalization and transfusions and, if the placenta covers all or most of the cervix, a cesarean delivery.

Premature Labor

Prematurity is the major cause of death and serious disability in the newborn. Although tremendous advances have been made in treating and saving premature babies, the cost, both economically and emotionally, is great and large numbers of very premature babies are left with lifelong physical and mental handicaps. Thus, a major goal of pregnancy is to deliver the baby at term—both too early and too late are detrimental.

Sometimes prematurity is caused by a weak, or incompetent, cervix. In this condition, the cervix is abnormally dilated and, when the fetus reaches a certain size (usually in the second trimester), a miscarriage takes place. This can be prevented by sewing the cervix shut early in the pregnancy; the stitches are then removed with the onset of labor and normal delivery can proceed.

The causes of premature labor are poorly understood, mainly because it is not known precisely what initiates labor, even at term. Premature labor happens in about five percent of all pregnancies. Of course, the risk for the baby depends upon how premature the labor is; of the babies born after twenty-eight weeks of gestation, by which time they weigh slightly less than two pounds, about half survive, provided they have intensive treatment in a neonatal unit. If the baby weighs three pounds, the chances of survival rise to ninety percent.

The first sign of premature labor is usually uterine contractions. Sometimes there is vaginal bleeding or an increase in vaginal discharge; in about twenty to thirty percent of cases, there is a premature rupture of the membranes, or amniotic sac.

If at all possible, steps should be taken to halt premature contractions unless the pregnancy is close enough to term to ensure that the baby's lungs are sufficiently developed to sustain normal breathing. The woman should contact her doctor immediately. Bed rest, sometimes for the remainder of the pregnancy, is mandatory. In addition, there are two possible ways to halt the contractions. Ritodrine (Yutopar) is a drug that stops premature contractions. Typically, the woman will be admitted to the hospital and a high dose of ritodrine will be given intravenously. After the contractions have stopped and the woman appears stable, she may be sent home and continue taking the drug in pill form.

Although the use of ritodrine has lowered the mortality rate from prematurity, it can be used in only about twenty-five percent of cases. The drug should not be taken by women with heart disease or certain other conditions, including toxemia, uncontrolled high blood pressure, or asthma that is being treated with a similar drug or with steroids. Ritodrine causes a rise in blood sugar; thus, if it is necessary to use this drug in a diabetic woman, the insulin doses need to be increased, sometimes even doubled. In addition, ritodrine causes a drop in potassium levels. Other possible side effects include increased pulse rate, palpitations, feelings of nervousness, nausea and vomiting, tremor and a skin rash. Although unpleasant, the side effects usually can be tolerated, especially with the knowledge that they are temporary and the baby's chances for survival are improving the longer the pregnancy can continue. Terbutaline (Brethine) is a drug similar to ritodrine which has also been used to treat premature labor.

Alcohol will relax the uterus, and taking a stiff drink of whiskey, gin or some other alcoholic beverage every few hours may be recommended for women experiencing premature contractions. Some women question this strategy since they have been cautioned not to drink alcoholic beverages during a pregnancy because of the possibility of causing congenital abnormalities. Since the baby is fully formed, this amount of alcohol will not cause birth defects. Premature labor is an instance in which the benefits of the use of alcohol outweigh the possible hazards to the fetus.

LABOR AND DELIVERY

As noted earlier, it is not known what initiates labor. Labor can be induced by giving a woman an infusion of the hormone oxytocin at or near term. At one time, it was thought that this hormone, which is produced by the pituitary gland, initiated labor, but further studies indicate that it acts more as a messenger to promote the progression of labor rather than one that actually starts it.

Animal studies seem to indicate that the signal starting labor may come from the fetus itself. (See Figure 13.) This has led to the theory that, when the fetal brain, pituitary and adrenal glands reach a certain stage of maturity, they produce hormones that are secreted into the fetal membranes,

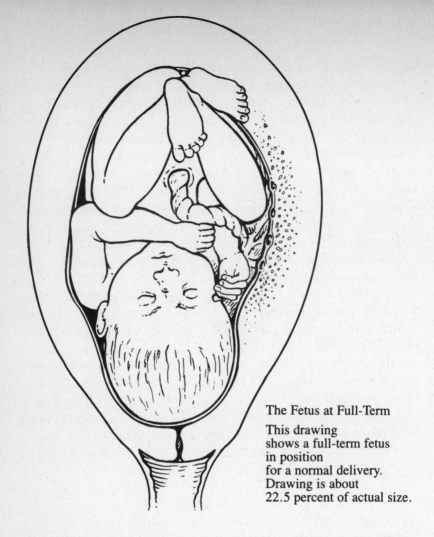

The Fetus at Full-Term

This drawing
shows a full-term fetus
in position
for a normal delivery.
Drawing is about
22.5 percent of actual size.

leading to an increased production of prostaglandins, which in turn soften the cervix and cause uterine contractions. While this theory may hold for some animal species, it is not clear that it applies to humans. Prostaglandins clearly play a key role in labor, but what prompts their increased production is unknown. Some researchers suggest that increased estrogen and lowered progesterone are factors.

Others speculate that the excessive stretching of the uterus and fetal membranes as pregnancy reaches term results in increased prostaglandins. Before the actual onset of labor, women experience painless contractions of the uterus. These are called Braxton-Hicks contractions, and are sometimes confused with the onset of labor. They produce a hardening of the uterus, similar to what occurs during labor contractions, but they do not become increasingly intense or frequent or change the character of the cervix. Braxton-Hicks contractions "prime" the uterus and soften the cervix in preparation for labor. Some researchers think that these contractions may increase prostaglandin production in the uterus and initiate labor.

Labor itself is divided into three stages. The first stage, which is characterized by the rhythmic contractions of the uterine muscle and gradual opening or dilation of the cervix, is usually heralded by the "show," the discharge of the mucous plug that has helped hold the cervix closed during pregnancy. There also may be a rush of water, signaling a rupture of the membranes. In the beginning, the contractions are usually mild and last ten to twenty seconds and may be twenty to thirty minutes apart.

As labor progresses and the cervix opens, the contractions become stronger and more frequent. Toward the end of this stage, the contractions may last up to fifty seconds, and be only a minute or two apart, until the cervix is fully dilated, or open, signaling the end of the first stage of labor. In all, this stage usually lasts twelve to fourteen hours, but may be longer with first babies and shorter in subsequent deliveries.

The second stage begins after the cervix is fully dilated and continues until the baby is born. After the cervix is fully dilated, the contractions are not as painful and the woman gets a "second wind." This is fortunate because now, after hours of enduring painful, but involuntary muscle work, the woman is asked to work with her voluntary muscles until the baby is born. The woman will be asked to push or bear down to help move the baby through the birth canal. The pushing effort must be exquisitely timed with contractions. The doctor, midwife, nurse or partner should help coach the woman, telling her when to push and when to rest and breathe deeply in between pushes. In the first stage of labor, breathing exercises are used to lessen the perception of pain; in the second stage, the woman needs to breathe deeply to fill her lungs for the period when she is pushing and not breathing.

By this time, many women are tired and find it difficult to push as instructed. It's a poor time to try to be a good student. Before the onset of labor, the woman's doctor or midwife should give her detailed instructions of what to expect and also, what will be expected of her. Most women find labor preparation classes and having a partner on hand to help coach her through labor and delivery helpful.

An episiotomy—an incision that usually goes from the vagina toward the rectum, may be done to prevent tearing of the skin and to shorten the second stage of labor. In the normal birth sequence, the baby's head emerges first, preferably facing downward. After the head has emerged, it is turned sideways, and the shoulders and the rest of the body quickly follow. The umbilical cord, which attaches the baby to the placenta, is clamped and cut. The baby usually takes a breath and begins to cry loudly on its own; sometimes a small catheter will be needed to gently suction the baby's nose and mouth to permit it to breathe. Within the first minute or so, the baby will be carefully checked to make sure that it is breathing properly and everything is normal. The baby may then be passed to the mother or placed in a bassinet.

The third and final stage of labor entails the delivery of the afterbirth, or placenta. This usually happens within a few minutes after the baby is born; if not, the doctor may have to remove it. If an episiotomy was made, it will then be stitched shut. The woman also may be given a shot of the hormone oxytocin to stimulate further uterine contractions and help stop the bleeding.

SPECIAL CONSIDERATIONS

In the last decade, there has been increased emphasis on so-called natural childbirth, a term that has come to describe delivery without anesthesia, forceps or other aids. Obviously, childbirth is a natural event, and there is some merit to arguments that a delivery free of anesthesia, forceps or a vacuum extractor may be safer for the baby. But there are instances in which these aids are needed, and a woman should not feel that she has somehow "failed" because she needed a painkiller or that the baby needed extra help in being born.

Fetal Monitoring

Early in labor, an external fetal monitor is usually attached to the baby and will remain in place until the baby is born. The monitor consists of a microphone to monitor the baby's heart rate and to measure the uterine contractions. The monitor will alert the doctor if there is a sudden drop in the baby's heart rate—a sign that the baby may be in trouble and that delivery should take place immediately.

Some advocates of "natural" childbirth object to fetal monitoring. In reality, the monitor does not interfere with normal labor and delivery. The mother is hardly aware that the monitor is in place and it offers added protection for the fetus in case something does go wrong.

Cesarean Section

Most cesarean sections are unplanned and are performed at the last minute because the baby or mother are in distress or some other problem develops that makes surgical delivery safer. In other instances, a cesarean may be planned almost from the outset of pregnancy because it is clear that a vaginal delivery will be unsafe. Increasingly, cesarean sections are done with a local anesthetic (an epidural block) so the mother can be awake for the delivery of her baby. Some hospitals also permit the father in the operating room during a cesarean.

At one time it was felt that if a woman had one cesarean, all her subsequent babies must be born by cesarean. Today, this is not necessarily true. Depending upon the type of incision on the uterus and the reason for the first cesarean, it is possible that future babies may be delivered vaginally. Therefore, a woman should ask for a copy of her hospital record, which will tell what type of incision she has on her uterus, so her doctor can determine if a future vaginal delivery is feasible. The scar on the abdomen does not necessarily reflect what type of incision was used on the uterus. A horizontal incision on the lower part of the uterus is less likely to rupture during a subsequent labor than the classic vertical one. Women who have this type of cesarean incision may be able to have a safe vaginal delivery, provided that the reasons for the first cesarean no longer apply.

In recent years, there has been a marked increase in the number of cesarean deliveries. Critics charge that many of these cesareans are unnecessary, and undoubtedly, some of them are. Cesareans today are safer than in the past, and some doctors feel that if there is any doubt about a vaginal delivery, it is better to opt for a cesarean. Fetal monitoring is better able to detect a baby in distress than in the past, and perhaps has contributed to the increase in cesareans.

The rise in malpractice suits over problems that arise during childbirth, such as brain damage due to a lack of oxygen, also is a factor; if a problem is suspected, the doctor is likely to go ahead with a cesarean rather than take a chance. For example, in the past, a breech position was not necessarily an indication for a cesarean; the doctor would try to turn the baby or do a breech delivery. Today, many obstetricians will not take the chance on a breech delivery and will do a cesarean instead.

Before selecting an obstetrician, it is a good idea for a woman to ask the doctor his or her approach to cesareans: Do you get a second opinion before doing a cesarean in nonemergency situations? (If the woman is hemorrhaging or the baby is in distress, obviously there is no time or need to get a second opinion.) What do you consider indications for a cesarean? Do you allow a woman who has had a previous cesarean to attempt a vaginal delivery? Answers to these questions give an indication of a doctor's attitude on cesareans.

In considering the possibilities of a cesarean, it is important to realize that ninety-five percent of the time, everything goes as planned and a woman can have a normal vaginal delivery. In three to five percent of cases, however, there are problems in which a cesarean is a better choice. Undoubtedly, some of these women would be able to deliver their babies if labor were allowed to proceed, while others would encounter major, even life-threatening problems. Although a cesarean is disappointing to a couple who has planned a vaginal delivery, and also entails a longer recuperation and greater risk of complications for the mother, not many doctors or parents want to take any chance that may be a risk to the baby.

Induced Labor

Artificial induction of labor is not as common today as in the past, but there are times when it should be done. For example, if a woman goes a week beyond her due date and there is no sign of labor, it may be induced. Just as it is in the best interest of the fetus not to be born too soon, it also is preferable not to let the baby go more than a few days beyond the due date. As pregnancy reaches its full term, the placenta begins to age, and the baby may not get adequate nutrition.

Some obstetricians will advise sexual intercourse as pregnancy nears term because the prostaglandins in the seminal fluid may help soften the cervix and promote uterine contractions. In the past, couples often were advised to avoid sex during the last part of pregnancy because of fears of infection. We now know that sex does not lead to infection, unless, of course, the membranes have been ruptured or the man has an infection that can be sexually transmitted. Sex also should be avoided if the woman is threatening premature labor; otherwise, it is safe and even advisable.

If indicated, labor can be induced by administering oxytocin, provided that pregnancy is full-term. Sometimes a gel containing prostaglandins may be inserted into the vagina to soften the cervix before giving oxytocin. An injection of oxytocin also may be given if labor seems to be slowing down or stalling; labor that goes on and on, but is not producing increased dilation of the cervix can pose serious problems for the baby. Even under normal circumstances, uterine contractions temporarily decrease the blood supply to the baby. This is acceptable if the contractions are producing progressive labor, but if they are not and are allowed to go on too long, the baby may experience too much oxygen deprivation.

If a woman who has had a previous cesarean section and is now planning a vaginal delivery goes beyond her due date, she may have to have another cesarean, even if all else appears normal. It is not safe to induce labor with oxytocin in this situation because it produces very strong uterine contractions and raises the risk of rupture of the uterus at the old scar site.

HORMONAL CHANGES FOLLOWING DELIVERY

During pregnancy, the placenta has served as a hormone-making factory, turning off the ovaries and pituitary from their normal hormonal roles. After delivery, a woman's hormonal state is comparable to that following menopause. Before her normal hormonal function returns, a woman may experience many of the symptoms commonly associated with menopause: hot flashes, sweating, irritability, mood swings and depression, among others.

Many women and their husbands are bewildered by these symptoms, especially the post-partum depression. A woman has experienced nine months of joyful anticipation of having a baby; now the baby is here, and the mother finds herself bursting into tears or feeling sad for no apparent reason. If she understands that these feelings have a hormonal rather than psychological basis, she may find it easier to cope. In rare instances, the depression becomes so severe that it requires treatment. Traditionally, doctors treat this severe post-partum depression with powerful drugs, such as chlorpromazine (Thorazine), instead of looking on it as an endocrine disorder that could be treated hormonally.

Fortunately, in most instances, the nonpregnant body adjusts to its new hormone state in a few days and the post-partum blues and other such symptoms subside to a more manageable state. But the body will require several months to resume its prepregnancy functions. It usually takes several weeks for the uterus to fully heal and for post-delivery bleeding to fully stop.

Biblical law offers an interesting insight into ancient observations and views concerning the post-partum period. The laws of Moses stipulate that, after having a boy, a woman shall be separated from society for seven days—the period of her infirmity—but on the eight day she can return for the ceremonial circumcision of the baby. However, she cannot have sexual relations with her husband for another thirty-three days. By this time, the uterus should be healed and the danger of infection past.

The situation is quite different if the woman has a girl: "Then she shall be unclean two weeks, as in her separation; and she shall continue in the blood of her purifying threescore and six days." (Lev. 12:5.) Although the Bible does not explain why a woman should be separated for eighty days after having a girl and forty for a boy, it seems reasonable to assume that it might have stemmed from observations regarding post-partum depression and maternal bonding. Giving birth to a boy was honored much more than having a girl. Since it would be unkind to banish a mother from her son's circumcision, she was allowed to return to society as soon as she had recovered from childbirth. But she still could not have sexual relations because of her bleeding, which the ancients associated with unwellness (infection?).

The period of separation was longer for a girl, to give the mother a chance to adjust to the fact that she had not had a boy, and to bond with the baby. When she returned to society, she still may have been chided for having a girl, but after a longer period alone with her baby, she would be more oblivious to the derision. Similarly, the longer separation from her husband would give him time to get over the fact that she had had a girl instead of a boy, and be more accepting of his wife.

Menstruation usually resumes in three or four months, but if a woman nurses, the high levels of prolactin needed to make breast milk act to suppress ovulation, so a woman may not have her period for six months. Undoubtedly, ancient wise men took note of this fact, and, in some societies, women nurse their babies far longer than is necessary as a means of birth control. Among some African societies, for example, a woman may nurse for three or more years and, during this time, she and her baby live apart from her husband, who may have several wives.

Bones and ligaments may require several months to regain their prepregnancy strength. For this reasons, doctors advise that women use caution in resuming vigorous exercise programs. Toning exercises, such as modified sit-ups, leg-lifts and Kegel exercises to improve bladder control and tone the vaginal muscles can start shortly after childbirth. But vigorous exercises, such as jogging, should be approached cautiously. All women are different, however, and this is an instance in which a woman should take cues from her body. If an exercise hurts, it's an indication to ease up and work up gradually.

Many women are distressed to find that when they come home from the hospital, they still have to wear maternity clothes. It often takes several months for a woman to regain her trim, prepregnancy figure. Toning exercises to strengthen sagging abdominal muscles will help, but a flat stomach doesn't return overnight.

Weight gained during pregnancy also may be difficult to shed, especially if a woman breast-feeds. On average, a woman can expect to very quickly lose twenty pounds following delivery, since this is the normal weight gain to support the pregnancy plus the weight of the baby (nine pounds for the baby, placenta and membranes; two pounds of amniotic fluid; three and a half pounds for extra fluid; one pound in breast enlargement; two and a half pounds in the enlarged uterus; and two pounds of extra body fluid). But the average recommended weight gain during pregnancy is twenty-five to thirty pounds, so many women find they have a few extra pounds to shed to achieve their pre-pregnancy weight. Women who breast-feed find this particularly hard to do, for several reasons. The oxytocin acts as an antidiuretic hormone to help the body conserve salt and water, which is needed to make milk. The satiety center in the brain responds to the body's need for extra food to feed the baby by sending out stronger hunger messages. As a result, most women find they have a ravenous appetite during breast-feeding, and that it takes almost superhuman will power to reduce food intake at this time. Since breast-feeding should be a happy time for both mother and baby, it may be a good idea to postpone trying to lose those few extra pounds until after the baby is weaned.

Menstruation usually resumes in three to six months, although it may take a month or two longer for women who breast-feed. The most common cause for failure to resume menstruation is another pregnancy; many women mistakenly think that if they breast-feed or have not yet had a period, they are safe from getting pregnant. This is not necessarily true, and if a woman wants to avoid pregnancy, she should practice birth control as soon as she resumes sexual relations.

Sometimes pituitary dysfunction is the cause of a woman's failure to resume menstruation. In these circumstances, hormone therapy may be needed to "wake up" the pituitary and restart normal menstrual cycles. Typically, the body will be depleted of estrogen because the ovaries have not been functioning. This can be overcome by giving estrogen replacement, followed by clomiphene to get the pituitary to release its hormones, which in turn will prompt the ovaries to start working again. After ovulation takes place, the monthly cycles should be reestablished.

PRACTICAL POINTERS

Almost from the moment of birth, a woman establishes a very special bonding with her baby. Recent studies confirm the importance of letting the mother hold and react with her newborn infant immediately after delivery. In instances where this is not possible—for example, cases in which the baby requires special treatment in a neonatal unit, sometimes at another hospital—other steps should be taken to let the mother hold or help care for the baby.

A number of other important decisions need to be made, either before or just after the baby is born. These include whether or not to breast-feed. Although modern formulas provide adequate nutrition, most pediatricians agree that breast-feeding, if only for a short time, is superior. Almost all women are capable of breast-feeding, but there may be circumstances that prevent it, or a woman may simply choose not to nurse. If this is the case, a woman may be given an injection of male hormones to "dry up" the breasts. These hormones will not have a lasting effect, but will halt milk production. Women who do not want to breast-feed, or who are trying to wean a baby, also should avoid breast stimulation for a few days.

Picking a pediatrician is another important decision that should be made either before or shortly after a baby is born. It is vital that parents have good rapport with a pediatrician, and feel comfortable calling him or her at any time. It is not necessary to pick a famous specialist, unless the baby is born with a problem. Instead, a pediatrician is someone who can help parents manage the inevitable day-to-day problems: what to do when the baby has a cold or colic or a bout of diarrhea. If a parent feels intimidated by the pediatrician—for example, being reluctant to wake him or her at three A.M. because the baby is sick—then it is not the right doctor. The important criteria in picking a pediatrician is whether or not the doctor will listen to a parent, ask the right questions, and judge what action should be taken. The primary pediatrician may not feel qualified to treat a serious or complicated problem, but will have a sufficient back-up system to make the proper referral. In short, parents with a normal, healthy baby do not need a noted pediatric cardiologist or other specialist; instead, they need a doctor who will listen and give them the day-to-day support and information they need to be good parents.

SUMMING UP

Pregnancy is a major milestone in any woman's life. It is also a time when her entire endocrine system undergoes profound change directed toward producing a healthy baby. Knowing what to expect and warning signs of possible problems further ensure that this goal will be met.

Chapter 6

Menopause

MENOPAUSE IS A WORD THAT MOST OF US DON'T EVEN LIKE
to utter. Women anticipate it with apprehension; both sexes
mistakenly regard it as a sign that a woman is "over the hill."
Fortunately, these attitudes are changing as an increasing
number of women in their fifties and beyond are demonstrating that they can hold their own in the boardroom and
the bedroom. Indeed, many of the world's most influential
and glamorous women are fifty and older. A few years ago,
when Gloria Steinem celebrated her fiftieth birthday, someone told her she did not look her age. Instead of the usual
response of "why, thank you," she quipped: "Well, I am fifty,
and this is what it looks like!"

Popularly referred to as "the change," menopause is the
stage in a woman's life during which ovulation and menstruation cease, thus marking the end of her reproductive years.
Menopause is also referred to as the female climacteric, a
term derived from the Greek word meaning "top rung of
the ladder." Although doctors assign a medical meaning to
climacteric, it has more of a psychosocial connotation than a
clinical one, and it highlights the fact that menopause is
both a biological and a sociological/emotional event. In discussing menopause, it is often difficult to separate the two.

Traditionally, menopause has been associated with endings—the end of menstruation, of childbearing, of youth and attractiveness—and the beginning of old age. However, as we move through life, our perspective of what is "old" changes dramatically.

To a young girl, age twenty seems like the beginning of being old. When she becomes a teenager, she changes her mind, and decides that thirty heralds the start of old age. As she celebrates her thirtieth birthday, she realizes that she is still very young and, once again, she readjusts her sights— this time labeling menopause as the time when her old age will begin. Happily, when menopause arrives, she finds she can be just as energetic, sexy and receptive to new adventures as she was at each of the preceding landmarks.

All of us change with experience and the passage of time, but no longer do we look upon menopause as heralding old age, as did our grandmothers or great-grandmothers. At the turn of the century, the average age of menopause was forty-six, and a woman's average life expectancy was fifty-one years. Today, the average age of menopause is about fifty-one, and a woman's expected life span has advanced to seventy-eight. So, when a woman enters menopause in the 1980s, she can anticipate that a third of her life still lies ahead.

Obviously, menopause is no longer the end point it once was; instead, it is the end of the reproductive years, and a continuation of productive life. This does not negate the fact that a woman does encounter change with menopause, and that these changes often bring troublesome symptoms and physical and emotional problems. Still, new insight and understanding can minimize the symptoms and emotional trauma.

The biological impact of menopause does not happen overnight; it is a gradual process that covers five to ten years, during which the ovarian function slows down and then stops completely. At birth, a baby girl has about two million follicles, or egg-forming cells, in her ovaries. Over the years, most of these follicles wither and die. By the time of puberty, about 300,000 follicles will be left; from then on, one or two of these follicles will mature, or ripen, during each menstrual cycle, and others will die. As a woman approaches menopause, she will have only about 8,000 remaining follicles. Even though the pituitary produces more follicle-stimulating hormone with each cycle, ovulation does not always take place. Thus, no progesterone, which is secreted following rupture of the egg from its follicle, will be produced, and this results in a change in the nature of the menstrual period.

It is important to remember that natural (as opposed to surgical) menopause is not a single event or an illness; instead it is a gradual process that is divided into three stages. The first is premenopause, during which the ovaries gradually decrease their function. Periods become irregular; in most women they are more infrequent, but others find they may have two periods two or three weeks apart, then go six or eight weeks without one.

The menstrual flow itself changes. Most women notice that their periods are lighter and more watery, with less clotlike substances. This is due to reduced progesterone. Others find they have a very heavy flow for one or two days, then several days of thin spotting. (Several days of spotting before menstruation also may be a sign of premenopause.) Still other women will have very heavy bleeding. All of these are consistent with a decline in ovarian function and changing hormonal levels, but not all women will experience them.

The second stage is menopause itself. Ovarian function declines further and periods stop completely. After a woman has gone for a full year without menstruating, menopause is complete and she enters the postmenopausal stage of life. The term "perimenopausal" is used to describe all three stages.

About 1.5 million American women enter menopause each year. The age at which this happens varies widely. Some women begin menopause in their early forties, others not until their mid-fifties. The average age for menopause among American women is now fifty-one, and by the age of fifty-five, ninety-five percent of women have gone through menopause. Just as the onset of menarche has been occurring in recent decades at younger ages among women in industrialized countries, menopause is happening at increasingly later ages. It is difficult to predict when menopause will occur, but generally, daughters of women who had an early natural menopause can expect to follow suit, and the same is true of a family history of late menopause.

SYMPTOMS ASSOCIATED WITH MENOPAUSE

Menopause varies from woman to woman. Some are barely aware of it until they suddenly realize that several months have passed since their last menstrual period. At the other extreme, some women suffer from frequent, almost incapacitating hot flashes, night sweats, depression, mood swings, irritability, insomnia and other symptoms which may continue for several years. Most women fall somewhere in between, but regardless of the lack or severity of symptoms, all women experience a marked change in hormonal status as they proceed through menopause.

Menopause may be accompanied by a wide range of symptoms, most of which are related to hormonal changes. (See Table 5.) As the ovaries cease to function, they no longer produce estrogen. In response, the pituitary sends out more luteinizing hormone (LH) and follicle-stimulating hormone (FSH) in a futile attempt to stimulate the ovaries into action.

Often, irregular or skipped periods are the first signs of menopause. Not uncommonly, a woman who misses one or two periods and has no other symptoms may think she is pregnant and use an at-home urine test. These tests are more likely to give a false positive result in women approaching menopause than in younger women, so further testing is needed before making the assumption that pregnancy is the reason for the lack of menstruation.

Although menopausal symptoms are frequently attrib-

Table 5. SYMPTOMS AND SIGNS ASSOCIATED WITH MENOPAUSE

Autonomic

Hot flashes
Sweating, including night sweats
Heart palpitations
Itching

Physical/Metabolic

Cessation of menstrual periods
Vaginal dryness, itching, shrinking
Bladder dysfunction, including incontinence
Bone thinning
Atherosclerosis
Bloating
Weight gain
Headaches
Joint pain and degeneration
Muscular weakness
Shrinking and sagging of breast tissue
Skin drying, wrinkling
Thinning of scalp and pubic hair; growth of facial hair (hirsutism)
Brittle, slow-growing and grooved nails

Psychological

Mood swings
Irritability
Depression
Insomnia
Anxiety or apprehension
Forgetfulness
Changes in sexual function and desire

uted to a lack of estrogen, in some women estrogen plays an indirect role, with the symptoms actually due to the high levels of LH or FSH.

Hot Flashes

A recent survey of women going through menopause found that three out of four experienced hot flashes, making them the most common menopausal symptom. During a hot flash, a woman experiences a sudden rush of heat to her upper body, starting in the chest area and rapidly spreading to the face, neck and arms. The skin reddens, her heart beats faster and breathing becomes more shallow. In some women, the hot flashes are accompanied by an itching sensation. As the episode passes, the woman will then begin to sweat, sometimes profusely. Afterwards, she may feel chilly and drained. The episode usually lasts for only a few minutes, and although the woman herself is very conscious of what is happening, people with her may not notice anything unusual.

Medically, hot flashes are referred to as vasomotor instability. They originate in the temperature-regulating center of the hypothalamus, and, for susceptible women, it appears that almost anything that affects temperature can trigger a hot flash. Many women report they feel a sudden chill just before a hot flash; others find it can be triggered by exercise, stress, entering a warm or cool room or lying under a blanket in bed. The temperature center incorrectly interprets the body as being too cool and sends out signals to constrict the small blood vessels in the skin, which then elevates temperature. Since the body really is not cold, it responds by opening the blood vessels in an attempt to cool down. This causes the rush of blood to the upper body and face.

Hot flashes are now thought to be due more to the rise in LH than to a lack of estrogen, although the precise mechanism is unknown. Studies have found, however, that women who were born without ovaries or women whose ovaries have never functioned do not experience hot flashes; however, if they are given estrogen, they may have hot flashes when it is withdrawn. It also has been well established that hot flashes can be stopped by taking replacement estrogen. The net result is that it does not matter whether the symptoms are due to low estrogen or high LH or FSH.

Some women never experience hot flashes at all, while others may have several each day or even every hour; still others experience them only at night. Night sweats are similar to those that may occur following childbirth—a time of abrupt hormonal change. Typically, the woman wakes up in a drenching sweat. They may happen several times in a single night, and may be responsible for the insomnia experienced during menopause.

For most women, the hot flashes end in three to five years, after the body has adjusted to its altered hormonal state. Again, their period of duration is unpredictable—in some women, they last for only a few months, while others may have them for five or more years. Sometimes the hot flashes end and then reappear years later. (Interestingly, older men also may experience hot flashes.)

Although hot flashes can be halted by taking estrogen, there are some women for whom hormone replacement therapy is contraindicated or who would prefer not to use it. If hot flashes are a problem, the symptoms may be minimized by such commonsense measures as wearing several layers of light clothing so some can be shed if the need arises, and, if possible, taking a tepid shower. Caffeine and alcohol seem to aggravate the symptoms in some women and should be avoided if they trigger hot flashes. Some medications, such as certain drugs used to treat high blood pressure, also may aggravate the vasomotor instability. If this is the case, an alternative medicine may be prescribed. Large doses of niacin, or nicotinic acid—a B vitamin that some people take in large amounts to lower cholesterol— also precipitate hot flashes. (In fact, men on high doses of niacin often say, after having a few hot flashes themselves, that they suddenly understand why women are troubled by them.)

Vaginal Symptoms

Vaginal itching and other changes are troubling symptoms experienced by many women. Vaginal symptoms usually do not appear until several years after menopause, and they are a direct result of a lack of estrogen. The vulvar skin, fat and tissues are particularly sensitive to estrogen; when hormone levels drop, the skin and tissues begin to atrophy or shrink. The external genitalia become smaller and pubic hair thins. The vagina also shrinks, and the tissue lining it thins out. Vaginal secretions become less acid and make the woman more prone to vaginitis, resulting in burning and itching. Many women also find that sexual intercourse becomes painful—a particularly distressing symptom since so many women worry that they will lose their sexual appeal as they grow older.

Studies have found that the vaginal symptoms are not as pronounced in women who have frequent intercourse and/or orgasms (defined as intercourse three or more times a month and orgasm at least once a week). Of course, this may be difficult for some women who lack sexual partners, or who already are troubled by vaginal symptoms. Sometimes the itching, burning and painful intercourse can be relieved by using a lubricating cream or ointment such as K-Y jelly. But, often, estrogen is needed, taken either orally or in the form of a cream, suppository or skin patch.

Urinary Tract

Lack of estrogen may cause changes in the urethra and urinary bladder, making a woman more vulnerable to cystitis. A tipping of the urinary bladder—usually the result of muscle weakness or damage from earlier childbirth—may exacerbate stress incontinence or other bladder control problems.

Palpitations

Many women complain of a rapid heartbeat, or palpitations, during menopause. Sometimes the palpitations accompany hot flashes, but, at other times, they occur independently. The rapid heartbeat is believed to be caused by the same vasomotor irregularity that triggers the hot flashes. The palpitations are harmless, but can be frightening and troubling. If palpitations are troublesome, they usually can be stopped by taking a low dose of a beta blocker, a drug that is often prescribed to treat angina and high blood pressure.

Mood Swings

Periods of irritability, crying spells, depression and other mood changes are common during menopause. Doctors debate whether these are due to organic causes or are rooted in emotional upheavals that a woman may be experiencing at this time. It may well be a combination of the two. Middle age is a time of change and reassessment for both men and women. By this time, children are growing up and leaving home. Career opportunities may be dwindling or at least leveling off. People also begin to notice undeniable signs of getting older: Parents age and die, the mirror reveals new wrinkles and graying hair, and they no longer have the stamina of youth. Coming to terms with these changes can be depressing, especially in today's youth-oriented society.

Still, it is doubtful that the mood swings are solely emotional. Many women liken the feelings to those they experienced immediately after childbirth, when the abrupt hormonal changes were similar to those of menopause. Others compare them to premenstrual symptoms.

Bloating

Many women complain of abdominal bloating, often accompanied by intestinal gas. The swelling is caused by fluid retention, and is similar to premenstrual bloating or that which occurs in early pregnancy.

Premenstrual and pregnancy bloating are attributed to a rise in progesterone; it is not known, however, what causes the bloating during menopause, since progesterone levels are reduced at that time. It is probably due to hormonal changes, but the precise mechanism is unknown. Reducing salt intake may help; avoiding tight-fitting clothing and foods that provoke intestinal gas also can lessen the discomfort. If the bloating persists or is troublesome, a mild diuretic may be prescribed.

Weight Gain

At about the time of menopause, most women notice that they are adding a few extra pounds. This added weight often is centered around the abdomen, leading to the so-called middle-aged spread.

There are several reasons for the tendency to gain weight at this time. As we grow older, our metabolism slows down and we do not burn up as many calories as before. Most people do not adjust their food intake according to their lowered energy needs, so, unless they increase their physical activity, they will gain weight without eating more.

This added weight tends to be concentrated in the abdominal area because fat here is more mobile. Recent studies have found that people with excessive abdominal fat have higher levels of blood cholesterol, blood glucose and a greater risk of heart attack than people with less fat or whose fat is concentrated in other parts of the body.

Poor muscle tone also may add to abdominal sagging. Women who have had children are particularly susceptible to this; pregnancy stretches these abdominal muscles. Toning exercises can bring them back into shape, but many women neglect these exercises after pregnancy. As they lose weight, they become less conscious of their sagging muscles, only to rediscover them years later when they add a few extra pounds.

Finally, estrogen causes weight gain in some women. Birth control pills with a relatively high estrogen content cause weight gain in some women; similarly, estrogen replacement therapy during menopause can have the same effect. But even women who do not take estrogen tend to gain abdominal weight. This is believed to be due to androgens, which promote abdominal fat deposits in both men and women.

Sexuality

Some women find that menopause decreases their interest in and enjoyment of sex, while others find that their sexual desire and responsiveness increases. These changes are likely due to a combination of psychological and hormonal factors. At about this time of life, many women experience loss of a sexual partner, either through death or divorce. Or a partner may be going through his own midlife crisis or have other problems that reduce his sexual interest or capabilities. As is so often emphasized, sexuality is a fragile thing that requires considerable attention and practice to keep alive and exciting. Thus, it is virtually impossible to separate the physical and emotional aspects of sex; many of the sexual complaints that accompany menopause may well have both a psychological and hormonal basis.

Loss of estrogen causes dryness and thinning of vaginal tissue, which may result in painful intercourse. Obviously, this will negate any pleasure, and many couples find they avoid sex simply because it is uncomfortable for the woman.

Contraception and worries about possible pregnancy also may be a factor. Although fertility is lessened as ovulation becomes more infrequent, so long as a woman is ovulating, pregnancy is possible.

Selecting an appropriate form of birth control can be troubling for an older woman. Sterilization is now the most common form of birth control used by married couples in this country. But there are millions of others who rely on reversible methods, with the pill being the most popular. Many doctors feel, however, that women over the age of forty should not use the combination pill because of the increased risk of high blood pressure, clotting and heart disease that comes with age. In addition, women over the age of thirty-five who smoke should not take the pill, since smoking in combination with estrogens may increase the risk of vascular disease. The mini- or progestogen-only pill is more appropriate for older women, but it causes a higher incidence of irregular or breakthrough bleeding, which may be troublesome.

Heretofore, the IUD has been a favored method of birth control for an older woman whose family is complete and who has a single sexual partner. But only one IUD is now available in the United States because of product liability lawsuits arising from problems associated with the device.

Since ovaluation is erratic among most menopausal women, rhythm or other so-called natural methods of birth control are even more unreliable. This leaves barrier methods, such as the condom, diaphragm or vaginal sponge, as about the only alternative means of birth control. As of this writing, there are threats to bar the sale of some of the spermicides used with diaphragms—a move that would further reduce birth control options, especially for the two groups for whom pregnancy poses the highest risk: teenagers and older women.

Of course, after menopause is firmly established (a year or more since the last menstrual period), birth control is no longer a worry, and many postmenopausal women find this a liberating factor that actually enhances their sex lives. Also, after menopause, women have higher levels of androgens—male hormones that are secreted by the adrenal glands and, in part, converted to estrogen in fatty tissue. The androgens also serve to increase libido, which explains why many menopausal women actually experience a heightened interest in sex.

Artificial Menopause

An ever increasing number of women never go through natural menopause; instead, they have a hysterectomy which prematurely ends their menstruating years. In recent decades, there has been mounting controversy over the number of hysterectomies performed in this country. More than 800,000 American women have hysterectomies each year, and up to a third or more of these have been called unnecessary. American women are up to four times more likely to have a hysterectomy than are women in other industrialized countries.

Some consumer advocates contend that a large number of questionable hysterectomies are motivated by money. Studies have found, for example, that a surgeon in a private, fee-for-service practice performs more hysterectomies than physicians who work with prepaid plans. Attitude also is a factor: Some doctors honestly feel that removal of the uterus, ovaries and other reproductive organs lessens a woman's chance of developing cancer. If she no longer plans to have children, and there are signs that point to a future risk, why not simply do a hysterectomy? Of course, this argument ignores the fact that many women feel a deep sense of loss after a hysterectomy. For many, their sexuality is affected, especially if the operation is a total hysterectomy (removal of the cervix and upper part of the vagina; most hysterectomies today are total, as opposed to subtotal, which entails removal of only the uterus).

Of course, if the ovaries also are removed, the woman immediately loses her female hormones and goes into an abrupt menopause that may carry more severe symptoms than a later, natural menopause. Some doctors recommend that the ovaries be removed during a hysterectomy if the woman is forty or older, reasoning that she will probably go into menopause in a few years anyway and that this spares her the risk of ovarian cancer. This argument can be countered by the fact that the risk of ovarian cancer is low— about one percent for women over forty. Also, the average age of menopause is still fifty-one; a forty-year-old woman who is castrated may have had more than a decade remaining of natural hormonal production. This is important, because women who lose their ovaries at an early age have a much higher risk of osteoporosis—a thinning of the bones. There is also evidence that the risk of a heart attack also rises.

In general, there are four indications for a hysterectomy: (1) cancer of the reproductive organs; (2) severe infection, or disease of the fallopian tubes or ovaries that cannot be treated by other means; (3) large fibroid tumors; and (4) excessive bleeding that is not controlled by other means, such as a dilation and curettage (D&C) of the uterus. But, as stressed by Jane Porcino in her book *Growing Older, Getting Better* (Addison-Wesley, 1983), these conditions account for only about twelve percent of all hysterectomies done in the United States. She also points out that if present trends continue, more than half of American women can expect to have a hysterectomy by age sixty-five.

If a woman has any doubt that she really needs a hysterectomy, she should get a second opinion. Questionable reasons for which a hysterectomy may be recommended include small, symptomless fibroids; bleeding that can be treated by other less drastic means; pelvic pain; prolapse of the uterus; and abnormal Pap smears that are not clearly cancer. In the past, hysterectomies have been done as a sterilization procedure, on the grounds that if the woman is going to be sterilized, she might as well have a hysterectomy so she can avoid having periods and reduce her risk of uterine cancer. This is no longer considered a justification for a hysterectomy.

Of course, there are instances in which a hysterectomy is the preferred treatment. There is no question if uterine or cervical cancer has been diagnosed. A woman who is severely anemic because she bleeds profusely for eight or nine days every month may indeed require a hysterectomy. The same may not be true of a woman who has heavy periods but is otherwise healthy; she may be treated with birth control pills or other more conservative means.

A hysterectomy because of a fibroid tumor may or may not be justified, depending upon the circumstances. Fibroid tumors are made up of smooth muscle cells and are also called myomas or leiomyomas (*myos* means "muscle", *leios* means "smooth"). They are most common after the age of thirty or thirty-five, with a prevalence of up to fifty percent in some ethnic groups. Most are small and slow-growing. They very rarely develop into cancer, and many women have fibroids without experiencing symptoms. There is no reason to do a hysterectomy because of these small, symptomless fibroids, which actually are a variant of what is normal.

A large, fast-growing fibroid that causes pain, bleeding, fertility problems and abdominal swelling is a different story, and there are circumstances in which it should be removed. For example, if left untreated, this type of fibroid can grow very large—some fibroids weighing more than a hundred pounds have been recorded. Fortunately, this is very rare; more commonly, the woman will look as though she is several months' pregnant.

Removal can sometimes be done surgically without taking out the uterus. The operation, called a myomectomy, entails making an incision in the uterine wall and cutting out the fibroid. It is a more complicated operation than a hysterectomy, and, not uncommonly, the fibroid will grow back. Still, a myomectomy is the preferred operation for a younger woman who wants to have a child, or for a woman who is experiencing fertility problems because of fibroids.

HORMONE REPLACEMENT THERAPY

The use of estrogen replacement therapy following menopause has been the subject of considerable controversy in recent years. On one side are the endocrinologists and others who contend that, following menopause, women experience an abnormal estrogen deficiency. (At one time, a woman's average life span did not extend many years beyond menopause, but today, a woman may expect to live another thirty years or more in this estrogen-deficient state.) On the other side are people who feel that menopause is a normal stage, and thus the hormonal changes that accompany it also are normal. Mounting evidence supports the rationale for hormone replacement, and new ways of combining estrogen and progesterone to mimic the body's normal levels of these two hormones are increasing its safety.

Hormone replacement therapy for menopausal and postmenopausal women has been advocated for nearly a hundred years, ever since Dr. Charles Edouard Brown-Sequard, a French physiologist, gave ovarian extract to women whose ovaries had been removed. Since then, a number of different forms of estrogen that can be taken orally or added to a cream or patch that is absorbed through the skin have been developed. Millions of women now take estrogens to ease menopausal symptoms, particularly hot flashes and vaginal dryness, and to help prevent the bone loss that is so common among older women.

Despite the fact that seventy-five to eighty-five percent of the forty million menopausal and postmenopausal women in this country suffer from symptoms that can be eased by estrogen replacement, many women are reluctant to take it, and their doctors hesitant to prescribe it, largely because of outdated research. In the 1950s and 1960s, estrogen replacement was routinely prescribed for almost all women going through menopause. The unrealistic promise of "Forever Feminine" (interpreted to mean "Forever Young") led many women to believe that if they took estrogen, they not only would get rid of their hot flashes and other troubling symptoms, but their skin wrinkles and other signs of aging as well. Obviously, estrogen cannot stop the clock, and it is not a miraculous "fountain of youth," but it does help maintain bones and perhaps protect against heart disease—important benefits that doctors in the 1960s and early 1970s felt justified routine, long-term use of hormone replacement. From 1970 to 1975, the number of prescriptions for estrogen replacement increased by thirty-five percent.

Then came several disturbing reports in the mid-1970s that women on continuous long-term estrogen replacement had a higher risk of endometrial cancer. The overall incidence of endometrial cancer among these women was still low, but significantly higher—5 to 13.9 times greater in some studies—than among women who did not take estrogen replacement. It was also noted that women who have high levels of natural estrogen also had an increased risk of endometrial cancer. For example, obese women have more endometrial cancer than their normal-weight counterparts. A certain amount of estrogen is manufactured in fat cells and overweight postmenopausal women have higher levels of circulating estrogen than women of normal weight. This fact has led some experts to hypothesize that the hormone may play a role in their increased cancer rate.

Almost overnight, there was a swing away from long-term hormone replacement, with the number of prescriptions dropping by nearly thirty percent. Doctors were advised to prescribe it only to treat severe hot flashes and other symptoms, and in the lowest effective dosages for a relatively short period of time—usually one or two years. In fact, many doctors hesitated to prescribe it at all, urging women to take Valium or other tranquilizers, or to seek counseling to ease their symptoms.

The cancer scare quickly reached the women themselves, who, understandably, reasoned that it was better to endure hot flashes than to risk cancer. For more than a decade, these fears have been kept alive by a number of popular writers who advise against taking estrogen replacement for any but the most severe symptoms. Meanwhile, a good deal has been learned about new ways of administering hormone replacement therapy to minimize the cancer risk. Today, the pendulum is swinging back as it is becoming clear that the lack of estrogen replacement is contributing to problems that may be even more serious than an increased risk of endometrial cancer.

In recent years, for example, we have become increasingly aware of the seriousness of osteoporosis, the gradual thinning of bones that is most common among older women. About one out of four older women in this country can expect to suffer at least one broken bone, largely as a consequence of osteoporosis. Each year, fractures or other complications of osteoporosis contribute to forty thousand deaths, mostly among older women—many times the number of women at risk of dying from endometrial cancer. Typically, a woman breaks a hip or leg bone, is hospitalized for surgery, and then during the prolonged bed rest, develops a pulmonary embolism (a blood clot that lodges in the lung), infection, pneumonia or some other complication that results in death.

In most instances, bone thinning is a gradual process that is thought to begin when a woman is in her thirties and accelerates sharply following menopause. The risk of osteoporosis is particularly pronounced in women whose ovaries have never functioned or whose ovaries were removed at an early age. Therefore, estrogen replacement is especially important for a woman who has a total hysterectomy in which the ovaries are removed before the age of forty. Other factors that increase the risk of osteoporosis include cigarette smoking, which interferes with calcium absorption, and consuming a diet deficient in calcium and vitamin D, especially early in life. People who are fine-boned—for example, white women of northern European extraction and Orientals—have more osteoporosis than those with more bone mass, such as black women. Hormonal imbalances or diseases that upset calcium metabolism also can cause osteoporosis.

For reasons that are not completely understood, estrogen helps maintain bone strength and prevent further thinning from osteoporosis. Hormone therapy does not reverse the process, although there often is an improvement in the early years of estrogen therapy. (For a more complete discussion, see Chapter 7.)

Estrogen is also thought to have a protective effect on a woman's cardiovascular system. Coronary disease and heart attacks are relatively uncommon among premenopausal women. In the decade or two following menopause, women gradually begin to catch up with men in developing heart disease, and, among older women, it is the leading cause of death. A number of factors in addition to estrogen may account for the sexual differences in heart disease. Until relatively recently, cigarette smoking—one of the major risk factors for a heart attack—has not been as common in women as in men. Nor have women been as subjected to stress in the workplace. This is changing, but it is too early to tell whether women are experiencing a concomitant rise in early heart attacks.

The mechanism whereby estrogen may protect the heart is unknown, although many experts feel that it involves cholesterol metabolism. Following menopause, the average woman's cholesterol level goes up. The level of LDL cholesterol—the type that contributes to the buildup of fatty deposits in the arteries—also rises. Estrogen replacement prevents the rise in total and LDL cholesterol that often occurs after menopause, which may explain its protective effect.

Recent studies by researchers at Erasmus University in Rotterdam, the Netherlands, indicate that estrogen replacement also may help prevent rheumatoid arthritis among older women. Researchers who compared the incidence of arthritis among women on hormone replacement with those who were not found a two-thirds reduction in rheumatoid arthritis among women taking estrogen. Again, the mechanism is unknown, but the researchers feel that the hormone may suppress the inflammation that damages the joint, or that postmenopausal hormone therapy may somehow mimic the protective effect against the disease that is seen among pregnant women, who routinely enjoy a remission in rheumatoid arthritis.

More study is needed before we can definitely say that the benefits of hormone replacement therapy outweight the risks. Many doctors now feel that the judicious use of hormones during and after menopause not only eases the immediate symptoms, but also has potential long-term benefits in maintaining bones and perhaps protecting against heart attacks. Still, women on hormone therapy should be particularly diligent about having regular check-ups, which include a Pap smear every six months.

Basics of Hormone Replacement Therapy

Over the last decade, there has been an increasing trend toward replacing both estrogen and progesterone, thereby mimicking what happens during a normal cycle. Taken alone, estrogen causes a buildup of the uterine lining, or endometrium. Some authorities believe this unchallenged proliferation of endometrial tissue is what increases the risk of cancer. By taking an estrogen for twenty days, and then adding a progesterone along with the estrogen for ten days, a woman will have a shedding of the excess endometrial tissue when she stops both pills for five days—similar to what happens in a menstrual period. Some endocrinologists also note that addition of progesterone also may help prevent excessive hormonal stimulation of the breasts. Although there is no strong evidence that estrogen replacement causes breast cancer, there are some types of cancer that are stimulated by hormones. Women who have had breast cancer with positive estrogen receptors are not advised to take estrogen replacement therapy. This stricture does not necessarily apply to a woman who has been successfully treated (five to ten years with no evidence of recurrence) for localized breast cancer with no estrogen receptors.

Some women may experience adverse side effects from hormone therapy, although this is relatively rare in the low doses used for long-term replacement therapy. Symptoms may include nausea, vomiting, bloating, weight gain, breast swelling and tenderness, headaches, dizziness, increased susceptibility to vaginal yeast infections, and breakthrough vaginal bleeding. These adverse reactions usually subside and disappear in two or three months, but if they persist or are severe, a lower dosage may be tried.

Conjugated estrogens (for example, Premarin), the most common estrogens used to treat menopausal symptoms, can be taken orally or applied directly to the vagina in a topical cream. In a typical regimen, a woman will take .625 mg. of Premarin a day for twenty days (a higher dosage may be given if hot flashes persist or if there is progressive osteoporosis), and then 5 to 10 mg. of a progesterone, such as Provera, for ten days, then nothing for the next five days. After stopping the Provera, she should have three days of light bleeding. (This ends in about two years for half of women treated.) She then starts the regimen over again.

There also is a newer method of administering estrogen, through a patch that contains .05 mg. of the hormone, which is gradually absorbed through the skin. The patch, marketed under the name of Estraderm, is changed twice a week, and progesterone pills are taken in the same manner as with oral estrogen. The main advantage to the estrogen patch is that it delivers a low, steady dosage of the hormone, and is therefore not as likely to produce adverse side effects as the pills, which give a larger dosage all at once. It is not yet known whether it will be as effective in preventing osteoporosis as estrogen pills, but early studies seem to indicate that the patch has the same protective benefits as oral forms.

Any unscheduled vaginal bleeding is a warning sign to see a doctor as soon as possible. This applies to all women, especially after menopause. Vaginal bleeding is the major sign of cervical and uterine cancers; the incidence of these cancers increases markedly with menopause. Before menopause is established, many women tend to have irregular bleeding. It may be difficult to tell if this bleeding is a period or a warning sign to see a doctor. If there is any doubt at all, it is better to err on the side of caution. All women should have a pelvic examination and Pap smear annually with the approach of menopause (as well as an annual breast examination and mammogram), and more often if they are on hormone therapy.

Some doctors recommend weaning a woman off hormone replacement after two to five years, unless she has osteoporosis. Others feel that so long as there are no contraindications, the hormones can be continued for life. The major side effects of estrogens are salt and water retention, which can cause bloating; nausea; and breast soreness. Estrogens can promote a tendency for blood to clot, but the dosages given in replacement therapy are so low that this is not likely. Women who have a history of abnormal clotting, which can lead to development of thrombophlebitis (the formation of a clot in a vein), or a thromboembolism (a piece of a clot that breaks away and travels through the circulation to the lungs, heart, brain or other vital organ) are not candidates for hormone replacement therapy. Thrombophlebitis frequently occurs as a complication of pelvic surgery; a woman undergoing an operation in this area should stop taking the hormones well in advance of the surgery to minimize the risk of abnormal clotting.

Hormone replacement may unmasks diabetes. If diabetes develops, the hormones should be stopped. A diabetic woman may take these hormones if her dose of insulin is increased to counteract the glucose raising effect of these hormones, and if she has no eye, kidney or foot problems. A good diabetologist should be consulted to help in treatment plans. In addition, any woman with a history of a previous stroke or heart attack should not take these hormones.

BEYOND HORMONE THERAPY

Although hormone replacement is important to a woman's health and well-being during and after menopause, it is not a panacea. Hormones will not restore youth and beauty, nor will they rejuvenate a moribund marriage, save a faltering career, help land a new job, or solve any of the myriad other problems of daily living. Midlife is a time of change and of coming to terms with many inevitable facts of life. Children grow up and leave home; age and gravity begin to take their toll on physical beauty; careers change or reach a plateau. How well we cope with and adjust to these changes depends more upon our emotional health and feelings of self-esteem than our hormones. Hormones relieve the physical symptoms that come with menopause, and probably have a protective effect against some of the ravages of old age. But they will not solve problems of the mind and soul.

Part III

Endocrine

Disorders

Chapter 7

Osteoporosis and Other Diseases Related to Calcium Metabolism

ALMOST OVERNIGHT, WOMEN ARE SUDDENLY CONCERNED over the specter of developing osteoporosis as they grow older. Tens of millions of Americans, especially women, are taking calcium supplements in the hope of warding off this disfiguring and debilitating disease, which is marked by a gradual thinning of the bones. Despite the new awareness of osteoporosis and widespread consumption of calcium, many misconceptions persist about this common bone disease and the many roles of calcium in maintaining health.

IMPORTANCE OF CALCIUM

As every schoolchild learns, calcium provides the foundation for strong bones and teeth. Less well-known are the essential roles of calcium in the proper functioning of muscles, nerves, the endocrine and exocrine glands, hormones and other body tissues. It also is needed to bind cells together, activate enzymes, and promote blood clotting and fertilization. Recent studies suggest that calcium may be useful in the treatment of high blood pressure, and that it may have a protective effect against colon cancer.

Calcium is by far the most abundant mineral in the

body: The average adult woman has about 875 grams (1lb. 14 oz.), and an adult man has about one kilogram, or just over two pounds. Of this, ninety-nine percent is in the bones and teeth; most of the remaining one percent circulates in the blood and a small amount, about ten grams, is contained in body tissues.

Calcium metabolism is a complex process that involves several organ systems and hormones. The diet provides the body with its calcium—the best sources are milk and milk products and green leafy vegetables (see Table 6). Each day, a certain amount of calcium is lost in the urine and feces. To replace this lost calcium, an equivalent amount should be absorbed from the intestinal tract.

Although most people think of bones as being com-

Table 6. DIETARY SOURCES OF CALCIUM

Food	Serving Size	Calcium (mg.)
Milk and Milk Products		
Milk (skim, whole, etc.)	8 oz.	300
Yogurt, whole milk	8 oz.	275
Yogurt, skim with nonfat milk solids	8 oz.	452
Nonfat dry milk	1 tbs.	57
Ice cream, vanilla	1 cup	208
Ice milk, vanilla	1 cup	283
Cheese		
American	1 oz.	195
Cheddar	1 oz.	211
Cottage, creamed	1 cup	211
Cottage, low-fat dry	1 cup	138
Cream cheese	1 oz.	23
Parmesan, grated	1 tbs.	69
Swiss	1 oz.	259
Fish/Seafood		
Mussels (meat only)	3 ½ oz.	88
Oysters	5–8 medium	94
Salmon, canned with bones	3 ½ oz.	198
Sardines, canned with bones	3 ½ oz.	449
Shrimp	3 ½ oz.	63

Fruit

Figs, dried	5 medium	126
Orange	1 medium	65
Prunes, dried	10 large	51

Nuts/Seeds

Almonds or hazelnuts	12–15	38
Sesame seeds	1 oz.	28
Sunflower seeds	1 oz.	34

Vegetables

Bean curd (tofu)	3 ½ oz.	128
Beans, red kidney	½ cup	110
Beans, garbanzo	½ cup	80
Beans, pinto	½ cup	135
Broccoli, cooked	⅔ cup	88
Chard, cooked*	½ cup	61
Collard greens, cooked*	½ cup	152
Fennel, raw	3 ½ oz.	100
Kale, cooked*	½ cup	134
Lettuce, romaine	3 ½ oz.	68
Mustard greens, cooked*	½ cup	145
Rutabaga, cooked	½ cup	59
Seaweed, agar, raw	3 ½ oz.	567
Seaweed, kelp, raw	3 ½ oz.	1,093
Squash, acorn	½ medium baked	61

*Foods high in oxalic acid, which hinders absorption.

posed of inert, static tissue, they actually are in a constant state of remodeling. Since the bones serve as the body's storehouse for calcium, they release the mineral in response to hormonal signals when calcium blood levels fall, and then resorb it to maintain strength and density. When the level of blood calcium falls to a certain point, the parathyroid glands secrete parathyroid hormone into the bloodstream. This signals the kidneys to return calcium that ordinarily would be excreted in urine to the blood instead and causes the bones to release some of their calcium. It also stimulates the conversion of vitamin D to its active form, the hormone 25 hydroxycholecalciferol. This hormone promotes absorption of dietary calcium from the intestines, and also increases the kidneys' reabsorption of the mineral. A third hormone, calcitonin, which is secreted by the thryoid gland, acts as a calcium-sparing substance to prevent excessive breakdown of bone tissue. Estrogen also protects the bones from excessive calcium loss by stimulating the secretion of calcitonin and promoting the conversion of vitamin D, as well as by other mechanisms that are not fully understood. In contrast, cortisone promotes bone loss, a factor that limits its use in treating people with arthritis, other inflammatory disorders, or asthma. Growth hormone increases bone formation, and thyroid hormone also plays a role in bone metabolism. A thyroid deficiency in children causes stunted growth, while an excess in children or adults promotes bone loss.

A number of other factors affect bone remodeling. These include:

Exercise

Bones require a certain amount of physical activity to maintain their strength and density. Like muscles, bones respond to the stress of exercise by growing larger and stronger. Exercise also increases the flow of blood to bones and it also may affect hormonal balance. For example, a study by Pennsylvania State University researchers involving older sedentary women found that their estrogen levels increased and adrenal hormones decreased after a six-week exercise program.

Cigarette Smoking

Women who smoke tend to have more osteoporosis than nonsmokers. The reason for this is unclear, although some researchers theorize that it is related to the fact that tobacco use lowers estrogen production.

Alcohol

Excessive intake of alcohol interferes with the intestines' ability to absorb calcium. Even young men who are alcoholics often have serious bone loss.

Drugs

A number of medications interfere with calcium metabolism or promote bone loss. These include steroids, diuretics, aluminum-containing antacids, thyroid supplements and anticonvulsant drugs.

Fluoridation of Water

Fluoride, which is added to water to help maintain strong teeth, appears to have a similar effect on bones. Fluoride supplements are often used in the treatment of osteoporosis and other bone disorders.

Dietary Factors

In addition to consuming adequate calcium (at least 1,000 mg. per day and more during pregnancy, breast-feeding or if there are signs of bone thinning), other components of the diet are important in maintaining strong bones. Calcium and phosphorus, which is also needed to harden bones, should be consumed in about equal amounts. But the typical American diet—which is high in meat and other high-protein, phosphorus-rich foods as well as soft drinks that contain large amounts of phosphorus—promotes bone loss. Excessive salt consumption promotes calcium excretion by the kidneys, as does drinking large amounts of coffee, defined as four or more cups a day. Excessive dietary fiber, or roughage, can hinder calcium absorption from the intestines. Oxalates—substances found in spinach, rhubarb, asparagus, beet greens and certain other green vegetables—bind to calcium and prevent its absorption. Excessive intake of vitamins A or D also stimulates bone loss, while a deficiency of vitamin D results in rickets—a softening of the bones.

OSTEOPOROSIS

Osteoporosis means porous bones. It is caused by a loss of calcium from the bones, which leaves them thin and brittle.

Although some men eventually develop osteoporosis, it is primarily a woman's disease. In this country, about ten million women have osteoporosis serious enough to require treatment. One out of every four women over the age of sixty suffers from some degree of it, and half of all women who have a surgically induced menopause develop the disease. In its early stages, there are no obvious symptoms. Many do not know they have osteoporosis until they suddenly break a bone, most frequently a vertebra or hip. By that time, the osteoporosis is in an advanced stage, with considerable bone loss.

All bones become somewhat thinner with age. There are two basic kinds of bone tissue: the outer cortical bone, which is dense and hard, and the inner trabecular bone, which looks something like a honeycomb. The vertebrae are mostly trabecular bone, surrounded by a thin shell of cortical tissue, while the leg and arm bones are mostly cortical, with trabecular bone at the ends. The honeycomb-like structure of trabecular bone has more surface area from which calcium can be released, and therefore is most affected by the remodeling process. This is why bones rich in trabecular tissue are the most vulnerable to osteoporosis. Typically, a person starts to lose small amounts of trabecular bone in his or her twenties; in contrast, cortical bone continues to build until the mid-thirties, and then gradually declines.

For unknown reasons, women lose bone at a faster rate than men. After menopause, the rate of bone loss in women is about twice that of men, with the most rapid thinning occurring in the first five or six years after menopause. Shortened height is the most visible sign of advanced bone loss; it is not unusual for a woman with osteoporosis to lose eight or more inches from her adult height (see Figure 14). This is caused by a collapse of vertebrae weakened by osteoporosis. Often, the process is slow and not noticeable until the woman realizes that her waist is thicker (although she may weigh the same), and her clothes no longer fit properly. In other instances, the change may be more sudden; if sev-

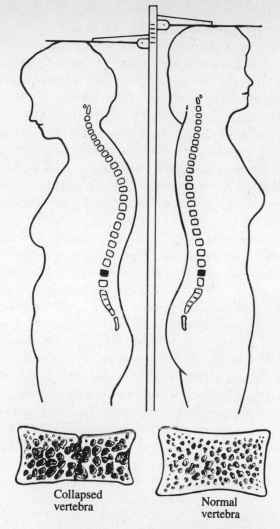

Collapsed
vertebra

Normal
vertebra

Height Loss Due to Osteoporosis

A height loss of three to eight inches is not unusual in advanced osteoporosis.

eral vertebrae collapse in rapid succession, a woman may
lose two or three inches in a few months.

As the vertebrae collapse, the woman will develop a

curved spine, the classic "widow's hump." Back pain, often severe, occurs at the time of the fractures; this may develop into chronic back pain caused by muscle spasms that result from inflammation and irritation around the collapsed vertebrae. Other fractures commonly accompanying osteoporosis are of the wrist and hip. Often a woman will break a wrist bone when she attempts to break a fall. Similarly, a woman with osteoporosis may break a hip in even a minor fall, although there are many instances in which the break seems to occur for no apparent reason. The woman will recall that she fell after experiencing a sharp pain; the fall was the result of the broken bone, and not the other way around.

Hip fractures are the most serious injuries suffered by women with osteoporosis. The fracture often leaves the woman disabled for her remaining life. About fifteen percent die shortly after their injury, and thirty percent die within a year. The broken bone itself is not usually the cause of death, but complications arising from it, such as a blood clot or a pulmonary embolism, often prove fatal. It is estimated that complications from fractures account for forty thousand deaths each year in this country, and the large majority of these are older women with osteoporosis.

In recent years, there has been increasing emphasis on preventing osteoporosis. Adequate calcium intake, especially early in life (when bone mass is being formed) and during pregnancy and breast-feeding—periods that require tremendous amounts of calcium—is important. Contrary to popular belief, pregnancy does not necessarily deplete a woman's bones. If her calcium intake is adequate, pregnancy actually helps increase bone mass. Calcium absorption increases when the body needs it most; this certainly applies to pregnancy, when the woman needs to provide enough calcium to build her baby's bones and teeth. The high levels of estrogen during pregnancy help stimulate the activation of vitamin D and increase calcium absorption, and the extra progesterone also has a protective effect on the bones.

The importance of calcium in preventing osteoporosis

is getting increased attention, both among doctors and the general public. At a 1985 National Institutes of Health (NIH) consensus meeting on osteoporosis, several experts suggested that the bone loss may be due to widespread calcium deficiency. They noted that the average woman in the United States consumes only about half of the Recommended Dietary Allowance (RDA) of 800 mg. of calcium per day. (See Table 7.) The panel urged that the RDA for calcium be increased from the present 800 mg. to 1,000 to 1,500 mg. for adult women, and that women be encouraged to consume more calcium-rich foods, especially early in life when bone mass is being built. The proposed RDA for calcium is comparable to the amount now recommended during adolescence, pregnancy and breast feeding—times of peak calcium need.

Table 7. RECOMMENDED DIETARY ALLOWANCES FOR CALCIUM

Age	Calcium (mg./day)
To 6 months	360
6 months–1 year	540
1–10 years	800
11–18 years	1,200
19-plus*	800
Pregnant women	1,200 +
Lactating women	1,200 +

*The National Institutes of Health has recommended that this be increased to 1,000 to 1,500 mg. per day for women over the age of 35 or 40.

The NIH panel also recommended estrogen replacement, especially in the years immediately following menopause. As noted earlier, exercise is an essential component in bone maintenance. Avoiding excessive alcohol and not smoking also are important. Since heredity appears to be a factor in determining risk, women with a family history of the disease should be particularly diligent about preventive measures. Women who are thin and small-boned are at much higher risk than heavyset, large-boned women. Other possible signs of susceptibility include thin, transparent skin, especially on the hands, and periodontal disease (a loosening of the teeth).

Diagnosis

Early detection of osteoporosis is important in preventing further bone loss. Unfortunately, many women are unaware that they have a problem until the osteoporosis already is in an advanced stage. Hip or spine X rays are often taken, but these are not sensitive enough to detect early bone thinning; in fact, about thirty percent of bone loss must occur before it shows up on conventional X rays. Enhanced X-ray techniques, such as radiogrammetry (which measures the width of cortical bone in a small area, such as the fingers) or photo-densitometry (which measures bone density) are better than conventional X rays, but still do not give an accurate picture of early bone loss, especially of the spine.

In some instances, dentists are the first to spot signs of bone loss. Often, simply looking at jaw X rays taken by a dentist over several years can help detect reduced bone density. Similarly, the loosening of teeth may be an indication of bone loss from the jaw. (One should not assume, however, that all cases of periodontal disease are caused by osteoporosis.)

The mineral content and width of bones can be accurately measured by single photon absorptiometry, a technique that has been used in research laboratories for many years. This test, which involves calculating how many gamma rays are absorbed by bone tissue, is capable of measuring very small amounts of bone loss. But, as with radiogrammetry and photo-densitometry, the arm and other bones that can be studied by this technique do not necessarily reflect what is happening with the spine, hip and other bones with a high proportion of trabecular tissue.

The single best examination is a CT (computed tomography) scan, which can precisely measure trabecular tissue in a vertebra. Unfortunately, the test is too expensive to be used widely for screening purposes. It also exposes a person to more radiation than other tests.

Treatment

The goal of osteoporosis treatment is to prevent further bone loss and, if possible, restore as much of the lost bone as possible. Some of the effects of osteoporosis, such as the shortened stature or widow's hump, cannot be reversed. But most women can achieve relief of their symptoms and arrest or slow the progress of the disease. The typical regimen involves hormone replacement therapy, exercise, and calcium supplements, perhaps with vitamin D or calcifediol, an activated form of vitamin D.

Fluoride is sometimes added to the regimen for its bone-building and strengthening properties. Of all the medications used to treat osteoporosis, fluoride is the only one that appears to increase bone mass. However, this happens in a relatively small number of patients; about a third derive no obvious benefit and another third have severe side effects that prevent its use—drawbacks that obviously limit its widespread application in treating osteoporosis. In addition, there are indications that the new bone formed as a result of fluoride treatment tends to be more brittle than ordinary bone, and may be more vulnerable to fractures.

Injections of calcitonin, a hormone which is secreted by the thyroid gland and acts to lay down calcium into the bone matrix, have been used experimentally to treat osteoporosis. Early results showed an easing of symptoms as well as small increases in bone tissue, but these effects tended to be temporary. Still, calcitonin is used in Europe, and some American researchers feel that it is worth trying.

OTHER DISORDERS OF CALCIUM METABOLISM

Blood levels of calcium that are too low (hypocalcemia) or too high (hypercalcemia) can pose serious problems. The most common sign of hypocalcemia is tetany, a convulsive muscle spasm, although it is not unusual for a person to have low blood levels of calcium without any obvious symptoms. The tetany may involve a number of muscles, but those of the forearm, hands and wrist are most commonly affected.

Hypocalcemia also can produce seizures, mental and emotional disturbances, diarrhea, malabsorption problems, abdominal pain and constipation. Long-standing hypocalcemia may produce abnormalities of the skin, hair, nails, teeth and eye lens. The skin may become dry and scaly, and conditions such as eczema or psoriasis may worsen. Hair, eyebrows and eyelashes may become scanty; there also may be a loss of pubic and underarm hair. Nails become thin, brittle and develop grooves. Teeth may develop yellow spots and grooves. Cataracts also are possible manifestations of hypocalcemia.

Causes of hypocalcemia include kidney disease, cirrhosis of the liver, a deficiency of parathyroid hormone or accidental damage to the parathyroid glands after neck surgery, lack of vitamin D, certain cancers, tumors that secrete calcitonin, pancreatitis and magnesium deficiency. Sometimes premature babies are born with hypocalcemia, but this usually disappears in a week or two.

Acute tetany can be eased by injections of calcium followed by oral calcium supplements, often with vitamin D in its activated form. The immediate treatment should be followed by diagnosis and correction of the underlying cause.

Hypercalcemia almost always is a sign of a serious underlying disease. Many of the symptoms are rather vague and could be caused by a number of illnesses; these include fatigue, lethargy, muscle weakness, loss of appetite, nausea and vomiting, weight loss, constipation, headaches and mental changes. More specific symptoms include thirst, excessive urination and dehydration. If allowed to progress to its most acute stage, hypercalcemia causes uncontrolled vomiting, severe dehydration, mental disturbances or unconsciousness, and, finally, death from widespread tissue destruction and calcification. Fortunately, this progressive form of hypercalcemia is rare.

About eighty percent of hypercalcemia cases are caused either by excessive production of parathyroid hormone or as a result of complications of cancer—especially multiple myeloma, lymphoma, leukemia, or advanced cancers of the breast, lung and kidney. Other causes include vitamin D toxicity; thyroid disease; sarcoidosis, a rare disease that resembles tuberculosis; and adrenal insufficiency. Extreme immobilization in a person who is in a high bone turnover state, such as might occur when a child or adolescent must be in a cast, may result in hypercalcemia. The use of thiazide diuretics, often used to treat high blood pressure, may cause elevated calcium in susceptible persons.

Ulcer patients who drink large amounts of milk and take calcium-based antacids may develop a disorder called milk-alkali syndrome, which is caused by excessive calcium intake. The risk of this type of hypercalcemia is increased if the person has pre-existing kidney disease.

Treatment of hypercalcemia entails diagnosing and correcting the underlying disorder that is causing the elevated calcium. Giving adequate fluids to overcome dehydration is essential, as is correction of other imbalances in body chemistry that result from hypercalcemia. For example, potassium depletion is common with elevated calcium, and must be corrected. Steroids also may be given to lower calcium levels; other drugs that work faster may be used in emergency situations.

OSTEOMALACIA AND RICKETS

Osteomalacia is defined as a softening of the bones due to a lack of mineralization, which gives bone tissue its hardness. If the osteomalacia occurs during periods of growth, the cartilage also will be affected, resulting in rickets and the characteristic bowed legs, thickening at the ends of long bones, pigeon breast and other deformities.

Traditionally, osteomalacia and rickets are caused by vitamin D deficiency, which prevents the body from using calcium. This is now rare in the United States because vitamin D is added to milk, baby formula and other foods. The most common causes in the U.S. today are intestinal malabsorption disorders; other intestinal disorders, including removal of the stomach; the use of anticonvulsant drugs in children or excessive aluminum gels in adults; a genetic defect in which the body does not utilize vitamin D and phosphate; and kidney disorders.

Recently it has been shown that young adolescent ballerinas who have delayed menses due to undernutrition lack the estrogen necessary to lay down bone during the adolescent growth spurt. These girls have a higher prevalence of scoliosis and fractures.

Bone softening and deformities usually can be prevented by recognizing the problem early and correcting the underlying cause. Rickets in young babies is not always apparent, however, and sometimes the problem does not manifest itself until deformities or failure to grow appear. Treatment usually involves giving large amounts of vitamin D, often with phosphorus supplements, to promote hardening of the bones. Care must be taken to prevent vitamin D toxicity. Treatment is more complicated if kidney disease is causing the problem; in such instances, removal of the parathyroid glands may be required.

KIDNEY STONES

Anyone who has ever attempted to pass a kidney stone knows that the pain caused by this common disorder is one of the most intense known to mankind. Kidney stones are more common in men than women, and, in ninety percent of cases, the cause is unknown. In the remaining ten percent, the cause may be structural problems in the kidney, gout, excessive parathyroid hormone (hyperparathyroidism), or intestinal disorders.

Kidney stones may be made up of calcium or uric acid.

Blood levels of these substances are usually normal, but, depending upon the type of stones involved, the urine will contain too much calcium or uric acid. After one passes a kidney stone, it should be retrieved so that its composition can be analyzed.

Traditionally, people with calcium kidney stones have been instructed to eliminate calcium-rich foods from their diets, although there is debate among doctors about the effectiveness of this strategy. The problem is not so much an excessive intake of calcium as it is the body's inability to properly metabolize the mineral. Recent studies also have found that reducing protein consumption—and thereby reducing urinary excretion of calcium, uric acid and phosphorus—is a more effective dietary strategy than eliminating calcium. Increasing fluid consumption to dilute the urine as much as possible also is important.

If dietary treatment does not prevent stone formation, drugs may be prescribed. In the case of calcium stones, a diuretic may be prescribed; allopurinol, a drug often taken by gout patients, will help prevent uric acid stones.

Often stones remain in the kidney for years without causing problems; others may be so small they are passed without notice. The major problems occur when a large stone becomes lodged in the ureter; this causes the pain, and also poses a risk of blocking the kidneys if it stays lodged for more than a day or two. When this happens, attempts may be made to remove the stone. Stones low in the ureter often can be snared out with a cystoscope and catheter with a basketlike tip. A newer treatment involves using underwater shock waves to disintegrate the stone. The patient is partially immersed in a tank of water and the shock waves are beamed at the stone. Surgery also may be used, but the operation is being replaced by these newer methods of stone removal.

Chapter 8

Hormones and the Breast

WE ARE BORN SEEKING OUT OUR MOTHER'S BREAST, BUT the attraction does not end with weaning; from the cradle to the grave, both men and women are preoccupied with the female breast. A woman's breasts are universally viewed as a symbol of beauty, sexuality and nurturing—the very essence of femininity. Anything that threatens a breast takes on a significance of its own. A mastectomy because of cancer, for example, is almost as dreaded as the disease itself. In the past, this dread of losing a breast has prevented many women who suspect they have breast cancer from seeking early medical treatment—a delay that can have tragic consequences. Fortunately, this is changing as women become more involved in treatment decisions and more knowledgeable about their bodies and health.

NORMAL BREAST ANATOMY AND FUNCTION
The breast is a glandular organ designed to produce milk. In women, each breast contains about twenty lobes arranged around the nipple (see Figure 15.) Each lobe branches into a number of lobules, which give rise to tiny milk-producing bulbs called acini. A network of ducts connects the lobe and

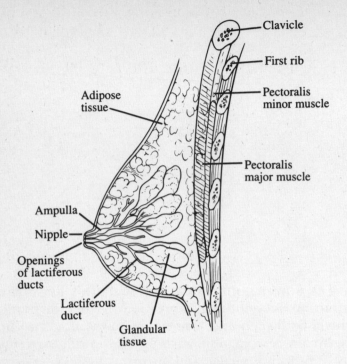

The Normal Breast

This drawing shows normal breast anatomy

its milk-producing structures to the nipple. The nipple is surrounded by a pigmented area, the areola, which contains special sebaceous glands, called Montgomery glands. These secrete the oily substance that lubricates the nipple. Sometimes these glands resemble small pimples, and some women mistakenly think they are abnormal growths; but they are really a normal part of the breast. Nipples also contain erectile tissue, which causes them to stand out when stimulated or exposed to the cold.

Breasts are very sensitive to hormones. This is often evident at birth; many babies are born with enlarged breasts due to the high levels of estrogen, prolactin and other hormones that circulate in the mother's blood during pregnancy. As these hormones are dissipated from the baby's body, the breast tissue shrinks and remains quiescent until puberty, when the rise in sex hormones stimulates the breasts to "bud" and start growing. Normally, only women develop breasts, but there are circumstances in which men's breasts enlarge. Pubescent boys sometimes develop enlarged breasts; they usually subside in a year or two, but can be very embarrassing to a young boy. Men who are markedly overweight (and as a consequence, have a high level of estrogen) may develop breasts. Certain drugs also can stimulate breast development.

Almost all adolescent girls are concerned about their breasts—they are developing unevenly, they are too big, too small, the nipples look strange, and on and on. Despite magazine ads to the contrary, there is not much short of surgery that we can do about the size and shape of our breasts. Breast size and contour are determined by heredity, weight and the amount of glandular tissue present. Very small breasts can be enlarged and very large ones can be reduced by plastic surgery, but this should be a course of last resort and is not recommended until adulthood. Frequently, having a baby or simply gaining or losing weight can have a major effect on breast size.

There are no creams, exercises or other remedies that can increase breast size. Body-building exercises can increase the size of underlying muscles and make the breasts look larger, but since the breasts themselves have no muscles, exercise will not make them bigger. Hormones can stimulate the breasts to grow, as evidenced by the fact that women taking birth control pills sometimes experience breast enlargement. But hormones should not be taken specifically to increase breast size because of the high risk of adverse side effects.

Breasts normally change with age. The developing breast is firm and the tissue is dense. During pregnancy, the breasts grow considerably, often doubling in size. As women grow older, their breasts feel lumpier. Following menopause, the lumpiness subsides and the breasts become softer and less glandular. There is a reduction in fatty tissue, and the supporting ligaments and skin lose some of their elasticity. This results in the sagging that is common among older women. These changes are not as pronounced in women who take hormone replacement.

Except during pregnancy, breasts are usually their fullest during young adulthood, but this varies considerably among women. Some women are relatively flat-chested until they have had a baby, and are pleasantly surprised to find that they have retained some of the size added during pregnancy. Others end up with smaller breasts after pregnancy. The same is true of breast-feeding; some women mistakenly think that nursing "ruined" their breasts. In reality, breast-feeding has very little effect on the size or shape of breasts; this is determined by the amount of glandular tissue, and some women retain more of this tissue following pregnancy, while others have less after childbirth and nursing. In either case, most experts agree that breast-feeding is highly beneficial to both the mother and child, and not an experience that should be missed because of its possible effects on breast appearance. The classic sagging breasts of African natives are more due to lack of bra support than breast-feeding.

HOW THE MENSTRUAL CYCLE EFFECTS BREASTS

During each menstrual cycle, breasts go through a series of changes that correspond with the rise and fall of hormones. These effects are most noticeable during the premenstrual phase, when the breasts become noticeably swollen and even tender. This swelling is due to the rise in estrogen and progesterone during the luteal, or premenstrual, phase. These hormones cause increased blood flow to the breast and promote retention of body fluid; they also stimulate swelling and proliferation of the milk glands. Many women find they need a larger bra size during the premenstrual phase, and even the slightest touch can be painful.

Women who have fibrocystic breasts may be particularly bothered by swelling and discomfort in the premenstrual phase. The increased retention of fluid in the premenstrual phase results in added swelling of the cysts—benign, fluid-filled sacs. Until recently, it was thought that women with fibrocystic breasts had an increased risk of breast cancer; studies conducted by researchers working with the American Cancer Society have found that fibrocystic conditions alone do not predispose a woman to breast cancer. Cysts do make breast self-examination difficult, however, and thus an abnormal lump might be hidden by "normal" cysts.

With menstruation and the fall in hormones, the breast swelling subsides and the extra glandular tissue begins to be resorbed. About seven to ten days after the start of menstruation, the breasts are at their smallest. This is the best time of the menstrual cycle for a woman to carefully examine her breasts, checking for any lumps, thickening, dimpling of the skin or other changes that may signal breast cancer. Even at this time in the menstrual cycle, most women will notice that their breasts have a somewhat lumpy feel. This is due to normal glandular tissue. Each woman, especially if she tends to have fibrocystic breasts, should get to know the normal feel of her breasts, so that she can be alert to a new lump or one that somehow feels different. Familiarity with the "normal" lumps will make it easier to find abnormal ones.

PREGNANCY AND LACTATION

Breast changes are among the first signs of conception. A woman often knows that she is pregnant simply by observing what is happening to her breasts at the time when she would normally expect to have her menstrual period. The breasts become more swollen and tender than usual and the areola becomes darker and enlarged. The breasts feel fuller than usual, and, as the pregnancy continues, the fullness becomes more pronounced though the tenderness characteristic of the first few weeks subsides. Even so, most women find they are more comfortable wearing a bra—a larger size is usually needed—that provides firm support. Some women prefer to wear a bra continuously, even while sleeping.

During the last half of pregnancy, there may be increased nipple discharge. This is usually in the form of clear or milky fluid, although sometimes there may be a drop or two of blood. This discharge is normal and should not be cause for concern; it is an indication of increased glandular activity resulting from the hormonal changes that are preparing the breasts to produce milk.

Women are often concerned about how pregnancy and nursing will affect the appearance of their breasts. The marked breast growth during pregnancy often leaves reddish stretch marks. Although a variety of preparations and creams are promoted as preventives, aside from softening the skin they do little or no good in preventing stretch marks. The marks never totally disappear, but they usually fade with time and often are barely noticeable.

As term approaches, the breast engorgement is more pronounced and there may be an increase in the nipple discharge. The breasts begin to secrete a thick, yellowish material called colostrum. This is a forerunner to milk, and is secreted for a day or two after childbirth. It is thought to contain antibodies that are important in giving the newborn baby immunity, but babies who are not breast-fed seem to do fine without colostrum.

The manufacture and release of breast milk is controlled by a finely tuned hormone feedback system. Shortly after the baby is born, he or she should be allowed to suckle. This breast stimulation signals the pituitary to release oxytocin. This hormone has several functions: It causes the uterus to contract, and is instrumental in labor and in the contractions that are needed to stop bleeding and restore uterine muscle tone following delivery. It also causes the milk ducts to contract and release milk to the nipple. While this is going on, the pituitary releases prolactin, the hormone needed to produce milk.

Many women worry that they will not produce enough milk for their babies, but this is very seldom a problem. By the end of the first week after birth, a nursing mother is producing about 500 ml., or about 17 oz., of milk. This amount doubles by the end of the third month, and increases as the baby's needs grow. In some societies, it is common for a mother to breast-feed for two or three years, and among certain isolated Eskimo tribes, women breast-feed their children until adolescence.

New mothers also may worry that their babies are not getting enough milk for proper growth. If the baby is gaining normally, it is safe to assume he or she is eating enough. On the average, a baby requires about 50 calories per day for each pound of weight. Thus a ten-pound baby will need 500 calories. An ounce of breast milk contains about 20 calories, so the baby should consume 25 ounces of milk.

Many women fear that they will not be able to nurse for a variety of reasons. For example, some women have inverted nipples and worry that they will not be able to breast-feed because of them. The baby's suckling usually draws the nipples out and the woman can nurse without problems. If not, she can wear a special device that will enable the baby to nurse. Occasionally, a woman will experience sore, cracked nipples. Washing them with warm water and a mild soap before and after feeding and applying a skin oil after nursing usually solves this problem. If inflammation occurs, a physician should be contacted to ensure that infection has not set in.

Any sort of breast stimulation can cause a flow of milk. Often, simply hearing a baby's cry is enough to prompt a release of milk. Inserting a clean cloth inside the bra will absorb this milk and prevent staining of clothes.

While nursing, a woman should be careful to consume adequate calories and nutrients, especially calcium, to fulfill the needs of both her and the baby. This is probably not the best time to try to lose the extra pounds that may have been added during pregnancy. The appetite and hunger centers of women who are nursing send out particularly strong messages, designed to ensure that a woman eats enough to make the milk needed by her baby. Breast-feeding itself uses calories; on the average, a woman who breast-feeds for six months will lose ten to twelve pounds. Since this should be a time of relaxation and enjoyment for the mother, it may be best to postpone any attempts to diet until after the baby is weaned. Otherwise, cutting back on calories requires almost superhuman will power.

Women who breast-feed should be particularly careful about taking medications, including birth control pills, antibiotics and even aspirin, illicit drugs, alcohol and other substances that are potentially harmful to the baby. Nursing mothers are advised not to smoke because the nicotine and other potentially harmful substances in tobacco enter breast milk. The same advice applies to marijuana, cocaine and other drugs. Small amounts of coffee and tea probably are not harmful, but caffeine does appear in breast milk and some pediatricians recommend using decaffeinated brands.

Although virtually all pediatricians recommend breast-feeding if at all possible as providing the best nutrition for a baby and antibody protection against the most common infections until the baby's immune system matures, not all women can or want to breast-feed. If a woman decides not to breast-feed, she should be assured that there are many excellent formulas that provide complete nutrition for the baby. A woman who knows from the beginning that she does not want to breast-feed usually will be given a hormone injection to halt milk production. Wearing a tight bra or binding the breasts to prevent nipple stimulation also helps stop milk production. When it comes time to wean the baby, most women find that if they simply reduce the number of nursings per day, and finally stop, they have no trouble with continued milk production. During this weaning period, a woman should refrain from breast stimulation during sex as this can promote the flow of milk.

BENIGN BREAST CONDITIONS

The finding of a breast lump is an understandably traumatic event for any woman, even though the large majority turn out to be harmless. Although about seventy percent of all breast lumps are benign, they all need to be checked by a doctor to make sure they are not caused by cancer or some other condition requiring treatment.

Fibrocystic lumpiness is the most common benign breast condition. It is frequently referred to as fibrocystic breast disease, but many breast specialists argue with this designation, pointing out that it is not a disease per se, but a variation of what is normal. By the age of thirty, most women have some fibrocystic lumpiness in their breasts. The lumpiness progresses until a woman reaches menopause, and then it begins to subside.

The lumpiness is caused by the cyclic hormonal stimulation of the breast during each menstrual cycle. Just as the female hormones cause the lining of the uterus to proliferate and grow each month in preparation for a possible pregnancy, the same hormones have a similar effect on the cells lining the breast ducts. If conception does not take place, the drop in hormone levels causes the uterine lining to break down; it is then shed in the menstrual flow. Similarly, the cellular growth in the milk ducts regresses, and the excess blood and water that makes the breasts fuller during the premenstrual phase also subside. But before the breasts can fully return to their previous state, another menstrual cycle is well underway and the rising hormones again stimulate a proliferation of glandular tissue. After years of repeated hormonal stimulation and regression, almost all breasts develop some degree of fibrocystic lumpiness.

Some women are barely aware of these changes, but many experience considerable swelling and tenderness, especially during the premenstrual phase (see Figure 16.) The symptoms tend to worsen with age, and as some women

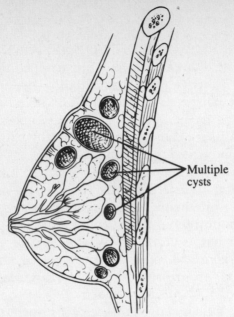

Multiple
cysts

The Fibrocystic Breast

This drawing shows cysts typical of a
fibrocystic breast during premenstrual phase, when hormonal influences are at their peak.

approach menopause, they find that their breasts are almost
constantly swollen and tender. This subsides after menopause, when the breasts are no longer subjected to repeated
changes. (However, postmenopausal women who take replacement hormones may continue to have fibrocystic
breasts.)

Women who have had the more routine fibrocystic tenderness for years are often alarmed by this more chronic
aspect. Many become fearful that the breast lumpiness has
turned into cancer. While it is true that there is a rise in the
incidence of breast cancer at this time in a woman's life, she
should rest assured that the fibrocystic lumpiness has noth-

ing to do with the disease. Thus, while it is important for a woman in her late forties and early fifties to be particularly diligent about breast self-examination and periodic examinations by her doctor (which include mammography), women with fibrocystic breasts should not assume that they have a higher risk of cancer.

Ordinarily, fibrocystic breasts do not require any special treatment. A mild painkiller such as aspirin is usually sufficient to relieve the discomfort. Wearing a well-fitted bra that gives adequate support also helps. A larger size may be needed for the premenstrual period, and some women find that wearing a bra all the time, including in bed, is helpful. Cutting down on salt intake may help reduce fluid retention and swelling; if this is not sufficient, a diuretic may be prescribed. A woman should not use diuretics unless specifically recommended by a doctor.

Some women find that abstaining from products that contain methylxanthines—substances found in coffee, chocolate, tea, some soft drinks and medications—helps in preventing premenstrual breast tenderness. It has not been proved that methylxanthines cause breast tenderness, nor are all women helped by abstaining from them. Still, enough women obtain relief to lead some doctors to recommend a trial period of avoiding methylxanthines.

Large doses of vitamin E also help some women. Since vitamin E is a fat-soluble vitamin that is stored in the body, chronic large doses may have a toxic effect, although this has not been proved. Still, a woman should check with her doctor before self-treating with this or any other vitamin.

If these conservative measures are inadequate to relieve the breast symptoms, a woman may be a candidate for hormone treatment. Women who use birth control pills often find that their breast symptoms subside or disappear. Tamoxifen (Nolvadex), an anti-estrogen drug, may reduce breast nodularity and relieve the swelling and pain. Bromocriptine (Parlodel), which inhibits prolactin secretion and the normal breast stimulation exerted by this hormone, may be prescribed, although its use for this purpose has not been approved by the Food and Drug Administration and is, therefore, considered experimental.

Another hormonal drug, danazol (Danocrine), also may relieve breast symptoms, but it carries a number of side effects that limit its use for this purpose. Since danazol is a synthetic androgen which works by suppressing the release of gonadotropins, thereby preventing the ovaries from producing their hormones, its use is akin to a chemical menopause. Women taking danazol will experience hot flashes and other symptoms associated with menopause. And, because it is an androgen, it also leads to acne, hairiness, increased muscularity, deepening of the voice, and other signs of masculinization.

In extreme instances, a woman with fibrocystic lumpiness and large, difficult-to-examine breasts, may be subjected to repeated biopsies. Under these circumstances, some women become very fearful of cancer, to the point that it becomes a preoccupation that interferes with normal activities. There have been instances in which women in this situation have undergone preventive mastectomies followed by breast reconstruction. Obviously, this is a serious undertaking and one that should be considered only as a last resort. The large majority of women who suffer from this extreme fibrocystic condition and cancer phobia can be helped by counseling, and certainly this should be undertaken before any surgery.

BREAST CYSTS

Frequently, a woman will develop a cyst that is not necessarily related to fibrocystic breasts. Cysts often appear suddenly—one day there is nothing, and the next a woman may be alarmed to discover a large lump. Typically, a cyst is round, smooth and firm, but can be compressed when squeezed. They are most common in the premenopausal years, but can develop at any age. A cyst usually can be drained with a hollow needle; if it does not disappear with drainage or reappears in a few days, it should be biopsied for possible cancer.

FIBROADENOMAS

Fibroadenomas are another relatively common benign breast condition that manifests itself with a lump. These are usually rounded, firm and painless. They move freely when examined with the fingers. Normally, they appear singly, but sometimes a woman will develop several and in rare instances, there may be twenty or more fibroadenomas scattered throughout a woman's breast. Typically, a fibroadenoma first appears when a woman is in her late teens or early twenties, but there are many exceptions in which they develop later in life. There have been reports that women using birth control pills are more prone to develop fibroadenomas, but this has not been proved.

Most breast specialists recommend that fibroadenomas be removed at an early stage, even though a needle biopsy (an office procedure in which a thin, hollow needle is inserted into the breast lump and a small amount of tissue removed for miscroscopic study) may show it is benign. The justification for removal rests with the fact that a fibroadenoma may, over time, grow to a large size, distorting the contour of the breast and also making the growth more difficult to remove. Also, it is not always possible to definitely diagnose a fibroadenoma on the basis of a needle biopsy alone; if there is any doubt at all, a surgical biopsy, which entails removal of the lump and a small amount of surrounding tissue, must be performed to rule out the possibility of cancer.

A rare breast tumor called cystosarcoma phyllodes is closely related to fibroadenomas. These tumors are usually benign, but sometimes are malignant. They tend to grow very rapidly and may occupy the entire breast. Since it is sometimes hard to distinguish a cystosarcoma from a fibroadenoma, that's all the more reason why these tumors should be removed.

NIPPLE DISCHARGE

All women have a small amount of nipple discharge, but most are not aware of these secretions, which keep the nipple ducts open. Women who use birth control pills or postmenopausal estrogen replacement often experience increased nipple discharge, but this is normal. Often, a woman will notice a yellow crusting that appears to clog her nipple openings. This is hardened discharge and is easily removed while bathing.

Abnormal nipple discharges always should be checked by a doctor. For example, sometimes a woman will start to produce breast milk, even though she is not pregnant and has not recently breast-fed. This is usually caused by a hormonal imbalance or a milk cyst.

Any discharge that contained blood, pus or yellowish liquid also should be checked by a doctor. Bloody discharges are usually caused by an intraductal papilloma—a benign wart-like growth in the lining of a milk duct—but they also may be a sign of cancer.

MASTITIS

As its name implies, mastitis is an inflammation of the breast. It occurs most often in women who are breast-feeding, but also may be caused by other conditions, such as an obstructed milk duct. Abscesses requiring drainage sometimes form, and the breast may be engorged with the skin taking on the appearance of an orange peel, a characteristic referred to as "peau d'orange." The axillary lymph nodes in the armpit on the affected side also may be enlarged. Since these symptoms also are characteristic of the rare, but highly lethal, inflammatory breast cancer, they should be checked as soon as possible.

FIBROSIS

Fibrosis is characterized by a gradual replacement of glandular breast tissue by inert, fibrous tissue. Typically, a woman will notice areas that feel firm and thickened, with indistinct borders. The fibrosis may develop at the site of a previous infection or surgical scar, but more often, there is no apparent cause. A biopsy should be done to make sure that the thickened area is, indeed, fibrosis; once this is established, no further treatment is required.

SCLEROSING ADENOSIS

In sclerosing adenosis, there is an overgrowth of glandular tissue, which eventually crowds out some of the normal connective tissue of the breast. In an attempt to block further production of the glandular tissue, the body will produce fibrous cells. In some instances, a distinct mass that feels like cancer will form; in others, the overgrowth will be spread throughout the breast. A biopsy will confirm that the tissue is not cancerous, and no further treatment is called for.

FAT NECROSIS

Fat necrosis, as its name indicates, is a condition marked by the death of fat cells. Usually, this is caused by an injury or inflammation, but sometimes, fat necrosis develops after rapid weight loss. It also may be related to natural breast changes that come with age. The dead cells eventually become calcified and fibrous tissue may grow around them, forming a hard, irregular lump that feels like it might be cancer. Mammography usually can distinguish between the calcification of fat necrosis and the calcium deposits that accompany cancer, but a biopsy to make sure of the diagnosis is advised.

NIPPLE PAPILLOMAS AND POLYPS

Papillomas are wartlike growths in a milk-duct lining near the nipple. They usually produce a bloody discharge, and may be felt as a small lump near the nipple. These growths are quite rare; when they occur, it is usually in premenopausal women. A papilloma usually can be diagnosed by a microscopic study of the bloody discharge, but a surgical biopsy also should be done. Some types of papillomas have been linked to a slightly higher incidence of cancer, but it is not known whether they are actually implicated in causing cancer.

Nipple polyps are small growths that form on the skin. They often resemble tiny mushrooms, with a thin stalk and rounded head. They are harmless, but women often want to have them removed because of their appearance, or because they may become irritated if they rub against clothing.

BREAST CANCER

Of course, breast cancer is the most serious of all breast diseases. Unfortunately, it is also one of the most common among women in the United States and other industrialized nations. Among American women, the breast is the most common cancer site, and, until 1985, breast cancer, which claims about forty thousand live a year, also was the leading cancer killer of women. (Lung cancer now holds this dubious distinction, thanks to the increased prevalence of smoking among women and the very high ninety-five-percent mortality of this disease.)

At some time during their lives, one out of every eleven American women will develop breast cancer. Although marked progress has been made in both the diagnosis and treatment of breast cancer, the overall mortality has not changed appreciably in the last fifty years. This is attributed to the fact that the disease strikes mostly older women, and the United States has an aging population.

Although hormones appear to play a definite role in many breast cancers, the cause of the disease is unknown. Several factors that increase the risk of breast cancer have been identified and include previous breast cancer, a family history of the disease, a long menstrual history marked by early menarche and late menopause and a high-fat, high-calorie diet. Women who are markedly overweight (more than twenty percent above ideal weight) have a somewhat higher incidence of the disease, as do women whose first full-term pregnancy was after the age of thirty.

These risk factors are by no means predictive or uniform. As has been noted by many breast cancer specialists, all women must be considered to be at high risk, and therefore must be very diligent about breast self-examination and regular check-ups by a doctor even if they have no family history of the disease. Early diagnosis and treatment afford the best chance of surviving breast cancer. Up to ninety percent or even more of all women whose cancer is detected and treated while it is still small and confined to the breast can be cured of the disease, which is defined as being alive and free of any evidence of cancer five years after treatment. This cure rate falls to less than fifty percent if the cancer already has spread to the lymph nodes, a sign that malignant cells may already have traveled to other parts of the body.

About ninety percent of all breast cancers are initially detected by the woman herself, which is why regular breast self-examination is so important. All women over the age of twenty should systematically examine their breasts each month. For women who are menstruating, this should be done a week to ten days after the start of a period, when the breasts are smallest and easiest to examine. Postmenopausal women should mark their calendars to remind them to examine their breasts on the first day of each month. Despite the widespread publicity given to the need for regular breast self-examination, a recent survey by the American Cancer Society found that only twenty-seven percent of the women responding said that they did it on a monthly basis.

One out of five conceded that they never examined their breasts, and a similar number said they did it only two or three times a year.

Some of this reluctance to do breast self-examination has been traced to cultural or ethnic taboos. Many Italian women, for example, mistakenly believe that breast self-examination is contrary to dictates of the Catholic church. Similarly, many black women shun breast self-examination as well as examination by a male doctor because they believe it may be immoral. Church leaders and black celebrities are working to try to overcome these taboos.

In addition to examining their own breasts, all women should have their breasts examined by a doctor annually. The American Cancer Society also recommends that all women have a base-line mammogram—a special X-ray breast examination—sometime between the ages of thirty-five and forty, then every one to two years between the ages of forty and fifty and annually thereafter.

Numerous studies have confirmed that mammography will detect many cancers that are too small to be felt even by the most experienced examiner. In the past, questions have been raised about the potential risk from the radiation administered during mammography. Experts now agree that the low doses of radiation used by modern mammography equipment do not pose a substantial risk, and that the benefits in increased detection of early breast cancer greatly outweigh any risks involved.

As any woman who has found a lump in her breast will testify, such a discovery is terrifying. Even though most breast lumps turn out to be benign, the immediate fear is that "I have breast cancer." Ironically, this fear is cited as a reason why many women delay seeing a doctor for an average of six months after discovering a lump in the breast. Many think that somehow, if they don't know the worst, the lump may go away. As a result, they subject themselves to months of needless worry if the lump is benign; others who do have a fast-growing cancer risk death by waiting until it is in an advanced stage before seeking treatment. Any woman who finds a lump or other suspicious sign, such as dimpling of the skin, distortion, engorgement or other change, *should see her doctor as soon as possible.*

The diagnostic procedure involves physical examination—often, a doctor can tell by a characteristic feel whether a lump is a harmless cyst or something that should be investigated further—and sometimes mammography and a biopsy, which may be done either with an aspiration needle or surgically. A biopsy, which entails removing a small amount of tissue and examining it microscopically, is always needed for a definitive diagnosis of any suspicious lump. A biopsy is not needed if there is no doubt that a lump is a harmless cyst (a fact that can be confirmed by withdrawing its fluid), or a normal part of breast anatomy. Most biopsies can be done on an outpatient basis with a local anesthetic. Exceptions include instances in which the mass is deep within the breast or is affixed to the chest wall, or when a suspicious area shows up in a mammogram but cannot be felt. The latter can best be done by using mammography and special dyes to mark the suspicious area before going to the operating room to have biopsy tissue removed.

There is another vital diagnostic test that should be done at the time of a biopsy of any suspected malignant tissue. This is a hormone-receptor assay to measure the sensitivity of the cancer to estrogen and, to a lesser degree, progesterone. This must be done on fresh tissue at the time of the biopsy. The results may not necessarily alter the initial course of treatment, but are important if the cancer recurs or if there is evidence of spread. If the cancer recurs, the hormone-receptor tests should be repeated because the new cancers are not always of the same cellular type as the original one.

HORMONES AND BREAST CANCER

The precise role of hormones in breast cancer is not fully understood, but it appears that the growth of some cancers is stimulated by the female sex hormones. Researchers think that this may explain why obese women have a higher incidence of breast cancer than normal-weight women—because the fat cells convert adrenal hormones to estrogen and this higher level of estrogen is thought to stimulate growth of hormone-dependent cancers. Also, overweight women are likely to have high cholesterol levels, which some researchers believe increase breast-cancer risk.

Hormone manipulation in the treatment of breast cancer is nearly a century old, but it is only in recent years that we have gained enough insight to more precisely target this treatment to the women most likely to benefit. Today, it is estimated that a third of all women with advanced breast cancer can be helped by hormone therapy.

The concept behind hormone therapy for breast cancer originated in the late 1880s with the observation that removal of the ovaries of a woman with breast cancer could cause the tumor to shrink. A half-century later, researchers set about trying to refine this approach. In a study that began in 1948, several hundred premenopausal women with breast cancer agreed to undergo radical mastectomies followed by radiation to their ovaries to make them stop producing hormones. The women who underwent this premature artificial menopause lived longer without recurrence than women who were treated with mastectomies alone.

At about the same time, other researchers observed that some women who received estrogen also experienced shrinking of their breast cancers—a seeming contradiction to the other findings. These early studies indicated that younger women who were still menstruating were the most likely to benefit from inducing an artificial menopause, while older, postmenopausal women were most likely to respond to additive hormone therapy, in which they were given hormones. But not all women in either group benefitted from these strategies, and with the development of anticancer drugs in the 1960s, chemotherapy gained favor over hormonal manipulation in the treatment of advanced breast cancer.

Today, thanks to hormone-receptor tests which help

identify women who are most likely to be helped by this therapy, hormonal manipulation is again a mainstay of breast-cancer treatment. Researchers have found that about two out of three women will have positive hormone receptors, indicating that their cancers are stimulated by estrogen, progesterone or both.

Premenopausal women are less likely to have estrogen-dependent cancers than older women who have gone through menopause. Among women whose cancers have recurred or metastasized to other parts of the body, about half will have positive hormone-receptor tests and sixty percent of these will improve with some sort of hormonal manipulation. The higher the level of receptors, the more likely a woman is to benefit from hormone therapy. The greatest improvement is seen among women who test positive for both estrogen and progesterone receptors; by the same token, women who test negative for both hormones are unlikely to improve under hormone treatment.

The form of hormonal therapy depends upon a woman's age and whether she has gone through menopause. Premenopausal women are likely to receive some sort of ablative treatment to reduce the amount of circulating estrogen. At one time, this usually meant removing the ovaries surgically or damaging them with radiation treatment to halt their hormone production. Today, a woman is more likely to take an anti-estrogen drug, usually tamoxifen (Nolvadex), which results in a chemical menopause.

Other possible hormonal treatments include taking a drug called aminoglutethimide (Cytadren) to block the adrenal glands from producing steroid hormones. The objective is to rid the body of androstenedione, which is secreted by the adrenal glands and converted by fat cells into a form of estrogen. Alternatively, the adrenal glands may be surgically removed. After this operation, the woman will have to take cortisone to replace that which is normally made by the adrenal glands.

In some instances, the pituitary gland may be removed to rid the body of prolactin, which may stimulate the growth of some breast cancers. The woman then must take replacement hormones to maintain proper fluid and salt balance.

In the past, male sex hormones were given to women with advanced breast cancer, a strategy that produced remission in about fifteen percent of women who were premenopausal or who had only recently gone through menopause. However, these hormones produced severe side-effects in women, including pronounced hairiness and virilization, and their use has been replaced by tamoxifen.

Sometimes the use of progesterone produces improvement in women with advanced breast cancer. It is not known how this hormone works against cancer; it is usually given along with estrogen following the failure of anti-estrogen drugs. Steroids also may be given, usually with anticancer drugs, to relieve symptoms of advanced metastatic cancer. These hormones do not appear to alter the cancer itself, but may produce relief from symptoms associated with metastases to the lungs, brain and bones.

Occasionally, hormonal manipulation may be combined with cancer chemotherapy, especially in dealing with a fast-growing type of tumor such as inflammatory cancer. It takes about four months to achieve a remission with hormonal manipulation, whereas cancer chemotherapy produces much faster results. Therefore, three or more chemotherapy agents are usually given immediately to initiate a regression of the disease.

MASTECTOMY—STILL THE LEADING TREATMENT

Although hormone manipulation is an important facet of treating breast cancer, it is by no means the initial or major treatment for this disease. Mastectomy remains the most common and most effective treatment, but in the last decade, the medical community has greatly revised its thinking regarding the extent of surgery needed to give a woman her best chance of overcoming breast cancer. Heretofore, a Halsted radical mastectomy, an operation named for the pioneering surgeon who developed it in 1882, was the favored operation. This procedure entails removal of the entire breast as well as the underlying chest muscle and the axillary lymph nodes from the adjacent armpit. The operation produces considerable deformity, but it also reduced the very high mortality rate that prevailed before its inception.

In 1948, a British surgeon, Dr. D. H. Patey, developed the modified radical mastectomy, in which he removed the breast and axillary nodes, but left the underlying chest muscle in place. Studies demonstrated that this operation lowered recurrence and mortality just as much as the classic Halsted procedure, but it did not produce as much chest deformity. Even so, American surgeons were reluctant to switch: A study by the American College of Surgeons in 1972 found that only twenty-six percent of the breast-cancer operations were modified radicals. An exception was Dr. George W. Crile, a famous surgeon and head of the Cleveland Clinic. He became a champion of less radical surgery, and even asserted that in instances of small, localized cancer, removal of the lump followed by radiation therapy was just as effective as a mastectomy.

This controversy within the medical community coincided with the growing awareness among women that they should have more control over their health-care decisions. Until that time, many if not most women were reluctant to talk about breast cancer or to admit that they had had a mastectomy. It was almost as if having had a mastectomy was a badge of shame, and a burden that women endured in silence. This changed as a number of respected and prominent women, most notably Happy Rockefeller and Betty Ford, "came out of the closet," and talked openly about their bouts with breast cancer.

This encouraged other women to follow suit, and at the same time, to demand more say in the way breast cancer was treated. At that time, the most common approach was to enter a hospital for a biopsy with the understanding that if the sample was found to be cancer, an immediate mastectomy would be performed. Typically, the biopsy was done under a general anesthesia and, with the woman still asleep, the tissue sample would be sent to the hospital pathology department for an immediate frozen section and microscopic examination. If cancer cells were detected, the surgeon would be notified and the operation would proceed. Thus, a woman entering an operating room for a biopsy would not know if she would waken to find her breast missing.

Understandably, this was a traumatic prospect for any woman, and was considered a major reason why so many women delayed seeking treatment for a suspicious breast lump. To many, the treatment was as dreaded as the disease itself. The surgeon's primary concern was in saving the woman's life, and little attention was paid to the emotional consequences. The formation of volunteer groups, such as the American Cancer Society's Reach to Recovery, helped somewhat, but women still were left to cope with their deformity, emotional problems, fears and other nonmedical aspects of breast cancer as best they could.

Happily, this has changed dramatically in recent years. Women now have more say in their treatment decisions, and most doctors are more sensitive to the emotional aspects of breast cancer for both the woman and her family. The most common operation is now the modified radical mastectomy, increasingly followed by breast reconstruction to overcome the deformity of losing a breast. For small (less than 4 cm.) cancers that are confined to the breast, a lumpectomy or partial mastectomy followed by radiation therapy may be just as effective as more extensive surgery. In this procedure, the cancer and a small amount of surrounding cancer-free tissue are removed and the axillary lymph nodes are dissected for evidence of spread. As soon as the wound has healed sufficiently, a woman will begin radiation therapy, which is aimed at killing any cancer cells that may have been missed in the operation.

Many breast specialists are still skeptical that this approach will produce as great a chance of a cure as a modified radical mastectomy, but several major studies suggest that it may be just as effective. The largest of these studies is the National Surgical Adjuvant Breast Project, which involved 1,843 women treated at more than thirty institutions in the United States and Canada. The women were randomly divided into three treatment groups: partial mastectomy alone, partial mastectomy plus radiation therapy and a simple mastectomy. Early results of this study were published in 1985 and showed similar survival for all three groups. However, there was a greater incidence of local recurrence among women who had only a partial mastectomy, which led Dr. Bernard Fisher, a University of Pittsburgh surgeon and head of the project, and his fellow researchers to conclude that women having a partial mastectomy should also have follow-up radiation therapy.

Even though many breast surgeons do not favor a partial mastectomy, most now agree that a woman should be more informed and allowed to participate in the decision-making process. The former one-step biopsy/treatment procedure is now seldom done, and if it is, a tentative diagnosis of cancer will have been made before the operation and a woman will be given an opportunity to get a second opinion and explore other treatment options. Some women may not want to participate in the decision-making process, but increasingly, they are the exceptions and not the norm, as in the past. Second opinions are encouraged and a woman also can meet with a plastic surgeon before her mastectomy to plan breast reconstruction.

Obviously, breast cancer is still a dreaded and difficult disease, but today's approach makes it easier for both the woman and her family to cope with its consequences. Improved reconstruction techniques make it easier for a woman to accept the loss of a breast. Although there is no cure yet for breast cancer once it has spread beyond the breast, an increasing number of women are enjoying many years of comfortable, productive life thanks to combinations of treatments that can produce remissions for large numbers of women. And today's increased emphasis on early diagnosis and treatment is paying off in improving chances of a cure.

SUMMING UP

A woman's breasts are more than milk-producing glands; they also are objects of sexual attraction and, to many, the embodiment of femininity and maternal nurturing. Breasts are particularly sensitive to hormonal changes, and many breast disorders are hormone-related. Breast cancer remains one of the most common and serious of all breast diseases. All women must be attuned to the early warning signs of breast cancer and seek prompt treatment, thereby giving themselves their best chance of overcoming this most dreaded of all female cancers.

Chapter 9

Ovarian Disorders

IN A VERY REAL SENSE, THE OVARIES ARE A WOMAN'S MASTER glands. These small, egg-shaped glands are tucked deep within the pelvic cavity, one on each side of the uterus and in close proximity to the fallopian tubes. They are formed during the embryonic stage—about four weeks after conception takes place—and by the fifth month of gestation, the fetal ovaries contain six to seven million immature egg follicles. No new follicles are ever formed; in fact this number declines to about two million by the time of birth. During a woman's reproductive years, only three hundred to five hundred of these follicles develop into mature eggs; the others wither and die.

Until puberty, a girl's ovaries are quiescent, producing only a very small amount of hormones. But as puberty approaches, the ovaries "wake up," thanks to stimulation of the pituitary gland's gonadotropin hormones. As the ovaries increase their output of estrogen, the girl develops the secondary female sex characteristics—breasts, pubic and axillary hair and the rounded curves of a woman's figure. The onset of menstruation is the culmination of this developmental process.

Theoretically, each month during her reproductive

years, one and sometimes more of the egg follicles ripens and is released, ready for fertilization. This process, referred to as ovulation, is controlled by the complex, finely tuned hormonal feedback system described in Chapters 1 and 3.

Scores of factors can interfere with proper ovarian function. The ovaries are exquisitely sensitive to what is going on elsewhere in the body and all systems have to be just right in order for them to function properly. If a woman weighs too little or too much, if her thyroid fails to produce the proper amount of its hormones, or if she is ill or under heavy stress, the ovaries may shut down. This sensitivity actually is protective and designed to ensure that, should conception take place, the developing fetus will have an optimal environment. Of course, the system is not foolproof; there are times when conception takes place under extremely adverse conditions, and others in which the ovaries fail to function for no apparent reason.

The hormonal feedback systems controlling ovulation and the menstrual cycle are described in detail in Chapter 4, and will be only briefly summarized here. After regular ovulation is established, usually one to two years after menarche, a woman can expect to have an average of thirteen cycles of twenty-eight to twenty-nine days each per year. Some women will have more, with cycles of twenty-one or twenty-two days, while others may have fewer, with cycles up to thirty-five days. Menstrual cycles of twenty-one to thirty-five days are considered normal. In addition, all women now and then have cycles in which they bleed but do not ovulate. Among younger women, this may happen only once or twice a year, but as a woman grows older, the number of anovulatory cycles increases.

During the first, or follicular, phase of the menstrual cycle, there is a steady rise in follicle-stimulating hormone, which prompts the ovary to prepare a follicle to mature. This causes a steady rise in estrogen during the follicular phase, with a rapid increase as the follicle nears maturity.

This rise in estrogen has a brief decline which signals the hypothalamus to tell the pituitary to increase production of LH and FSH. The surge in these gonadotropins results in raising the estrogen level again. Up to this point, the level of circulating progesterone has been very low; just before ovulation, the follicle begins to increase progesterone production, and blood levels of the hormone rise sharply. Other hormones, including prolactin, growth hormone, ACTH-cortisol, parathyroid hormone, calcitonin and androgens, also rise during this midcycle period.

The surge of FSH and LH prompts release of the mature egg from the follicle that then develops into the corpus luteum, which refers to the yellowish fat of this structure. The corpus luteum secretes large amounts of progesterone, the hormone that prepares the endometrium for the fertilized egg and maintains the pregnancy if conception takes place. If the egg is not fertilized by the time it reaches the uterus—a journey that takes four to six days—there is a sharp drop in progesterone and estrogen and the endometrium begins to break down. Fourteen days after ovulation, menstruation—the shedding of the uterine lining—takes place. Prostaglandins secreted by the uterus are thought to help facilitate menstruation by causing contractions of the uterine muscles. Excessive prostaglandins are believed to cause the painful cramping experienced by many women during the first day or two of their periods.

The hormonal changes that occur at different points of the menstrual cycle are responsible for varied physical and emotional changes. The many symptoms of the premenstrual syndrome are by now well-known (see Chapter 4). Many women note that they experience a rise in sexual desire at about midcycle; this is thought to be due to a rise in androgens at this time. Androgens, male hormones that are produced by a woman's adrenal glands, are responsible for female libido. (Androgens also control male libido, but in men, the testes are the major source of these hormones.) The role of estrogen in sexual desire is unknown. Taking extra estrogen does not increase libido in a normal healthy woman, but removing the ovaries will lower sexual drive, while giving replacement estrogen will restore it.

During the premenstrual phase, many women experience diminished interest in sex. This is thought to be due to increased progesterone and perhaps aldosterone. Contrary to popular belief, orgasm and the ability to achieve it is not controlled by hormones; instead, it is an involuntary reflex during which there is a sudden release of muscular tension and congested blood vessels produced by sexual stimulation. Women of all ages are capable of orgasm, regardless of their hormonal status. In fact, many older women find that they actually are more sexually responsive and achieve orgasm easier than when they were younger. The reasons for this are probably both psychological and physical.

AMENORRHEA

Amenorrhea, or failure to menstruate, is one of the most common signs of ovarian failure. As noted earlier, the ovaries respond to almost all of the other endocrine glands, and any hormonal imbalance can result in failure to menstruate. Most often, however, amenorrhea is not associated with any disorder. Undiagnosed pregnancy is one of the most common causes for amenorrhea; menopause, both artificial and natural, is another. Other causes include emotional stress; the use of birth control pills and certain other drugs; weight loss, often due to anorexia nervosa or rigorous exercise training; diabetes and other illnesses; tumors; infection; ovarian cysts; irradiation of the reproductive organs; and congenital abnormalities, including obstruction of the cervix or vagina. Many of these are discussed in Chapter 4; in this chapter, we will concentrate on specific ovarian disorders.

Unless there are other signs of abnormalities, such as failure to grow or develop secondary sexual characteristics, it is acceptable to wait until a girl is sixteen years old before being concerned over primary amenorrhea, which is failure to start menstruating. This is relatively rare; when it happens, about sixty percent of the cases can be traced to congenital defects that affect ovarian or genital development. The remaining forty percent are due to hormonal disorders, cystic ovaries and other ovarian or uterine disorders.

In attempting to track down the cause of primary amenorrhea, a doctor will start by reviewing prior medical history, with special attention to growth and development during puberty. If, for example, there has been a normal onset and progression of puberty, including development of breasts and other sex characteristics, it is a sign that the ovaries are functioning and that the problem probably lies in some sort of structural abnormality, such as lack of a vagina. If a young woman has normal breasts but little or no axillary or pubic hair, the problem may be due to a chromosomal abnormality in which a person develops female characteristics but has a male genetic makeup.

CHROMOSOMAL ABNORMALITIES

All body cells with nuclei have forty-six chromosomes with the exception of the egg and sperm, which have twenty-three each to make a total of forty-six when they unite. The female genotype carries two X (female) sex chromosomes, while the male genotype has an X and a Y (male) chromosome. Thus the female egg always carries the X, or female characteristic, while the sperm may carry either male or female characteristics. If an egg is fertilized with a Y chromosome, the baby will be a boy; an X sperm will produce a girl. The Y chromosome carries a gene that controls formation of testes in the embryo. These embryonic testes secrete hormones that further develop the male reproductive tract.

In rare instances, something goes amiss at the moment of conception. For example, an abnormal sperm lacking the X or Y chromosome may fertilize an egg; instead of an XX genotype, the baby will have an XO. Similarly, an XO genotype can be produced by a normal X sperm fertilizing an egg lacking an X chromosome. (An X chromosome is needed to produce a viable fetus; there are no recorded instances of a YO fetus, which would have only the male genotype, surviving.) Since an XX genotype is required to form normal ovaries, babies born without this combination (e.g., XO) may have female characteristics, but they will lack properly functioning ovaries. An XO genotype occurs about once out of every 2,500 females, and is referred to as Turner's syndrome.

Typically, a woman with Turner's syndrome is short, has a thick, webbed neck, underdeveloped breasts, immature genitals, and the ovaries are absent and replaced by only streaks of tissue. A number of other congenital abnormalities also may accompany Turner's syndrome, such as autoimmune diseases, thyroid disorder, diabetes, hearing loss, a possible increased susceptibility to cancer, growth disorders, kidney abnormalities and hypertension.

Sometimes the defect may be apparent at an early age, but usually it is not evident until puberty. Not uncommonly, a girl with Turner's syndrome will develop breasts, but she will have sparse or absent pubic and axillary hair. After Turner's syndrome has been confirmed, estrogen therapy is started at some point during adolescence. Care should be taken not to give estrogen too early as it will further diminish growth. With estrogen therapy, a woman with Turner's syndrome will develop normal female secondary sex characteristics and, if she has an intact uterus, she will menstruate if she also is given progesterone.

In the past, women with Turner's syndrome have been hopelessly infertile, even though they may have a normal uterus. Recent advances in in vitro fertilization and embryo transplants now make it possible for some of these women to become mothers by obtaining donor eggs that are fertilized with their husbands' sperm and then transferred to the woman who will carry the baby to term. Obviously, in order for this to be successful, the woman with Turner's syndrome will have to have the proper hormonal therapy to support a pregnancy.

In about one out of every five hundred births, a baby will be born with poorly differentiated sexual characteristics. In very rare instances, the baby may be a hermaphrodite, with both internal ovarian and testicular tissue. The external genitals may be mixed, but male characteristics usually dominate. This sexual ambiguity is usually treated by surgically removing the nonpredominating sexual characteristics.

More commonly, the baby will be a pseudohermaphrodite, defined as having different external genitalia and internal reproductive organs. In order for the male embryo to develop the right reproductive organs for its sex, its testes must produce the right hormones during the embryonic stage. Until about the eighth week of gestation, the gonads of males and females are indistinguishable, and without male hormones, they will develop into female reproductive organs regardless of the genotype. Thus, if a male embryo at this stage does not receive the necessary male hormones, it will develop what is called testicular feminization. The baby will be born with testes (often hidden inside the body), and female external genitalia (a vagina but no uterus or fallopian tubes). Typically, these individuals are reared as girls; with the onset of puberty, breasts may develop, but there will be little or no sexual hair. Fortunately, this type of defect is quite rare.

Typically, the child will be allowed to enter puberty, and then undergo surgical removal of the testes. If the testes are removed earlier, estrogen is given at the time of puberty to stimulate development of breasts and sexual hair. Obviously, women with these chromosomal abnormalities are infertile, and there is no treatment that can correct the condition. They usually have a vaginal canal, however, and can have normal sexual relations.

Occasionally, the use of hormone preparations by a woman during the first trimester of pregnancy can cause sexual abnormalities in the developing fetus. At one time, progestogens were given to women to prevent a miscarriage; nearly three percent of the baby girls born to these women had some degree of masculinization of their external genitalia. Danazol, a drug derived from testosterone that is used to treat endometriosis, has sometimes been taken by women who did not realize they were pregnant, resulting in baby girls being born with male genitalia. Large amounts of stilbestrol, a synthetic estrogen that also was once given to prevent miscarriage, also can cause masculinization.

In unusual cases, a mother may have a tumor that produces male hormones; these not only cause virilization in the woman but also can result in masculinization of a female fetus should the tumor be present during early pregnancy. Although these events may be very distressing to the parents, the problem is usually easily corrected. The effects are usually confined to the external genitalia, and these can be surgically corrected at the appropriate time. The girls usually are born with the proper internal reproductive organs and, with the onset of puberty, will develop into normal women. However, the occurrence of these abnormalities underscores the importance of avoiding hormonal drugs if there is any chance that a woman may be pregnant or that conception may take place while they are being used.

OVARIAN CYSTS

Polycystic ovaries are one of the more common causes of menstrual irregularities and failure to ovulate. As its name indicates, this disorder is characterized by the formation of multiple estrogen-producing ovarian cysts. What initiates the syndrome is unknown, but once it is set in motion, it perpetuates itself with increasing hormonal imbalances.

Normally, the rise of estrogen in the first phase of the menstrual cycle signals the pituitary to increase secretion of FSH and LH. In response to these gonad-stimulating hormones, one or more ovarian follicles begin to mature. One or two of them outpace the others, growing to one-half to three-quarters of an inch in diameter. When the egg is mature, it bursts from its sac and the large follicle in which it grew is replaced by the corpus luteum, which begins secreting large amounts of progesterone to build and maintain the lush uterine lining that has been primed by the earlier surge of estrogen.

In polycystic disease, however, the egg is not released from its sac; instead, the follicle thickens and continues to produce estrogen. This results in menstrual irregularities; the period may be delayed, or come every two weeks for a cycle or two and then not occur for several cycles. Bleeding may be heavier than normal—a characteristic of menstruation without ovulation. There may be abdominal pain caused by pressure from the expanding cysts.

Most commonly, the cyst will disappear in a month or two, and no treatment is required. In fact, a woman may not be aware that she had an ovarian cyst. But, in some women, the condition becomes chronic, and is referred to as polycystic disease or Stein-Leventhal syndrome. The ovaries will become enlarged with white cysts and thickened thecal cells that secrete large amounts of estrogen and androgens. The egg cannot escape from these thickened thecal walls, and ovulation does not occur. Because of the large amounts of androgens being produced, a woman with polycystic ovaries often will become hairier than normal, and may also be troubled by acne. (See Figure 17.)

Polycystic ovarian disease can be treated by taking hormones to stimulate ovulation. Alternatively, a part of the ovaries containing the thickened cysts may be removed. This was once the most common treatment of polycystic ovaries; today, it usually is reserved for women who desire to conceive and do not get an adequate response from hormonal manipulation to cause spontaneous ovulation.

TUMORS

A variety of tumors also can lead to ovarian failure. Many of these tumors produce hormones that interfere with normal ovulation and also may produce a variety of other symp-

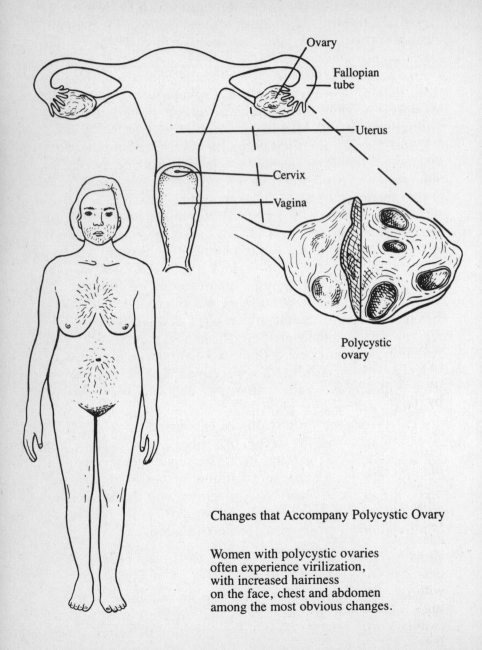

Ovary

Fallopian tube

Uterus

Cervix

Vagina

Polycystic ovary

Changes that Accompany Polycystic Ovary

Women with polycystic ovaries
often experience virilization,
with increased hairiness
on the face, chest and abdomen
among the most obvious changes.

toms, depending upon the hormones that are being secreted. Among the more common hormone-secreting tumors are:

Granulosa-Theca Cell Tumors

The most common of the ovarian hormone-producing tumors, the granulosa-theca cell tumor derives its name from the types of cells that predominate. The tumor secretes estrogen, androgens and progesterone. The most common symptoms are related to excessive estrogen, but in some women, there also are signs of virilism from the excessive androgens. These tumors can occur at any age, but are most common after the age of thirty. About ten to twenty percent are malignant.

Androblastomas

Androblastomas usually originate in the Sertoli-Leydig cells, and are the most common of the androgen-secreting ovarian tumors. Even so, they are quite rare, accounting for only one percent of the solid ovarian tumors. They, too, can occur at any age, but seventy percent are in women twenty to forty years old. About twenty percent are malignant. The most common symptom of androblastomas is virilism caused by the excessive androgens.

Lipid (Lipoid) Cell Tumors

Lipid cell tumors also are virilizing tumors that fall into one of two categories: adrenallike tumors that secrete estrogens, or hilar or Leydig cell tumors that produce androgens. The adrenallike tumors have a twenty percent rate of malignancy and often produce symptoms similar to Cushing's disease—for example, accumulation of fat on the face and shoulders, giving a moon-faced, hump-back appearance; easy bruising; and muscle weakness, among others—but without the increased levels of cortisol seen in true Cushing's. These tumors are most common among women twenty to fifty years old, and are often associated with diabetes.

The hilar cell tumors are rarely malignant. They occur most commonly after the age of forty-five.

Germ-Cell Tumors

Germ-cell tumors secrete non-steroidal hormones. The two that secrete chorionic gonadotropin (hCG)—dysgerminomas and choriocarcinomas—are cancerous and are most commonly seen among children or young adults. Carcinoids produce serotonin, strumas produce thyroxine and a mixed carcinoid and struma produce both hormones. These are rarely cancerous, and occur most commonly in middle-age or after menopause.

All of these ovarian tumors are relatively rare. Some of the malignant tumors are a result of metastases of cancers elsewhere in the body. Surgical removal is the primary treatment; cancers may also require radiation therapy or anticancer drugs. However, these cancers continue to grow even with treatment.

OVARIAN CANCER

Cancer of the ovaries is the third most common gynecological cancer (preceded by cancers of the cervix and uterus/endometrium). About eighteen thousand new cases are diagnosed each year, and more than eleven thousand deaths result. The high death rate is attributed to the fact that the cancer usually is not diagnosed until it reaches an advanced stage. Unlike cervical cancer, which can be detected by a simple, inexpensive Pap smear, there is no simple screening examination for ovarian cancer. Nor are there likely to be symptoms in the early stages. Sometimes X rays of the pelvic area will show a growth, but this is relatively rare in the early stages.

The most common symptoms are abdominal swelling and discomfort. Frequently, the swelling is so extreme that the woman looks like she is in the advanced stages of pregnancy. Other symptoms include weight loss (except for the distended abdomen), nausea, vomiting, urinary urgency or retention, constipation and other gastrointestinal problems caused by the rapidly expanding growth and accumulation of fluid.

Whenever a doctor feels an ovarian growth during a pelvic examination, a biopsy should be done, especially if the woman is past menopause—the time of life in which ovarian cancer is the most common. Although four out of five ovarian growths turn out to be benign, there is no way of telling for sure without doing a biopsy. This can be done by using a laparoscope—an instrument with viewing devices that is inserted into the pelvic cavity through a small incision below the navel.

About eighty-five percent of ovarian cancers arise in the epithelial tissue that covers the ovaries. The others originate in other types of cells; in addition, the ovaries are a common site for metastatic cancers that have spread from other parts of the body.

The role of hormones as a possible cause of ovarian cancer is unknown, although some studies have reported a somewhat higher incidence of the disease among postmenopausal women who take estrogen. The ovary has estrogen receptors, but these are not found in the epithelium, the most common site in which ovarian cancers originate. The cancers themselves have been found to contain receptors for both estrogen and progesterone, and the use of progesterone has produced response rates of up to thirty-eight percent in some studies, but this is not a universal finding.

Recent epidemiological studies have found that women who have had several children are less likely to develop ovarian cancer than women who are childless or who have had small families. A British researcher, Dr. Valerie Beral, and her colleagues have found that Catholic women with large families have a lower incidence of ovarian cancer than Protestant or Jewish women with smaller families. The reasons for this are unknown, but Dr. Beral suggests that pregnancy or some other aspect of childbearing may protect a woman from this type of cancer. Treatment involves removal of the ovaries and other reproductive organs. If the cancer has spread to surrounding tissue, this too will be removed if possible. Surgery may be followed by radiation therapy and, depending upon the type of cancer, chemotherapy. However, these treatments do not adequately keep the cancer from recurring.

HYSTERECTOMY

Obviously, no discussion of ovarian function is complete without a mention of hysterectomy. As noted in Chapter 6, millions of American women have had hysterectomies. In a very large number of women over the age of forty, the operation includes removal of the ovaries. This creates an abrupt menopause that is invariably accompanied by hot flashes, mood swings and other menopausal symptoms. Since there has been no opportunity for a gradual tapering off of hormones, the symptoms frequently are more severe than those experienced with natural menopause.

Increasingly, women who must undergo a hysterectomy are demanding that their ovaries be left intact unless there is a good medical reason for their removal. Cancer elsewhere in the female reproductive tract often spreads to the ovaries, and this is justification for their removal. But there is no reason to remove the ovaries of a woman who is having a hysterectomy due to benign fibroids or other such conditions. Studies have found that women who have their ovaries removed at an early age are much more likely to develop severe osteoporosis than women who enter a later natural menopause. A second opinion is advised before any woman consents to removal of her ovaries for a benign condition.

SUMMING UP

The ovaries serve as a woman's major source of sex hormones, and also are essential in normal reproductive function. These glands are extraordinarily sensitive to their environment and a large number of circumstances can lead to ovarian failure. Some of these are relatively easy to detect and correct; others may require considerable medical detective work to pinpoint the cause. Fortunately, chromosomal and other uncorrectable abnormalities are uncommon. However, recent advances in in vitro fertilization and embryo transfers now make it possible for some women without ovaries but with normal uteruses to experience pregnancy and childbirth.

Chapter 10

Diabetes and
Hypoglycemia

Diabetes, a chronic disease marked by the body's inability to properly metabolize carbohydrates and other foods, is the most common endocrine disorder in the world. In the United States, more than ten million people have diabetes, and, for reasons that are not clearly understood, their number is rising by about six percent per year. The disease is the direct cause of about 40,000 deaths a year, but when diabetic complications such as kidney failure and cardiovascular disorders are added, the total number of diabetes-related deaths soars to more than 300,000, making it the country's third leading cause of mortality. In addition, it is a very costly disease; diabetes adds more than $10 billion to the nation's total medical bill each year, and this does not count the indirect costs of time lost from work and other such expenses. Of course, it is impossible to put a price tag on the human suffering for both patients and families caused by diabetes.

Although these statistics are grim, there is a more optimistic side to diabetes. Over the last decade, our knowledge of how to control diabetes has progressed remarkably, and with proper management, today's diabetic patient can lead a normal, productive life. However, this requires a thorough knowledge of the disease and diligent attention to virtually every detail of living; a person with diabetes must monitor day-to-day activities that most of us never give a second thought to. Diet, exercise, infection, stress, the menstrual cycle and myriad other factors can alter blood sugar and make diabetes worse.

There are two different forms of diabetes. In one, which has at least three names—Type 1, juvenile-onset, or insulin-dependent diabetes—the pancreas ceases to produce insulin—the hormone the body needs for a number of functions, especially utilization of blood sugar, or glucose, its major fuel. This type of diabetes requires daily injections of insulin and close attention to balancing the intake of fat, protein and carbohydrate.

In the other form, which is known as Type 2, adult-onset or non-insulin-dependent diabetes, the pancreas may produce insulin, but the body is unable to make proper use of it. Type 2 diabetes often can be treated by weight loss and exercise and, although it is a serious disease, it is not as life-threatening as uncontrolled Type 1 diabetes. Before the discovery of insulin by two Canadian scientists—Frederick G. Banting, a medical student, and Dr. Charles H. Best—in 1921, a person with Type 1 diabetes usually succumbed to the disease within a few months or a year or two.

ROLES OF INSULIN

Insulin is needed to regulate the amount of glucose that circulates in the blood. Almost all carbohydrate and fifty to sixty percent of protein is converted to glucose; that which is not needed immediately is stored, mostly in the liver, as glycogen, which is converted back into glucose as the body needs it. Any rise in blood glucose is quickly sensed by the pancreas, which secretes extra insulin to take care of it. (See Figure 18.) If there is not enough insulin or if the body is unable to use the insulin it has, the blood becomes overloaded with glucose, a condition referred to as hyperglyce-

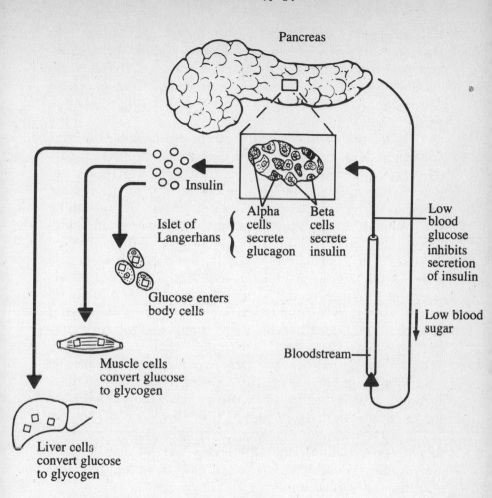

Insulin Metabolism

mia. Some of the excess glucose spills over into the urine, resulting in the sweet urine that the ancients recognized as a hallmark of diabetes.

Insulin is also needed for proper fat metabolism. Excess fat is stored as triglycerides in the adipose, or fat tissue. Excess carbohydrate calories also are used to form the triglyceride molecule. Insulin helps prevent the breakdown of triglycerides, but when the hormone is lacking, the liver metabolizes these triglycerides, forming highly acidic substances called ketones. The muscles can utilize a certain amount of ketones, but if they are produced in an excessive amount, they will build up in the body, upsetting the body's chemical balance.

The causes of diabetes are unknown, although several risk factors have been identified that appear to make a person more vulnerable to the disease. In Type 1 diabetes, genetics seems to play a role; a family history of the disease increases the risk. The immune system is also thought to be instrumental. In susceptible people, the disease often develops following a viral infection, an observation that has led researchers to speculate that the immune system somehow destroys the insulin-producing cells (the Islets of Langerhans) in response to the viral infection. Type 1 diabetes usually develops in childhood or young adulthood, but there are exceptions in which it is diagnosed in older people.

In Type 2 diabetes, the pancreas may produce insulin in varying amounts; in fact, some patients have higher-than-normal levels of insulin, while others have sharply reduced insulin production. Most people with this form of the disease are middle-aged or older, and the majority are overweight. It is thought that the extra weight may make a person more resistant to insulin, or may increase the body's need for the hormone.

Pregnancy is another precipitating factor for diabetes. About two to six percent of all pregnant women develop gestational diabetes, a form of the disease that appears during pregnancy and disappears with childbirth. As noted in the chapter on Pregnancy and Childbirth, gestational diabetes is particularly serious for the fetus and is a major cause of stillbirths or death shortly after birth. Women who have had gestational diabetes also are more likely to develop diabetes later in life.

SIGNS OF DIABETES

As early as 1500 B.C., doctors recognized the classic symptoms of diabetes. Greek physicians named the disease diabetes mellitus: *Diabetes* means "fountain" or "siphon," referring to the excessive urination that is a common sign of the disease, and *mellitus*, which means "honey," refers to the sweet smell and taste of urine caused by the excessive glucose in it. The most common early symptoms of diabetes are insatiable thirst accompanied by copious urination, hunger, weight loss and weakness. Mood swings are common. People with diabetes are more susceptible to infection; for many women, one of the first signs is an increased vulnerability to vaginal infections. Male impotence also is common in diabetes.

Diabetes affects virtually every organ system in the body. Leg cramps or pins-and-needles sensations resulting from nerve damage may occur. The disease also may cause eye problems and kidney damage. High blood pressure, elevated cholesterol, and atherosclerosis (hardening of the arteries from fatty plaque) all are made worse by diabetes, but these usually are later effects of the disease.

THE SELF-CARE CONCEPT

The concept of diabetes self-care has evolved over the last decade and has meant new freedom and greater control, not only of their disease but also over their lives, for many people with the Type 1 form. Of course, self-care has always been an important part of diabetes treatment, since it is the patient who must learn to inject insulin and be alert to symptoms that indicate blood glucose is too low or too high. In the past, this meant testing urine at least daily for the presence of sugar (glycosuria). Although urine tests provide useful information about diabetes control, they do not necessarily reflect the immediate picture, and consequently, do not tell a patient what he or she should do at that moment to correct any imbalance. This shortcoming has been remedied by the development of new blood tests that enable a person to measure his or her own blood glucose within a minute or two, and to take whatever action is appropriate to normalize sugar levels. By keeping careful daily records of blood sugar levels, food and insulin intake, exercise and other factors that affect the body's metabolism, a diabetic patient can avoid dangerous swings in blood glucose, and, most experts agree, prevent many of the serious complications of diabetes.

Successful diabetes self-care requires balancing the amount of insulin that is injected with the intake of food. Exercise and other circumstances that affect the body's uptake of insulin also must be taken into consideration. For example, a person who engages in regular vigorous exercise will not need as many units of insulin as a more sedentary person. A diabetic woman will require extra insulin during the premenstrual phase of her monthly cycle to overcome the anti-insulin effects of the female hormones that are high at that time. Stress and infection also make blood glucose more difficult to control.

After diabetes has been diagnosed by blood tests following a sugar drink, it is important that the patient learn how to measure his or her blood sugar and how to balance insulin dosages against food intake, exercise and other factors. This may involve intensive education sessions with a doctor, nurse, diabetes educator or other health professional who has been assigned this role. At first, some people have difficulty giving themselves insulin injections or pricking a finger to draw the drop or two of blood that is needed to measure glucose levels. But the large majority of people find that, in a week or two, they have mastered not only the injection routine, but that they also can measure blood glucose in a couple of minutes. A variety of automated glucose meters are now widely available that remove much of the guess work from measuring blood sugars; instead of the earlier methods that required matching color strips to determine the level of blood glucose, the newer meters give a digital reading and are much easier to use.

Type 2 diabetes may be optimally managed with a diet and exercise program, or an oral drug to stimulate insulin secretion and uptake may be prescribed if these conservative measures are not effective. The medication helps the glucose to be metabolized and thus overcome the "barrier" or insulin-resistance which characterizes Type 2 diabetes.

People with diabetes need to pay special attention to keeping their toenails trimmed and groomed to avoid developing ingrown toenails. These can lead to serious foot infections, especially if circulation to the lower limbs is impaired.

THE PREGNANT DIABETIC

Diabetes self-care is particularly important for a woman with the disease who wants to have a baby. Only a few years ago, a pregnant woman with diabetes faced very discouraging odds for both herself and the baby. Studies conducted in the 1960s and early 1970s found that one out of five babies born to diabetic women died; among the survivors, up to eighteen percent had congenital malformations, twenty to thirty-six percent had brain damage, and two to nine percent were born with respiratory disorders. The "big, sick baby syndrome" was particularly common; sixteen to forty percent of the babies weighed nine or more pounds—a factor that increases the likelihood of complications for both the mother and baby.

This began to change in the late 1970s with the realization that a woman's chances of having a healthy baby increased if she could keep her blood glucose in the normal range throughout pregnancy. To achieve this, a woman must be extraordinarily motivated and attuned to her body; she also must know how to adjust her insulin dosage to meet her changing needs.

Ideally, a woman will have mastered the concept of successful diabetes self-care before attempting pregnancy. She should discuss her plans with both the doctor who treats her diabetes and with her obstetrician, who, ideally, should be experienced in the care of diabetic pregnancies. Since pregnancy often extends some of the more common complications of diabetes—especially eye and kidney problems, high blood pressure and heart disease—extra caution must be exercised by a woman who already has any of these.

Even if there is no prior evidence of complications, a woman should realize that pregnancy itself has profound effects on diabetes and the body's need for and utilization of insulin. The placenta manufactures anti-insulin hormones and enzymes and the high levels of estrogen and progesterone during pregnancy alter carbohydrate metabolism. If a woman's levels of blood glucose are too high, the fetus will respond by increasing its own insulin production. Since insulin acts as a fetal growth hormone, this can result in an oversized baby. Every now and then, the media exuberantly report the birth of a fifteen- or twenty-pound baby as though this were a marvelous feat. In reality, these big babies are likely to be very sick at birth, and those who survive often have serious birth defects. Maintaining a normal blood glucose level throughout pregnancy can prevent excess fetal growth and the other congenital abnormalities associated with diabetes.

High levels of insulin also lower the fetus's potassium level. This can lead to the development of weak, flaccid muscles and also can result in fatal heart arrhythmias—a major cause of fetal death in late pregnancy.

For several months before a diabetic woman attempts pregnancy, she should make sure that her blood sugar levels are normal and that other possible complications, such as high blood pressure, are under good control. If she is not already keeping daily blood glucose charts (see Figure 19), she should do so. While this kind of meticulous record-keeping may seem like a lot of bother at first, it is important for both the woman and her doctor because it provides a day-to-day overview of the state of the diabetes as well as a basis for corrective steps.

During pregnancy, a woman should plan to measure her blood glucose six to eight times a day: upon rising, before and after meals and at bedtime. Daily urine tests also are advised to make sure that the body chemistry is normal; blood glucose can be normal even when the body is breaking down fatty tissue and producing ketones, which pass into the fetal blood supply.

The woman should know how to adjust her food and insulin dosage to keep her blood glucose normal. It is particularly important that a pregnant diabetic woman eat on a regular schedule. Typically, this means three meals and three or four snacks a day, but some women may need to eat even more often. For example, if a morning urine test shows ketones, a woman may need to wake up in the middle of the night for a snack.

Because diligent self-monitoring and constant adjustment of insulin, food and exercise are so important during pregnancy, a session with a diabetes educator or doctor experienced in pregnancy and diabetes is advisable. Nondiabetic women often marvel at the dedication and amount of work a diabetic patient puts into carrying her pregnancy to term; aspects of daily living that most of us take for granted must be carefully calculated and monitored. But diabetic mothers universally agree that the outcome—a normal, healthy baby—is worth the considerable effort.

GESTATIONAL DIABETES

Two to six percent of pregnant women develop a temporary type of diabetes that disappears almost immediately after delivery. Heretofore, this gestational diabetes often went undiagnosed and was the leading cause of late fetal death and stillbirths. Today, most obstetricians test for gestational diabetes and, if it is diagnosed, the woman must monitor her blood sugar and take insulin as though she had regular Type 1 diabetes.

The routine screening tests for gestational diabetes usually are administered in the twenty-sixth week of preg-

DATE AND WEIGHT.	INSULIN				AM Ketones		BREAKFAST		LUNCH		DINNER		Bed Time	During Night	EXPLANATIONS: Activity, illness, time and change of eating patterns, time of insulin reactions with blood sugar and treatment.
	Morning	Lunch	Supper	Bed Time			Before	2 Hrs. After	Before	2 Hrs. After	Before	2 Hrs. After			
S						B/G									
I						S/A									
Supp. Insulin															
S						B/G									
I						S/A									
Supp. Insulin															
S						B/G									
I						S/A									
Supp. Insulin															

URINE AND BLOOD GLUCOSE TESTS

SANSUM MEDICAL RESEARCH FOUNDATION
2219 BATH STREET
SANTA BARBARA, CALIFORNIA 93105

B/G

S/A

B/G

S/A

B/G

S/A

B/G

S/A

S

I

Supp.
Insulin

S

I

Supp.
Insulin

S

I

Supp.
Insulin

S

I

Supp.
Insulin

nancy. A woman is asked to take a drink containing fifty grams of glucose and her blood sugar is measured an hour later. If it is elevated (more than 140 mg./dl.), a three-hour glucose tolerance test, which involves drinking 100 grams of glucose and then measuring blood sugar hourly for the next three hours, will be administered. Women who are at a high risk for gestational diabetes should be tested more often, for example, during the twelfth, eighteenth and thirty-second weeks of pregnancy. Factors that increase the risk include obesity, a family history of diabetes, a history of sugar in the urine, glucose intolerance or previous gestational diabetes, personal birthweight of more than nine pounds, and recurrent urinary infections during pregnancy. A poor obstetrical history, such as previous miscarriages, stillbirths, large babies, toxemia, excessive amniotic fluid, or congenital defects, also indicates an increased risk of gestational diabetes. (For more details, see Chapter 5.)

As a diabetic woman approaches the end of her pregnancy, extra-careful monitoring is required to ensure that the baby is not in distress. At one time, doctors were reluctant to let a diabetic woman proceed to full term and a natural labor and delivery—an understandable caution given the large number of late fetal deaths and stillbirths. With the development of self-monitoring and improved blood glucose control, more obstetricians are now willing to let a pregnant diabetic go to full term and normal delivery, but from the thirty-fourth week on, the woman will be asked to be particularly attuned to fetal movements; any drop in kicking and other activity is a warning sign to call the obstetrician immediately. A drop in insulin requirements or other changes also warrant immediate investigation. During these last few weeks before delivery, the doctor also may want to check the baby's heart rate more often.

If there are any signs of fetal distress, tests should be done to assess the baby's status and its degree of maturity. If the baby's lungs are fully developed, many doctors will go ahead and induce labor or do a cesarean section on the theory that, by this time, the baby will probably be better off on the outside. As soon as the baby is full-term, most obstetricians would prefer to induce labor if it does not start on its own. More commonly, however, if a woman has managed to keep her diabetes in good control throughout her pregnancy, she is likely to have a normal labor and delivery.

REACTIVE HYPOGLYCEMIA

Periodically, women's magazines and other popular media "discover" a new disease, often with vague, troubling symptoms that most people experience from time to time. Typically, physicians are at a loss to find a cause from the symptoms, and the frustrated patient, convinced that something really is wrong, goes from doctor to doctor in search of a diagnosis and treatment. Then an article appears in which the symptoms are described and the malady is given a name. Almost overnight, thousands of people make a self-diagnosis and rush to their doctors, article in hand, to announce that they have finally found the answer. Hypoglycemia is a classic example of symptoms in search of a disease.

Hypoglycemia, which is the medical term for low blood sugar, or glucose, can occur in diabetes and other conditions when the amount of insulin circulating in the blood is more than is needed to metabolize available sugar. Among diabetic patients, it occurs most often when too much insulin has been injected, resulting in a rapid depletion of available blood glucose. Signs of this kind of insulin reaction include tingling sensations, particularly in the mouth and fingers; buzzing in the ears; a cold, clammy feeling; pallor, excessive sweating; feelings of weakness, dizziness, or faintness; headache; hunger; abdominal pain; irritability and mood swings; palpitations; trembling; impaired vision; and sudden drowsiness or sudden awakening from sleep, especially accompanied by other symptoms. In a person with diabetes, an insulin reaction should be treated by administering a rapidly absorbed source of sugar. If ignored, an insulin reaction can progress to a coma and even death. Diabetes self-care includes careful education on how to recognize and handle hypoglycemia.

Among non-diabetics, clinical hypoglycemia is rare because the hormonal feedback systems that control the body's release of insulin are very efficient. When the body senses that blood glucose is low, the pancreas reacts by halting insulin secretion and other systems aimed at maintaining an adequate supply of glucose come into play. But it is possible by dietary manipulation to "trick" the body into producing too much insulin and consequently experience some of the symptoms associated with hypoglycemia. This occurs most often among women who consume a low-calorie, high-carbohydrate diet.

Typically, the woman will have a carbohydrate breakfast—for example, orange juice, coffee and a Danish or sweet roll. The pancreas will secrete a large amount of insulin to handle the large amount of glucose produced by this meal. But since the breakfast contained very little protein and fat, which take longer to metabolize than simple carbohydrates, by lunchtime the glucose from breakfast has been burned up and the woman may well experience some of the symptoms of hypoglycemia, most commonly headache, hunger, shakiness, lightheadedness, irritability and palpitations. If she eases her hunger with a sweet snack or more simple carbohydrate, the pancreas will again respond by pumping out insulin; by late afternoon, the blood glucose may again be below normal and the symptoms will return.

This woman does not have a disease, per se; instead, her body is reacting normally to poor dietary habits. And although her blood sugar falls significantly, this type of reactive hypoglycemia is a normal variation rather than a clinical disorder. The symptoms can be avoided by adding protein and fat to her breakfast or by eating a snack in the midmorning to take care of the large amount of insulin produced by the high-sugar breakfast. But instead of making the proper dietary adjustments, many women end up going from doctor to doctor to find a diagnosis for their symptoms. Many eventually undergo a five-hour glucose tolerance test, which will show the low blood sugar that has resulted from an unbalanced high-carbohydrate diet, and they will be diagnosed as "hypoglycemic."

OTHER CAUSES OF HYPOGLYCEMIA

Hypoglycemia is a component of a number of diseases, but unlike in reactive hypoglycemia, the symptoms do not occur in response to eating carbohydrates; instead, they may appear at unpredictable times, including when fasting. Drugs are the most common cause of hypoglycemia; in addition to insulin, low blood glucose can be caused by sulfonylureas (oral anti-diabetes drugs) which increase insulin secretion and lower blood glucose.

Alcohol also produces hypoglycemia by interfering with the liver's ability to make glucose. Alcohol-induced hypoglycemia is particularly common among people who drink heavily for several hours without eating. Other drugs that can lower blood glucose include large amounts of aspirin, acetaminophen, colchicine (a drug used to treat gout), MAO inhibitors, beta blockers, and some of the anti-psychotic medications.

Insulin-secreting tumors also can produce hypoglycemia through their abnormal hormone production. Most of these tumors are insulinomas, which are small, usually benign, growths of pancreatic islet cells. Some types of cancer cause hypoglycemia, particularly cancers of the liver and adrenal glands, carcinoid tumors, lymphoma, sarcoma and other relatively rare diseases. Liver and kidney diseases, severe infection and congestive heart failure also may produce hypoglycemia.

Sometimes the excessive insulin is due to a faulty regulatory mechanism; instead of the body sensing that it has enough insulin, the signals get mixed up and the pancreas continues to secrete the hormone. Hormonal imbalances, such as deficiencies of growth hormone or cortisone, also may cause hypoglycemia.

Prolonged fasting, especially in infants, can cause hypoglycemia. Newborn babies are particularly susceptible to hypoglycemia, especially in the first few hours of life before the glucose regulatory systems are fully operational. Babies born to women with poorly controlled diabetes also may have problems regulating blood sugar because their pancreases have been producing large amounts of insulin to compensate for the high level of glucose in the mothers' circulation. Infant hypoglycemia also may be caused by congenital deficiencies in enzymes needed to metabolize glucose.

It should be stressed that hypoglycemia from these miscellaneous causes should not be confused with the reactive hypoglycemia that is most commonly associated with a diet high in carbohydrates and low in protein and fat. Since hypoglycemia that is unrelated to food absorption is potentially life-threatening, its cause should be identified and treated as soon as possible. Fortunately, these are uncommon disorders.

SUMMING UP

Diabetes is the most common of all endocrine disorders. It is also one of the most serious. Increased understanding of how to match insulin to diet and life-style, along with simple self-monitoring tests, have improved diabetes control. Most experts believe that better long-term control of diabetes will help prevent many of the common complications of the disease. Hypoglycemia that is unrelated to the treatment of diabetes is not as common as many people have been led to believe; most cases are not caused by a clinical disorder, but instead can be traced to poor dietary habits.

Chapter 11

Thyroid Disorders

THE THYROID, A BUTTERFLY-SHAPED GLAND THAT RESTS atop the windpipe, is the body's equivalent to a car's accelerator. Thyroid hormones control the body's metabolic rate—when levels are too high, body processes are speeded up, making a person feel he or she is constantly running in high gear. In contrast, when thyroid hormone levels are too low, body functions slow to a crawl.

Normally, the thyroid weighs about 20 grams, or .7 ounces, but when diseased, it may grow to many times this size. Many people have the mistaken notion that thyroid overgrowth, or goiter, is either a thing of the past or confined to certain parts of the world, such as the Alps, where the soil is lacking in the iodine the body needs to make thyroid hormones. Actually, thyroid disorders still are very common; more than ten million Americans have some form of thyroid dysfunction, although in two million, the problem is undiagnosed.

Even so, thyroid disease was more common in the past before we understood its causes or how to treat it. Ancient Chinese physicians observed that seaweed could cause a goiter to shrink, but they did not know that this was probably due to the iodine in the seaweed. Ancient Romans looked upon the development of a goiter in a young wife as a sign that she was pregnant, attesting to the fact that thyroid disease often appears during pregnancy. The prevalence of thyroid disease played an important part in the failure of Switzerland and other alpine countries to emerge as leading powers. Soil in these mountain regions lacks the iodine that the body needs to make thyroid hormones; as a result, the population fell under the dominance of healthier and stronger invaders.

During the Middle Ages, an enlarged thyroid was so common, especially among women, that people looked upon it as a mark of feminine beauty and thought that women had goiters to make the neck contour more graceful. Rubens and other artists of the period frequently chose female models who had goiters and other visible signs of thyroid disease. Of course, the deformities that accompany more advanced thyroid diseases are anything but beautiful, and the effects upon the body are even more devastating.

THE THYROID HORMONES

There are two active thyroid hormones: triiodothyronine, or T_3, and thyroxine, or T_4. The numbers refer to the number of iodine atoms on each molecule, but it is not known how the two hormones differ in their actions in the body. It is thought that T_3 is the more active hormone, and that a large portion of T_4 is converted to T_3. But how the hormones exert their actions on the cells is unknown—it is not clear if T_3 needs a second or third messenger to produce the net result.

The hormones are stored in the thyroid until needed by the body. When blood levels of thyroid hormones fall too low, the pituitary secretes thyroid-stimulating hormone, or TSH, which signals the thyroid to increase hormone secretion and production. (See Figure 20.)

Thyroid hormones are instrumental in almost all metabolic processes, controlling the rate of metabolism and also the body's consumption of energy (calories). Thyroid hor-

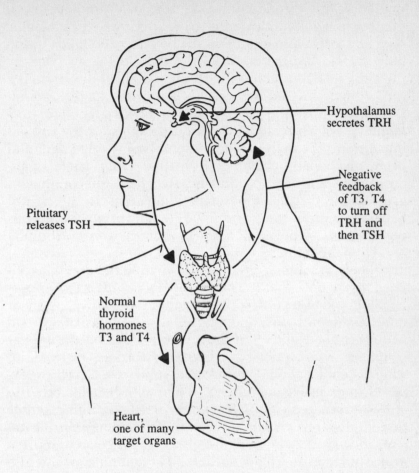

The Normal Thyroid, Its Controls and Actions

mones also stimulate growth, lower cholesterol and are essential for normal development of the central nervous system. They enhance the action of the adrenal's stress hormones and speed up the action of insulin.

There are several types of thyroid disease, and virtually all of them are more common among women than men. Hyperthyroidism is characterized by high levels of thyroid hormones, while hypothyroidism refers to a deficiency of thyroid hormone, and both conditions may promote development of a goiter. However, the mere presence of a goiter does not necessarily mean that the body has too much or too little thyroid hormones. Since the thyroid is controlled by the pituitary's secretion of TSH, high levels of this hormone can promote thyroid overgrowth. For example, if the pituitary senses that the thyroid is not making enough hormones, it will increase TSH production to spur the thyroid into action. The thyroid may respond by growing larger and producing more hormones. Even if it is incapable of increasing its hormone production, the gland will continue to grow due to increasing pituitary stimulation. In the case of hyperthyroidism, the gland enlarges and produces increasing amounts of hormone even though there is no stimulation from the pituitary.

There are numerous causes of thyroid diseases. Historically, iodine deficiency was a major cause. This is less important today due to widespread addition of iodine to salt or other common foods, and the wider availability of seafood and other good sources of the mineral. Many people appear to inherit a susceptibility to thyroid disorders. People with this susceptibility may develop thyroid disease when exposed to excessive amounts of iodine or when subjected to undue stress. Female sex hormones are thought to promote thyroid diseases, explaining why it is nine times more common in women than men and also why pregnancy so often unmasks latent thyroid disorders. The immune system also plays an important role in thyroid disease; certain antibodies are believed to have an effect similar to that of TSH on the thyroid, prompting it to overproduce its hormones.

The thyroid is especially sensitive to radiation. Exposure to X rays or other sources of ionizing radiation can reduce the thyroid's ability to produce hormones; it also increases the risk of later thyroid cancer.

THE HYPERACTIVE THYROID

Also referred to as Graves' disease or diffuse toxic goiter, hyperthyroidism is characterized by speeded metabolism, which has many different effects. In this classic 1835 description of a woman with hyperthyroidism, Dr. Robert J. Graves wrote:

A lady, aged 20, became affected with some symptoms which were supposed to be hysterical [and] after she had been in this nervous state about three months,... her pulse had become singularly rapid,... she complained of weakness... and began to look pale and thin.... The eyeballs were apparently enlarged, [and] in a few months, a tumor of horseshoe shape appeared... in exactly the situation of the thyroid gland....

The symptoms noted by Dr. Graves in this young Dublin woman are characteristic of the most common type of hyperthyroidism, a condition that doctors still refer to as Graves' disease. Several characteristics distinguish Graves' disease from other forms of hyperthyroidism. (See Figure 21.) There appears to be a strong hereditary tendency to develop Graves' disease; most patients can recall other family members who had thyroid disease. Patients with Graves' disease have thyroid-stimulating antibodies. Over the years, there appears to be a slowing of the hyperthyroidism, and in their later years, many Graves' patients actually become hypothyroid.

Typically, a person with Graves' disease complains of feeling jittery or nervous and irritable. Weight loss, muscular weakness and fatigue are common. The hyperthyroidism causes intolerance to heat; many women recall that even before noticing other symptoms, they felt especially uncomfortable during warm weather and kept turning down the furnace thermostat, even when others insisted a room was

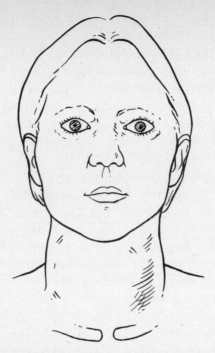

Development of a Goiter

This drawing shows the characteristic
neck swelling and mildly protruding
eyes, both hallmarks of Graves' disease.

too cool. The hyperthyroidism also causes excessive sweating.

The speeded metabolism and body processes are reflected in digestive function. Stools become looser and more
frequent. Patients complain of feeling more hungry than
usual, and although they eat as much or more than ever,
weight loss is common. High levels of thyroid hormone
cause the heart to beat faster; many women with hyperthyroidism consult their doctors because of palpitations or a
rapid heart beat. Shakiness or tremors may occur.

The speeded metabolism also causes a greater turnover
in hair, and, as more hairs enter the resting and shedding

phases, women will notice a thinning of scalp hair; some people even develop bald spots. The skin becomes very soft, thinner and more transparent; fingernails grow more rapidly and with uneven margins that make them more difficult to clean. The skin over the front of the lower legs may become thicker and reddened, a condition called pretibial myxedema.

The "enlarged eyeballs" referred to by Dr. Graves really are not caused by a growth of the eyes, but instead, by a swelling of the tissue behind the eyeballs. The upper eyelids also become elevated, further adding to the bulging appearance. Sometimes the protruding eyes become inflamed; the bulging also can damage the optic nerve and interfere with vision.

Women frequently develop menstrual abnormalities; the interval between periods may be shorter or longer than normal, and fertility problems may develop. Sometimes ovulation stops, although there still may be periodic menstrual bleeding.

A simple blood test will confirm whether there is a high level of thyroid hormone, but this will not determine whether the problem is in the thyroid gland itself or due to excessive TSH from the pituitary. Thus a blood test for TSH is necessary. Now we have a monoclonal antibody test which can measure down to zero TSH. Thus thyroid causes of hyperthyroidism have a TSH of zero. Pituitary causes of hyperthyroid have a TSH that is sky high. A thyroid scan using radioactive iodine may be done to determine if the entire gland is overactive, or whether the problem rests with hormone-producing nodules. The iodine will concentrate in areas of hormone production and show up on a scan.

In a young patient who has only mild symptoms, extra thyroid hormone may be given to determine whether this will reduce TSH production and thereby lower the thyroid's hormone output. A newer test that is gaining in popularity takes advantage of the fact that the pituitary and indirectly, the thyroid, are controlled by the hypothalamus, which produces TSH-releasing hormone (TRH). By administering a synthetic TRH and noting its effect on the pituitary and thyroid, a doctor can determine whether the problem is in the pituitary or the thyroid.

OTHER TYPES OF HYPERTHYROIDISM

Although Graves' disease is the most common cause of excessive thyroid hormones, there are several other types of hyperthyroidism. Sometimes a thyroid will develop one or more "hot nodules" in which specific areas of the gland become overactive. About thirty percent of hyperthyroidism falls into this category. In about five percent of cases, the hyperthyroidism will be caused by a single nodule; in the remaining twenty-five percent, multiple nodules will develop. The nodules usually show up on a thyroid scan. As they secrete increasing amounts of hormones, the rest of the gland gradually stops functioning. Thus, when a doctor examines the thyroid, one part may feel enlarged and the rest smaller than normal, or if there are several nodules, the gland will feel enlarged and lumpy.

Inflammation of the thyroid also can cause hyperthyroidism. Typically, a patient develops flulike symptoms with a very sore throat. The thyroid becomes tender and inflamed, and excessive hormones may be secreted into the blood. Blood tests will show high levels of thyroid hormone, and the gland may feel enlarged, but there will be a low uptake of radioactive iodine and scans will be normal. Other tests, such as a red blood cell sedimentation rate, will indicate the presence of inflammation, and help establish a diagnosis.

This inflammatory form of hyperthyroidism usually resolves itself in a few weeks, although there may be a period of hypothyroidism during which the gland gradually recovers and resumes normal functioning.

Tumors are another relatively rare cause of hyperthyroidism. Excessive TSH can stimulate the thyroid into hyperactivity. There also are rare hormone-producing cancers of the reproductive tract that can cause hyperthyroidism.

Treatment of this type of hyperthyroidism entails detecting and removing the source of the abnormal hormone production.

Consuming too much iodine in the diet can produce hyperthyroidism in some susceptible people, such as those with thyroid nodules. Initially, researchers thought this phenomenon was limited to people whose diets had heretofore been deficient in iodine, and who abruptly started to consume large amounts of it. More recently it has been found that some people who ordinarily consume normal amounts of iodine will develop hyperthyroidism if they suddenly start eating large amounts of kelp—a popular item in some fad diets—or undergo an X-ray examination that entails using a dye containing iodine. Often the hyperthyroidism will disappear when the excessive iodine is removed from the diet.

Overuse of thyroid pills also can cause hyperthyroidism. This is most common among people with an underactive thyroid who are taking an improper dosage of replacement hormone. It also may occur among overweight people who have been led to believe that thyroid pills will help them lose weight. This improper use of thyroid pills was more common in the past than today, but there are still people—mostly overweight women who were started on thyroid medications when they were teenagers—who misuse thyroid pills for weight control.

TREATMENT OF HYPERTHYROIDISM

After it has been determined that the source of the hyperthyroidism is indeed the thyroid gland, treatment may be with antithyroid drugs, radioactive iodine or surgery. The choice of treatment depends upon the nature and severity of the disease and the age of the patient.

Antithyroid drugs which act by preventing the gland from manufacturing thyroid hormone are usually the treatment of choice in children with hyperthyroidism. Typically, the drugs—either propylthiouracil (PTU) or methimazole (Tapazole)—will be given for a year and then stopped to see if the youngster's thyroid is capable of functioning normally. This tactic also may be tried in an adult with mild Graves' disease, although the chances of a remission are not as high as in children and many doctors feel that a year's trial on antithyroid drugs for an adult is a waste of time.

Radioactive iodine has become a favored treatment for an overactive thyroid in recent years. The purpose of this treatment is to, in effect, destroy the thyroid with radiation. The patient consumes a drink containing radioactive iodine. The iodine carries the radiation directly to the thyroid, and in a few days, the radioactive isotopes disappear from the body, either in the urine or through natural decay into nonradioactive substances. Although there has been concern that the isotopes may themselves cause cancer, follow-up studies have not found this to be the case. If an adequate dosage is given, the thyroid gland will be destroyed by the radiation, leaving no tissue in which cancer can develop. The iodine is so specific for the thyroid that the radiation does not pose a major threat to other parts of the body. It should not, however, be given to a pregnant woman because of possible harm to the fetus. The same restriction applies to nursing mothers, since the radioactive substances can pass into the breast milk. Otherwise, it appears to be a safe and effective treatment without long-term danger. Usually, only one treatment is needed, but if the initial dosage is too low to destroy the thyroid, a second treatment may be needed.

Of course, after the thyroid is destroyed, the patient will need to take thyroid replacement hormones to prevent becoming hypothyroid. This therapy must be continued for life.

Surgical treatment of hyperthyroidism entails removal of part of the thyroid gland. The objective is to remove enough thyroid tissue to cure the hyperthyroidism, but to leave enough to produce adequate thyroid hormones. Surgery is not recommended for very ill patients since the operation itself may prove fatal to a person with uncontrolled hyperthyroidism. Typically, a candidate for thyroid surgery will be given antithyroid pills for several weeks to bring the symptoms under control. The surgeon should be experienced in thyroid removal because the operation should spare parathyroid glands—whose hormones are needed for proper calcium metabolism—and nearby nerves that are instrumental for proper speech. If the parathyroid glands are damaged or destroyed, replacement parathyroid hormone will be needed for proper calcium metabolism.

A beta-blocking drug, such as propranolol, should be given during treatment for hyperthyroidism to help control some of the symptoms, especially the palpitations and feelings of nervousness. Beta blockers do not alter the thyroid function itself, but block some of the action of the elevated hormones.

The eye problems that often accompany Graves' disease are best treated with steroid drugs, which reduce the swelling behind the eyeball and lessen the bulging. Steroids will also counter any eye inflammation.

Any patient undergoing treatment for hypothyroidism should be diligent about yearly examinations to ensure that proper levels of thyroid hormones are being maintained. Frequently, patients who experience a remission of Graves' disease with antithyroid drugs will eventually develop hypothyroidism, and require replacement hormones.

THE UNDERACTIVE THYROID

Hypothyroidism, or a deficiency of thyroid hormone, can be an insidious disease that may take years to develop, producing increasingly troublesome symptoms. Once diagnosed, it is easily treated with replacement hormone.

Hypothyroidism is most serious in infants and very young children. Babies born without enough thyroid tissue to produce adequate thyroid hormones will develop cretinism—an irreversible form of mental retardation—unless their hypothyroidism is detected and treated early in life. Thyroid hormone is necessary for normal growth and development; children who develop hypothyroidism may have stunted growth and delayed sexual development. Because congenital hypothyroidism causes such profound mental and developmental abnormalities, the umbilical cord blood of all babies should be tested for thyroid hormone at birth.

Symptoms of hypothyroidism are the opposite of those of hyperthyroidism. All bodily processes slow down, resulting in fatigue and listlessness. Often, the first sign is development of a goiter, a result of the pituitary producing large amounts of TSH in an effort to stimulate the thyroid into action.

Increasing weakness, lethargy and sleepiness are almost universal early symptoms of hypothyroidism. Patients complain of feeling exhausted by climbing a flight of stairs or too weak to lift a bag of groceries. Intolerance to cold becomes more pronounced; a woman will often realize that she is the only one in a room that is wearing a sweater and that she needs extra blankets at night.

Women notice that their skin becomes coarser, very dry and scaly. Skin over the elbows and on the legs becomes especially thick and scaly. The skin will feel cold and clammy to the touch, and there is a lack of sweating. Nails are slow-growing, dry and brittle; the hair thins and becomes coarser. Premature graying (before the age of thirty) is common among hypothyroid patients; so is vitiligo—patches of white, unpigmented skin. Constipation is common.

Many patients complain of loss of appetite, but they still may gain weight despite eating less. The eyelids and face often become puffy, an early sign of hypothyroidism, or myxedema. A woman may be conscious that her voice is deeper and husky, symptoms that are often mistaken for laryngitis. Heavy menstrual periods and infertility, both caused by a lack of ovulation, are common. Both men and women may experience a loss of interest in sex, and most other activities as well.

Impaired hearing or loss of balance may occur. Some patients complain of palpitations, but slow heart rate is more common. Joint stiffness, especially in the morning, also is common and may be mistaken for arthritis or rheumatism. As the hypothyroidism progresses, full-blown myxedema may develop. This is characterized by a thickening of facial features, overgrowth of the tongue, generalized swelling or edema, and extreme lethargy and mental dullness. Impaired memory is common. If untreated, the disease may progress to a myxedema coma and even death.

At one time, iodine deficiency was the most common cause of hypothyroidism. This is no longer true, especially in the United States, where this deficiency has virtually been eliminated by adding iodine to salt and certain other staples in the diet. Sometimes over-consumption of iodine can cause thyroid problem. There are instances in which a pregnant woman who consumes too much iodine will have a baby with a goiter and hypothyroidism. Lithium, a drug used to treat manic-depression, can produce hypothyroidism. People whose thyroids are very sensitive to iodine may become hypothyroid after X-ray examinations using iodine-containing dyes.

Today, one of the most common causes of hypothyroidism is intentional, namely removal or destruction of the thyroid in the treatment of hyperthyroidism. This is easily treated with replacement thyroid, but sometimes the dosage may be inadequate or the condition may go unnoticed until serious symptoms appear.

One of the most common causes of hypothyroidism in older children and adults is Hashimoto's disease, named for the Japanese doctor who first described it. Hashimoto's is characterized by a chronic inflammation of the thyroid gland without evidence of infection. The thyroid becomes enlarged, and, in many patients, this is the only sign of Hashimoto's. Many women first notice that they have a developing goiter when a favorite necklace suddenly feels too tight.

The disease appears to be inherited, and is much more common among women than men. It is an autoimmune disease, in which the body produces antibodies against its thyroid tissue. In fact, Hashimoto's is distinguished from other forms of hypothyroidism by the presence of antithyroid antibodies.

TREATMENT OF HYPOTHYROIDISM

The preferred treatment of hypothyroidism entails giving thyroid pills that contain only T_4, or thyroxine. The original thyroid pills—desiccated thyroid or Proloid—which are still available, are made from animal thyroid glands. These drugs contain both T_3 and T_4, and cause surges in T_3. This can be dangerous for people with underlying heart disease. The T_3 works more rapidly than T_4 (which the body converts to T_3 as it needs it) and T_3 surges can cause palpitations and other adverse effects on the heart.

Desiccated thyroid and generic thyroxine are less expensive than the brand-name drugs Synthroid and Levothroid. However, this is one instance in which it pays to spend extra money for the brand-name products, since laboratory tests have found that the generics tend to be unreliable in potency and bioavailability (the degree to which the body is able to absorb a drug). Patients who require thyroid pills should talk to their doctors about dosage and reliability of the pills they are taking. Both Synthroid and Levothroid are color-coded according to dosage, which helps avoid confusion.

THYROID CANCER

Thyroid cancer is relatively rare, but has been increasing in recent years. This is due to the large number of children and adolescents who received X-ray treatments between the 1920s and early 1960s for a variety of ailments, including tonsilitis, acne, ringworm and other throat or skin conditions. People exposed to radiation fallout from atomic bomb tests or other nuclear incidents also have a higher rate of thyroid cancer.

Efforts are being made to locate people who had earlier X-ray treatments that increase their risk of thyroid cancer.

Many hospitals have searched through back records and contacted patients to let them know they should have periodic thyroid examinations. If a person thinks he or she may have had such treatments, it is a good idea to contact either the hospital or doctor to confirm the date and type of X-ray exposure. Some doctors recommend that anyone who has a history of X-ray head and throat treatments undergo periodic thyroid scans, and that suspicious thyroid nodules be biopsied to rule out cancer.

SUMMING UP

Thyroid disease that results in either too much or too little thyroid hormone affects virtually every body system and process. Often the problem goes undiagnosed for long periods because the symptoms often are vague or easily mistaken for other conditions. Since many of these disorders tend to be hereditary, anyone with a family history of thyroid disease should be particularly attuned to early warning signs.

Chapter 12

Disorders of the Adrenal Glands

THE ADRENALS ARE A PAIR OF TRIANGULAR GLANDS THAT rest on top of the kidneys. The outer yellowish portion, the adrenal cortex, manufactures cortisone and other steroid hormones. The inner, reddish brown portion is called the adrenal medulla, and it secretes catecholamines, norepinephrine and epinephrine—the so-called stress hormones. Both the adrenal cortex and medulla functions are regulated by intricate feedback systems that control numerous body functions.

THE STEROID HORMONES

Three different groups of steroid hormones are secreted by the adrenal cortex: the corticosteroids, which include hydrocortisone; the mineralocorticoids, primarily aldosterone; and the sex steroids, namely, androgen, estrogen and progestogen. (These latter sex hormones are produced in larger quantities by the male testes and the female ovaries.)

All of the steroid hormones are synthesized from cholesterol. In recent years, the general public has come to believe that cholesterol is a detrimental substance that should be avoided at all costs. The truth is, cholesterol is essential to all animal life—so much so, in fact, that the liver is capable of manufacturing all that the body needs from essential fatty acids. Cholesterol becomes a problem only when the body manufactures too much, or when an excessive amount is consumed in the diet. In either instance, the body may not be able to handle the excess cholesterol, and it builds up in the blood, forming the fatty deposits that lead to hardening of the arteries and clogging of the coronary blood vessels.

Proper function of the adrenal cortex depends upon extremely sensitive hormonal feedback interactions with other glands. The secretion of the adrenals' glucocorticoids and sex steroids, for example, is controlled by the pituitary's production of ACTH, while the production of aldosterone, which is instrumental in controlling the body's salt and water balance, is regulated by the renin-angiotensin system.

Corticosteroid secretion is closely linked to our individual biorhythms or internal clocks. Steroids are secreted in pulses throughout the day. Secretion is lowest during the four hours before going to bed and the first two hours of sleep. During the remaining hours of sleep, there are increasing pulses of hormone secretion, peaking at about wake-up time. Blood levels of corticosteroids are highest in the early morning, gradually falling during the day, with periodic pulses that coincide with our feelings of renewed energy. This internal biological clock is closely tied to light/dark, sleep/wake and feeding cycles. We are perhaps most acutely aware of our biological clocks, or diurnal rhythm, when we fly from one continent to another or across several time zones. The jet lag we experience is a function of our diurnal rhythm, and it usually takes several days to reset our internal biological clock to coincide with the new time zone.

Many factors can alter secretion of adrenal steroids. Illness, psychological stress, infection, fever, exposure to cold or heat, increased physical activity, certain drugs, and any kind of trauma are but a few of the many factors that affect the adrenal glands and their pituitary controls. Whenever the body is subjected to any kind of stress, the adrenal glands respond by increasing output of corticosteroids as well as stress hormones. If the adrenal glands fail to produce the needed hormones to counter the stress, blood pressure will fall dangerously and cardiovascular collapse or shock will result—a situation that can quickly lead to death. This is why a person who has been on long-term steroid therapy, such as chronic prednisone treatment of asthma, cannot abruptly stop taking the drugs.

Topical steroids that are applied to the skin may be absorbed in sufficient amounts to affect normal adrenal function. Whenever steroid medications are given over a period of time, the pituitary gland becomes accustomed to the high levels of steroids and stops producing ACTH, which signals the adrenals to secrete their corticosteroids. If the drugs are then stopped and the person is subjected to a stress that the body ordinarily handles quite well, such as an infection, burn or surgery, the sluggish adrenal glands which have gone to sleep from lack of ACTH stimulation may not respond by secreting the needed hormones and the patient will go into shock. Studies have found that this complication of steroid therapy can be avoided by using a short-acting drug, such as prednisone, and administering it at 8 A.M. every other day instead of daily. This administration of the drug follows the body's normal early morning peak pulse of hydrocortisone secretion, and the every-other-day administration is not as likely to suppress the normal feedback system.

A woman's normal hormonal fluctuations that accompany her menstrual cycle are reflected in adrenal function. In the premenstrual phase, the high levels of progesterone are associated with increased secretion of aldosterone, which in turns promotes retention of sodium and fluid. This leads to the bloating that many women experience before their periods.

Birth control pills that are high in estrogen raise steroid levels, which can also lead to bloating and increased blood pressure from the excess sodium and fluid. These side effects were more common with the earlier pills, which contained more estrogen than today's pills. The hormonal changes of pregnancy are similar to those of birth control pills, only more exaggerated because of the higher hormone levels. In some women, the adrenal glands produce very high levels of corticosteroids, which can lead to symptoms similar to those seen in patients with Cushing's syndrome— reddish stretch marks, a rounding of the face, fluid retention and mild glucose intolerance (see section on Cushing's syndrome below). Overproduction of adrenal hormones also may be related to toxemia of pregnancy, but this has not been proved.

An imbalance of any of the adrenal steroids also can have profound effects on many other body functions. For example, there are several congenital errors that result in over- or underproduction of adrenal hormones. One of the most common is an enzyme deficiency that causes an overgrowth of the adrenal cortex and excessive production of androgen. This causes virilization of females and false precocious puberty in males. Another inborn metabolic error is one that results in inadequate aldosterone; people with this defect may develop excessive loss of salt and water and low blood pressure. Defects in glucocorticoid production, especially hydrocortisone, interfere with the metabolism of food and numerous other body functions.

Secretion of corticosteroids is closely related to production of growth hormone. Growth hormone is suppressed in people with chronically high levels of steroids, which is believed to explain the stunted growth in children who are treated with long-term steroids for asthma, juvenile arthritis and other chronic disorders. The other explanation of stunted growth in children taking steroids is that the body sees the cortisone as similar enough to a sex steroid hormone that it is "tricked" into thinking that the child has become an adult and therefore should stop growing. The steroid acts by closing the growth plates of the long bones.

CUSHING'S SYNDROME

Cushing's syndrome, named in 1932 for Dr. Harvey Cushing, a famous neurosurgeon who described a group of patients with the disease, is caused by excessive hydrocortisone, either from drugs or a disease of the adrenal glands. It is one of the most common disorders of the adrenal cortex, occurring more often in women than men. The disease can appear at any age, but is seen most often between the ages of twenty and forty, frequently during or immediately after pregnancy.

Excessive hairiness, unexplained weight gain and changes in the distribution of body fat are the symptoms that usually prompt a woman with Cushing's to see her doctor. Typically, the face becomes moon-shaped and body fat accumulates on the trunk, especially on the abdomen and upper back—the characteristic "buffalo hump" associated with Cushing's. The skin becomes very thin, bruising easily and disfigured by purplish stretch marks. Muscle weakness, menstrual irregularity and infertility also are common symptoms of Cushing's.

Laboratory tests usually show abnormal glucose metabolism, and many people with Cushing's develop diabetes. The body's chemical balance is upset: Excessive sodium retention causes bloating and hypertension, while a loss of potassium accounts for the muscle weakness. People with Cushing's also notice that cuts and other wounds are very slow in healing. Abnormal calcium metabolism leads to thinning and weakening of the bones, explaining why stress fractures are common among Cushing's patients.

There are numerous causes of Cushing's, and successful treatment requires tracking down the source of the excessive hydrocortisone. A common cause of Cushing's involves overuse of steroid medications to treat asthma, arthritis and other chronic diseases. In such cases, treatment involves a gradual weaning away from the steroids.

A hormone-producing tumor or overgrowth of the

adrenal gland can result in overproduction of hydrocortisone. Treatment entails surgical removal of the source of the abnormal hormone production. This may mean removal of a diseased adrenal gland, followed by hormone treatments to restore the pituitary's normal production of ACTH, which will eventually "wake up" the remaining adrenal gland and stimulate it to produce hydrocortisone.

Sometimes the problem is in the pituitary and hypothalamus, resulting in an overproduction of ACTH, which in turn stimulates the adrenals to secrete too much hydrocortisone. This is treated by identifying and correcting the pituitary-hypothalamic disorder.

After hormone levels are restored to normal, patients with Cushing's syndrome gradually lose many of the symptom effects, but some of the changes caused by long-standing disease may be permanent. In time, the moon-faced appearance, truncal obesity, acne, easy bruising and menstrual irregularities will lessen or disappear. The hirsuitism also will subside, but electrolysis is needed to remove the hairiness that already has occurred. Further thinning of the bones may be prevented, but established osteoporosis is difficult or impossible to reverse.

ADDISON'S DISEASE

Addison's disease, the opposite of Cushing's syndrome, is caused by a chronic deficiency of adrenal hormones. In more than half of Addison's patients, the adrenal cortex has atrophied and ceased producing its hormones. Most commonly, this is caused by an autoimmune disorder in which, for unknown reasons, the body produces antibodies against one or more organs, resulting in their destruction. The second most common cause is infection, usually tuberculosis, which causes death and calcification of the adrenal tissue. Most of these patients have never been diagnosed as having tuberculosis, but careful medical investigation often will turn up signs of an inactive infection, usually in the lungs.

Other possible causes of adrenal failure include various fungal infections—such as histoplasmosis, coccidioidomycosis or blastomycosis—or cancer. Sometimes meningitis (meningococcemia) can result in adrenal failure due to exhaustion from the stress of overwhelming infection. Failure of the pituitary to produce ACTH also can result in adrenal failure. About ninety-five percent of the gland must be destroyed before symptoms occur. These include increasing weakness, fatigue, severe muscle cramping, weight loss, darkening of the skin, low blood pressure, loss of appetite, low blood sugar, abdominal pain, nausea and vomiting. Extreme fatigue, lightheadedness when standing and unexplained weight loss are usually the symptoms that prompt a person to consult a doctor. Other early signs include a darkening of the skin (a summer tan may not fade, and instead, persist well into the winter). Women often notice that the pigmented mucosal lining in the genital area takes on a dark blue-gray color; they also may have dark creases on the palms and an increased number of dark freckles or moles on the upper body. Sometimes the darkening skin may be made even more noticeable by patches of unpigmented white skin; these areas of vitiligo—the medical term for lack of pigmentation—usually develop on areas exposed to the sun.

Addison's disease also affects sexual function. Sexual desire may decrease and some men experience impotence. Women often notice a thinning of pubic and armpit hair due to the decreased androgens. Menstrual irregularity and infertility also are common.

After Addison's disease is properly diagnosed, patients can expect to live a normal life with daily hormone replacement. Prednisone is the drug used most often. When given to replace the deficient adrenal hormones, this drug has few side effects; the most common being weight gain, bloating from fluid retention and heartburn. Aldosterone replacement also may be needed to maintain normal blood pressure and fluid balance.

CONN'S SYNDROME

Also referred to as primary aldosteronism, Conn's syndrome is marked by an overproduction of aldosterone due to a benign tumor of the adrenal gland. The major characteristics are high blood pressure, excessive urination and potassium depletion. The hypertension is most often mild, and usually does not cause the enlarged heart and other cardiovascular problems associated with high blood pressure. Most of the symptoms are related to the loss of potassium, which causes numbness, muscle weakness, and sometimes paralysis or severe muscle spasms (tetany).

Although only a few people with hypertension have Conn's syndrome, it should be considered in cases of high blood pressure and low potassium that is not due to thiazides, birth control pills or other medications that may produce this combination. To make a proper diagnosis, a doctor must determine whether the problem is due to an adrenal tumor or a kidney disorder. A narrowing of the renal artery, for example, reduces the blood flow to the kidney. This activates the finely tuned renin-angiotensin system, which is instrumental in controlling blood pressure. To compensate for the lowered blood flow to the kidney, the renin-angiotensin system signals the adrenals to produce more aldosterone, which will raise blood pressure. Thus, the diagnostic test for Conn's disease will include studies of kidney function. If the kidneys and renal arteries are normal, further studies will focus on finding an adrenal tumor that is producing the aldosterone. Treatment then requires an operation to remove the tumor, which often is very small and entails skillful surgery to find and remove.

VIRILIZING SYNDROMES

Normally, the adrenal glands in both sexes produce small amounts of androgen, which the body converts to testosterone. Even a small overproduction of testosterone can result in virilization—a condition in which girls develop male characteristics and boys experience premature sexual development and other abnormalities.

Most of these virilizing syndromes are caused by congenital defects that upset normal production of the enzymes needed to synthesize certain hormones. The most common of these deficiencies interfere with the synthesis of hydrocortisone; the pituitary responds by increasing ACTH secretion in an attempt to get the adrenals to make more corticosteroids. The high levels of ACTH in an attempt to make more cortisone only succeed in building up the precursors to the hormone because the patient lacks the enzyme to convert the precursor to cortisone. The precursors have androgenlike properties. The high levels of ACTH also promote excessive production of androgens, which are then converted into testosterone. Baby boys born with these congenital enzyme deficiencies will show signs of a false premature puberty in which the penis enlarges, pubic hair develops and other such signs of early sexual development appear. Since the testosterone is coming from the adrenal glands and not the testes, true puberty in which the testes grow and start producing hormones does not occur. Girls born with this syndrome will have masculinized genitalia. About a third of these youngsters also will have insufficient mineralocorticoids, and will suffer from low blood pressure and dehydration due to excessive salt and water excretion.

Sometimes the androgen overproduction does not show up until adolescence or adulthood. A period of stress may provoke symptoms in a person who has a partial deficiency of an enzyme. Hormone-producing tumors may be responsible for the imbalance, which is more apparent in women than men because of the abnormal masculinization. In other instances, no cause can be found and it is assumed that the excessive androgen production is due to a mild enzyme deficiency that was not complete enough to cause virilization during infancy and early childhood. This type of imbalance can be controlled by taking prednisone to suppress the excessive adrenal activity.

DISORDERS OF THE ADRENAL MEDULLA

The major hormones secreted by the adrenal medulla—norepinephrine and epinephrine—are responsible for our fight-or-flight response. Whenever the body perceives that it is in danger, either from an external threat or from undue internal stress, the adrenal medulla responds by secreting these catecholamine hormones, which provide the extra surge of energy needed to either escape from danger or fight it off. They cause the heart to beat harder and faster and the smallest arteries to constrict, raising blood pressure. Some of the blood flow also is diverted from the gastrointestinal tract and other internal organs to the muscles. Oxygen uptake is increased and the liver and muscles convert stored glycogen to glucose for immediate energy. At the same time, insulin secretion is suppressed, which helps ensure a high level of blood glucose.

Studies have found that people who are hyperreactors, such as time-driven, overly competitive Type A personalities, secrete large amounts of catecholamines in response to even very minor stresses. Some researchers theorize that this chronic overreaction and consequent surge of stress hormones may account for the increased incidence of heart attacks among people with Type A personalities; their cardiovascular system is frequently subjected to sharp rises in blood pressure and other changes that may in some way damage the vessels and give rise to the buildup of fatty deposits along the artery walls.

Although catecholamines are usually thought of in terms of stress hormones, they have numerous other functions that influence almost all body tissues. These hormones play a role in regulation of the body's fluid and electrolyte balance, cell growth and division, regulation of the nervous system and muscle function, secretion of various proteins and fat metabolism. Catecholamines are also instrumental in generating body heat. When we feel cold, for example, catecholamines promote shivering; this involuntary muscular activity generates heat and helps the body maintain its normal temperature. During exercise, cathecholamines help mobilize stored fuel for use by the muscles.

ORTHOSTATIC HYPOTENSION

Normally, when we stand up after sitting or lying down, the body adjusts almost instantly by increasing blood pressure sufficiently to ensure a steady supply of oxygen to the brain. This automatic response is regulated by the effects of catecholamines on the nervous system. If something goes awry to upset this feedback system, we may experience a temporary drop in blood pressure when assuming an upright position, a condition referred to as orthostatic hypotension. This may occur in a number of nerve disorders, including the nerve degeneration that sometimes accompanies diabetes. Drugs that are used to treat high blood pressure also may cause orthostatic hypotension.

Usually, the dizziness or faint feelings that are characteristic of orthostatic hypotension can be controlled by avoiding abrupt changes in posture. Getting out of bed in stages—rising to a sitting position and then waiting a minute or so before slowly standing up—can prevent the occasional dizziness that many people experience when rising in the morning. Sleeping with the head elevated or even in a semi-sitting position also may be advised. Standing slowly after sitting for a long period also may help. If the problem is related to medication, switching to a different drug or lowering the dosage may be necessary.

In more serious instances in which the drop in blood pressure cannot be controlled or is disabling, other treatment strategies may be tried. Wearing elastic stockings to prevent a pooling of blood in the legs and to promote return circulation to the upper body may help in mild cases. Taking a mineralocorticoid drug (fludrocortisone), along with a high intake of salt to expand blood volume, also may be recommended. To avoid excessively high blood pressure while lying down, patients on such a regimen may be advised to sleep in a semi-sitting position.

PHEOCHROMOCYTOMA

Pheochromocytoma is a tumor, usually benign, that produces catecholamines, resulting in high blood pressure. These tumors are quite rare, accounting for only one percent of all cases of hypertension. Even so, their detection is important because this is one form of hypertension that can be readily cured by removing the tumor. Sometimes the hypertension caused by these tumors is very severe, progressing rapidly (a condition referred to as malignant hypertension) and causing severe eye and kidney damage. Frequently, the high blood pressure is not lowered by conventional antihypertensive drugs. This should signal a doctor to consider pheochromocytoma as a possible cause. Erratic hypertension, often accompanied by orthostatic hypotension, is also a characteristic of high blood pressure caused by a pheochromocytoma. In some instances, the excess catecholamines make a person more susceptible to shock during surgery or in response to a serious injury.

The excessive catecholamines produced by a pheochromocytoma also can result in a number of other symptoms, including angina and even a heart attack, without other evidence of coronary disease. Other troubling symptoms associated with pheochromocytoma include: severe headaches, excessive sweating, palpitations, nausea and vomiting, tremor, weakness, fatigue, feelings of nervousness or anxiety, indigestion, hot flashes, numbness or tingling sensations, blurred vision, dizziness or fainting, and a variety of pains. Sometimes this stress is associated with mild diabetes because catecholamines act against insulin.

The excess catecholamines also can promote adverse, even fatal drug reactions, especially to opiates, such as codeine, and other painkillers or anesthetics. Other drugs that may produce severe reactions include histamines, ACTH, saralasin and glucagon. The contrast substances used in some X-ray examinations also may provoke a catecholamine crisis. Over-the-counter cold medications and decongestants, and certain prescription drugs, such as guanethidine and tricyclic antidepressants, may provoke a severe rise in blood pressure, and should be avoided by anyone with a suspected pheochromocytoma. Sometimes pheochromocytomas accompany other disorders, particularly a rare type of inherited tumor affecting the thyroid and other endocrine glands, as well as neurofibromas. More commonly, however, the tumor develops in the adrenal medulla itself and is independent of other tumors. The large majority, about ninety-five percent, are benign, but the remaining five percent are malignant, with metastases to the bone and liver being common.

Occasionally, the tumor can be felt or detected on X ray. More commonly, diagnosis is made by challenging the tumor with glucagon or other substances that stimulate catecholamine release and then observing whether the challenge affects blood pressure. After a pheochromocytoma has been diagnosed, the preferred treatment is surgical removal. This can be complicated, however, because the excessive catecholamines make a patient more susceptible to shock and other complications. Blood pressure must be monitored very carefully both during and after the operation. Once the tumor is removed, most patients recover fully and again have normal blood pressure.

SUMMING UP

The adrenal glands produce a number of hormones that affect virtually every body system and function. The release of these hormones is controlled by intricate feedback systems, but may also be influenced by stress, both internal and external, and many other circumstances. Diagnosing an adrenal disorder often involves considerable medical detective work, but once a diagnosis is established, most can be successfully treated.

Chapter 13

Eating Disorders

WEIGHT—EITHER TOO MUCH OR TOO LITTLE—IS ONE OF our most common health problems. More than thirty million Americans are obese, which is generally defined as being more than twenty percent over their ideal weight. Excessive thinness is far less common; still, it is estimated that up to five percent of adolescent girls and young women in this country suffer from anorexia and bulimia. Anorexia is a severe eating disorder characterized by self-starvation, often to the point where it becomes life-threatening. Bulimia involves uncontrolled food gorging, usually followed by purging—either voluntary vomiting or laxative abuse—to avoid weight gain. Anorexia nervosa, one of the most severe disorders, is believed to be a psychiatric illness, but its true cause has not been established.

Although most cases of obesity and anorexia/bulimia are not directly caused by hormonal imbalances, enough are to warrant considering an endocrine disorder in the absence of other obvious causes. In addition, both excessive overweight and underweight can have profound effects on a woman's endocrine system, resulting in menstrual irregularity, infertility and other hormonal problems.

OBESITY

Medical textbooks describe a variety of methods to determine whether a person is obese. These include skin-fold tests, weighing a person underwater to determine percentage of body fat, or complicated formulas to calculate body mass index, uptake of inert gases, total body water or potassium, among others. While these tests may be important in research studies or other unusual instances, for the vast majority of people they are unnecessary. Most of us can tell if we are overweight simply by looking in a mirror or by standing on the bathroom scale and comparing weight registered with a standard weight/height table (see Table 8).

Table 8. DESIRABLE WEIGHT FOR HEIGHT

WOMEN			
Height	Small Frame	Medium Frame	Large Frame
4'10"	92–98	96–101	104–119
4'11"	94–101	98–110	106–122
5'	96–104	101–113	109–125
5'1"	99–107	104–116	112–128
5'2"	102–110	107–119	115–131
5'3"	105–113	110–122	118–134
5'4"	108–116	113–126	121–138
5'5"	111–119	116–130	125–142
5'6"	114–123	120–135	129–146
5'7"	118–127	124–139	133–150
5'8"	122–131	128–143	137–154
5'9"	126–135	132–147	141–158
5'10"	130–140	136–151	145–163
5'11"	134–144	140–155	149–168
6'	138–148	144–159	153–173

Although weight gain itself is a simple matter of mathematics—namely, consuming more than is expended—there are many puzzling aspects to obesity. There is considerable debate among nutrition experts over whether obesity is genetically determined or a result of environmental influences. Undoubtedly, both are involved, but recent studies of twins, both fraternal and identical, seem to indicate that some people do, indeed, have a genetic tendency to gain weight. Researchers at the University of Pennsylvania studied military records of more than two thousand pairs of twins, and then sent them questionnaires to determine their weights some twenty years later. They found that the weights of the identical twins tended to be closely correlated with each other, even into middle age, when their environments were likely to be different. The weight of fraternal twins, who presumably share the same early environment but are genetically different, frequently varied.

Of course, millions of overweight people have long maintained that their weight problems are caused by "fat genes." This is based on observations that people can eat virtually identical amounts, and some will gain weight and others will remain slim. Studies have documented that many of these overweight people have highly efficient metabolisms, which may well be inherited. Still, even if a person has an inherited tendency to be overweight, the excess weight comes from consuming more calories than are expended. People with an inherited tendency to gain weight may not require as many calories as those with "thin" genes, but this does not mean they are necessarily doomed to be fat. Unless a person has a serious endocrine or other medical problem, he or she can maintain ideal body weight through a combination of calorie-counting and physical activity, making sure that the two are in balance.

Ideally, this balance is achieved early in life. It has long been observed that overweight children are likely to grow into obese adults and have life-long weight problems. Exercise is still another important component of successful weight control. Numerous studies have found that overweight people are more sedentary than their normal-weight peers; in fact, many obese people actually consume fewer calories than slender counterparts, but they are not as physically active.

Psychological factors also may be involved. Overweight

people tend to respond more positively to external cues to eat, and their eating habits often contribute to obesity. For example, overweight people tend to eat rapidly, barely chewing their food. In contrast, thin people are likely to eat slowly, which gives the satiety center in the brain time to react to the food intake and signal the body that its hunger has been satisfied.

Psychological profiles of very obese people have found that some have a distorted self-image of themselves as needing to be fat. These people may find it difficult to adjust to a slimmer body—a problem that can be overcome through counseling or by devices that will prepare a person to welcome a new body image. Dr. Herbert Spiegel, a New York psychiatrist who counsels many overweight patients, uses a particularly ingenious device: a special mirror that can be adjusted so a person can see how they will look at different weights.

HOW MANY CALORIES DO YOU NEED?

Nutritionists have long recognized that the basis of successful weight management requires calorie-counting, and any diet that promises you can forget about calories is automatically suspect. A calorie is simply a unit of energy—specifically, the amount required to raise the temperature of one gram of water one degree centigrade.

Everyone requires a certain number of calories per day to provide the energy or fuel needed for basic bodily functions—breathing, circulation, maintenance of body temperature, digestion, metabolism and so forth. This is referred to as a person's basal metabolic rate. The Food and Nutrition Board of the National Academy of Sciences has estimated that the average woman weighing about 130 pounds requires somewhere between 1,300 and 1,600 calories a day to support her basic metabolic needs. To arrive at an approximate figure for your needs, you can use this formula: Multiply your weight by ten and add your weight to the result. For each decade over the age of thirty, reduce the total by two percent. For a forty-year-old woman weighing 135 pounds, the calculation would be:

$$135 \times 10 = 1350 + 135 = 1485 - 4\%$$
$$(1485 \times .04 = 59) = 1426$$

Of course, everyone burns more calories than the amount required for their basal rate, unless they are confined to bed and sleeping most of the time. How many calories depends upon the level of physical activity. (See Table 9 for approximate amounts of energy consumed by various physical activities.) To calculate approximately how many calories a person requires to support both basal metabolism and physical activities, use the following:

Activity level	Calories needed per pound
Very sedentary	12
Moderate	15
Vigorous	20

Thus, if the forty-year-old woman described above is moderately active, her daily calorie requirements are about 2,025. But everyone is different. Some women eating this much may lose a small amount of weight while others will gradually gain. Remember, too, that metabolism gradually slows with age so as we grow older, the amount of calories needed per day drops.

Arriving at your daily requirements may require some adjustment in either the amount of food eaten or exercise level. (Table 10 shows average caloric needs as calculated by the Food and Nutrition Board of the National Academy of Sciences.)

In general, weight alone is not the only criterion in determining whether a person is obese; the amount of body fat also must be taken into consideration. When we eat more than we burn up, the excess is stored as fat. There are two types of obesity: hyperplastic, in which the number of fat cells increases; and hypertrophic, in which the fat cells themselves become enlarged. Animal studies have found that, for some species, patterns of infant feeding determine

Table 9. CALORIE EXPENDITURES FOR PHYSICAL
ACTIVITIES

Activity	Calories Used Per Hour
Strolling at 1 mph	150
Walking at 2 mph	200
Walking at 4 mph	350
Race walking	500
Jogging	600
Running	800–1000
Ballet exercises/calisthenics	300
Cycling at 5 mph	250
Cycling at 10 mph	450
Tennis (doubles)	350–450
Tennis (singles)	400–500
Swimming (breast or backstroke)	300–600
Aerobic dancing	600–800
Swimming-crawl	700–900
Handball	650–800
Cross-country skiing	700–1000

the number of fat cells and presumably lead to hyperplastic
obesity. For example, overfed baby rats develop a greater
number of fat cells than those fed a normal diet. Some researchers have postulated that this also applies to humans,
but it has not been proved.

Studies have found that overweight babies have larger
than normal fat cells, and that very obese adults have an
increased number of fat cells, but it is not known when this
increase takes place. Once a fat cell forms, it stays for life,
although it will shrink with weight loss. However, the
"starved" fat cell may send forth hunger signals, which
would explain why most people resume overeating after losing weight—their shrunken fat cells in some way stimulate
the appetite so that they can regrow to their former size.

Total body weight does not necessarily reflect the percentage of body fat because bone and muscle weigh more
than fat. A person who is very muscular and large-boned
may weigh much more than what is recommended on a

Table 10. DAILY CALORIE NEEDS

Age	Calories Per Day	Range
Birth-6 months	Weight (lb.) × 53	43–66 (per pound)
6 months-1 year	Weight (lb.) × 48	36–61 (per pound)
Children (Both Sexes)		
1–3 years	1300	900–1800
4–6 years	1700	1300–2300
7–10	2400	1650–3300
Males		
11–14	2700	2000–3700
15–18	2800	2100–3900
19–22	2900	2500–3300
23–50	2700	2300–3100
51–75	2400	2000–2800
Over 75	2050	1650–2450
Women		
11–14	2200	1500–3000
15–18	2100	1200–3000
19–22	2100	1700–2500
23–50	2000	1600–2400
51–75	1800	1400–2200
Over 75	1600	1200–2000
Pregnant	normal + 300	
Lactating	normal + 500	

Adapted from recommendations by the Food and Nutrition Board
of the National Academy of Sciences-National Research Council
for average healthy people. Individual requirements vary
according to weight, height and activity level.

standard table and still not be obese. Professional athletes,
particularly football players, are the classic example of this.
A football player's weight may be more than twenty percent
above that listed for his height on a weight table, and still be
below average in total body fat. On the average, fat will

make up five to ten percent of the weight of a lean man, and ten to twenty percent of the weight of a lean woman. A man who carries more than twenty percent of his weight in fat is generally considered obese, while for a woman, the figure is thirty percent.

HEALTH RISKS OF OBESITY

Insurance company statistics and long-term health studies, such as the thirty-year Framingham (Mass.) Heart Study, repeatedly show that overweight people die earlier than their ideal-weight counterparts. Obesity increases the risk of heart attacks, strokes, high blood pressure, diabetes, respiratory disorders, gallstones, and certain cancers, especially those of the breast and uterus. Studies have found that overweight people are more accident-prone, perhaps because they tend to be more awkward and have slower reactions than those who are normal weight.

An overweight condition also carries a psychological impact, resulting in low self-esteem and, not uncommonly, emotional problems. The notion that fat people are jolly, happy people is untrue—psychological testing has found that obese people are more likely to be unhappy and to perceive themselves as being weak-willed and unattractive. These feelings are likely to be compounded by the fact that our society puts a great premium on being slim. Fashions are designed for a svelte figure; a thin person is more likely to be hired and promoted than an equally qualified fat person; and surveys have found that thin people tend to be paid more than those who are overweight.

Women in particular are likely to feel miserable about being overweight and, all too often, turn to crash or fad diets to lose unwanted weight. At any given time, it is estimated that more than 20 million Americans are on a weight-loss diet. Many succeed in losing weight, but studies have found that ninety-five percent or more quickly regain what they lost while dieting. In addition, this sudden weight gain not only makes the fat cells fat again, but actually causes them to multiply. The major reason for diet failure is well-known: Most weight-loss schemes are based on a calorie-restricted eating plan that is difficult to maintain for very long and they do not address the basic problem—namely, faulty eating habits that have been built over a lifetime. In addition, the body's protective mechanisms quickly respond to a diet that calls for a sharp reduction in calories by increasing hunger signals and resetting the basal metabolic rate to conserve energy.

Hunger is a powerful instinct intended to ensure that the body has a steady supply of energy to carry out its vital functions. If the appetite/hunger center in the brain senses that the body is running low on fuel, it will send out powerful hunger signals that are almost impossible to ignore if food is available. Typically, a dieter will get by on very little food for a few days, or, with tremendous motivation and will power, stick to a diet until the desired amount of weight has been lost. But most will eventually succumb to their hunger drive, and will return to their former eating habits.

However, while the body is being forced to get by on a reduced amount of calories, it also tries to protect itself from starvation by lowering its energy requirements. As far as the body is concerned, there is no difference between voluntary calorie reduction to lose weight and involuntary starvation, such as might occur in a concentration camp or during a famine. In either instance, it will reduce its metabolic rate to conserve as much energy as possible. It also will start to break down lean body tissue, mostly muscles, and convert this into blood glucose—another good reason why fasting and extreme low-calorie diets should be avoided unless carried out under very close medical supervision.

As tedious as it may sound, the safest and most effective way to lose excessive weight is a moderate reduction in calories and an increase in exercise. This may be more difficult than going on a crash diet that requires following a set regimen for a set period of time, and then "going off the diet," which all too often means returning to the former eating habits that produced the initial obesity.

Experts agree that a dieter should not attempt to lose more than two or three pounds a week. In order to lose a pound, a person must burn up 3,500 more calories than consumed. So, by eating 700 fewer calories a day and increasing exercise enough to burn up an additional 300 calories a day, a person can lose almost two pounds a week. But a dieter should plan to consume at least 1,000 calories a day, and include a variety of foods from the four basic food groups to ensure adequate nutrition. Simply cutting portion size, reducing the amount of fat in the diet (a gram of fat contains nine calories compared with four calories per gram in carbohydrates and protein), and increasing the amount of complex carbohydrates and fiber (which has a filling effect and helps prevent feeling hungry), is usually sufficient for most people who want to lose a moderate amount of weight. (See Model Weight-Loss Plan, Table 11.)

Table 11. BASICS FOR WEIGHT-LOSS MENU PLANNING

	Total Calories/Servings per Day			
List	*1,000*	*1,200*	*1,500*	*1,800*
1—Free foods	Unlimited	Unlimited	Unlimited	Unlimited
2—Vegetables	2	2	2	2
3—Fruits	3	3	3	3
4—Starches	3	5	7	9
5—Proteins	6	6	7	7
6—Milk	2	2	2	3
7—Fats	2	2	6	7

FOOD CHOICES

List 1—Free foods *(no specific amounts)*		
Bouillon	Gelatin,	Pickle, sour or
Chicory	unsweetened	unsweetened dill
Chinese cabbage	Lemon	Radishes
Clear broth	Lettuce (all kinds)	Tea
Coffee	Lime	Soy sauce
Endive	Mustard	Vinegar
Escarole	Parsley	Watercress

List 2—Vegetables (*½ cup cooked or 1 cup raw, except as indicated*)

All leafy greens, except those in List 1	Cabbage (all kinds)	Onions
	Carrots	Peppers, red or green
Asparagus	Catsup (2 tbs.)	
Bean sprouts	Cauliflower	Rutabaga
Beans, green or wax	Celery	Sauerkraut
	Cucumbers	Summer squash
Beets	Eggplant	Tomato or vegetable juice (6 oz.)
Broccoli	Mushrooms	
Brussels sprouts	Okra	Tomatoes

List 3—Fruits

Apple, ½ med.	Fruit cocktail, canned, ½ c.	Prunes, dried, 2
Applesauce, ½ c.		Raisins, 2 tbs.
Apricots, dried, 4 halves	Grapefruit, ½ small	Strawberries, ¾ c.
	Grapes, 12	Tangerine, 1 large
Apricots, fresh, 2 med.	Honeydew, ⅓ med.	Watermelon, 1 c. cubed
	Mango, ½ small	
Bananas, ½ small	Nectarine, 1 small	Juices:
Blueberries, ½ c.	Orange, 1 small	Grapefruit, Orange, ½ c.
Cantaloupe, ¼ med.	Papaya, ⅓ med.	
	Peach, 1 med.	Apple, Pineapple, ⅓ c.
Cherries, 10 large	Pear, 1 small	
Dates, 2	Pineapple, ½ c.	Grape, Prune, ¼ c.
Figs, dried, 1 small		

List 4—Starches

Breads	*Cereals*	Angel food cake, 1½″ square
Any loaf, 1 slice	Hot cereal, ½ c.	
Bagel, ½	Dry flakes, ⅔ c.	*Vegetables*
Dinner roll, 1, 2″	Dry puffed, 1½ c.	Beans or peas (dried), ½ c. cooked
English muffin, ½	Bran, 5 tbs.	
Bun (hamburger or hot dog), ½″	Wheatgerm, 2 tbs.	Corn, ⅓ c. (½ ear)
	Pasta, ½ c.	Parsnips, ⅔ c.
Cornbread, 1½″ cube	Rice, ½ c.	Potato, white, 1 small or ½ c.
	Desserts	
Tortilla, 1, 6″ diameter	Fat-free sherbet, ½ c.	Pumpkin, ¾ c.
		Winter squash, ½ c.

Crackers
Graham, 2, 2½"
Matzoh, 4 × 6"
Melba toast, 4
Oyster, 20

Pretzels, 8 rings
RyKrisps, 3
Saltines, 5
Alcohol
Beer, 5 oz.

Whiskey, 1 oz.
Wine, dry,
2½ oz.
Wine, sweet,
1½ oz.

List 5—Proteins

Beef, dried,
chipped, 1 oz.
Beef, lamb, pork,
veal, lean only,
1 oz.
Cottage cheese,
uncreamed, ¼ c.

Poultry, no skin,
1 oz.
Fish, 1 oz.
Lobster, 1 small tail
Oysters, clams,
shrimp, 5 med.
Tuna (in water),
¼ c.

Salmon, pink,
canned, ¼ c.
Egg, 1 med.
Hard cheese, ½ oz.
Peanut butter,
2 tsp.

List 6—Milk

Buttermilk, fat
free, 1 c.
Skim milk, 1 cup

Yogurt, plain, made
with nonfat milk,
¾ cup

1%-fat milk, 7 oz.

List 7—Fats

Avocado, ⅛ of 4"
diameter
Bacon, crisp, 1 slice
Butter, margarine,
1 tsp.
French dressing,
1 tbs.

Mayonnaise, 1 tsp.
Oil, 1 tsp.
Olives, 5 small
Peanuts, 10

Rouquefort
dressing, 2 tsp.
Thousand Island
dressing, 2 tsp.
Walnuts, 6 small

From *Nutrition and Health* Vol. 1, No. 2 (1979) Columbia University Institute of Human Nutrition.

HORMONE-RELATED CAUSES OF OBESITY

Several hormones affect metabolism and may promote weight gain. Steroid hormones, for example, promote weight gain and a redistribution of fat deposits. Both people with Cushing's syndrome and those who are on long-term steroid drugs will develop a rounded, moon-shaped face; a layer of fat on the upper back (often referred to as a buffalo hump); and weight gain on the trunk and upper body, which contrasts with a thinning of the arms and legs. People on steroids complain of feeling ravenously hungry; the hormones also promote fluid retention, which adds to bloating and weight gain.

Thyroid disorders frequently affect weight; a deficiency of thyroid hormone may cause a moderate weight gain from fluid retention. The slowed-down metabolism also can result in weight gain because not as many calories are burned up and instead are stored as fat. In contrast, an overactive thyroid may cause a loss of weight, even though food consumption may be increased. (Some women, however, actually gain weight because they are hungry all the time and end up eating more calories than their bodies can burn up.)

Marked obesity in children may be caused by a variety of genetic disorders affecting the endocrine system. Mental retardation and other defects often accompany many of these syndromes, which tend to be quite rare. Brain tumors or infections affecting the hypothalamus and pituitary also can cause childhood obesity, but these usually are accompanied by other telltale symptoms.

ENDOCRINE EFFECTS OF OBESITY

Obesity can have a marked effect on hormonal balance, and can result in serious endocrine diseases. Type 2 or insulin-resistant diabetes is one of the most common. It is not fully understood how obesity promotes diabetes, but most experts feel the excessive fatty tissue somehow causes increased insulin resistance. Many people with Type 2 diabetes actually produce an excessive amount of insulin, but the hormone is not utilized.

Overweight women frequently develop menstrual irregularity and infertility due to increased conversion of androgen to estrogen in fatty tissue. Increased androgen conversion also causes the hairiness seen in many overweight women. After menopause, the excessive androgens, and their conversion to estrogens, are believed to account for the increased risk of uterine cancer found among obese women.

Obesity lowers production of growth hormone, but does not appear to alter production of other pituitary hormones. Among men, obesity lowers testosterone levels and increases estrogens. These changes usually are not apparent, although there are instances in which they prompt the growth of breast tissue, impotence and feminization.

WEIGHT-LOSS STRATEGIES

Obesity that is due to hormonal imbalances is relatively easy to treat, correcting the underlying endocrine disease usually will resolve the weight problem, although dieting may be necessary to lose the accumulated fat. But secondary obesity is uncommon; most overweight is due to overeating and underexercising.

It cannot be overemphasized that the preferred treatment of ordinary obesity is a program of reduced calories and increased exercise. This is often slow and tedious, and people looking for a quick, easy way to shed pounds are particularly vulnerable to fad diets or abuse of diuretics, appetite suppressants, or laxatives. Laxative abuse has been shown not to decrease the calories absorbed. Thus binging followed by a laxative does not stop the calories from entering the body and causing weight gain.

Occasionally, a new treatment appears on the scene that seems to have promise, but later proves to carry serious complications. Gastric bypass surgery, in which varying amounts of the stomach or intestines are removed, was popular a few years ago until it was found that patients who underwent this operation suffered serious diarrhea, nutritional deficiencies and other problems. More recently, less drastic operations have been developed that involve temporary stapling off of a portion of the intestinal tract. These are not advised for the average obese person; instead, they are intended for people whose massive overweight is virtually life-threatening and who have been unable to lose weight by less drastic means.

A new procedure in which a balloon is inserted into the stomach and then partially inflated to give a feeling of fullness has shown initial promise in helping people lose weight. However, this gastric balloon device can cause serious problems if it suddenly deflates, and the manufacturer cautions that it should not be left in place for more than three months. Also, this strategy should be accompanied by a program to change eating behavior to help ensure that the weight is not regained when the balloon is deflated and removed.

Surgical removal of layers of fat is sometimes done, but these are complicated operations that may cause permanent damage to nerves and blood vessels. The so-called "tummy tuck," in which plastic surgeons remove a certain amount of abdominal fat and tighten sagging muscles, is an increasingly popular operation, but this should not be considered an effective treatment for obesity. Similarly, fat suction operations, in which a saline solution is injected into a layer of fat which is then vacuumed out, has become a common plastic surgery technique in the U.S. and in France, where it was developed. This procedure does not seem to have as many potentially serious complications as surgical removal of fat, but it works only on relatively small areas, may be less effective in older individuals and is not recommended for people who are more than a few pounds overweight.

Over the last few years, a number of group weight-loss programs have been organized and these often enjoy a high success rate. Many of these, such as Overeaters Anonymous, are patterned on the techniques used by Alcoholics Anonymous, in which people turn to the support of fellow sufferers to overcome their own problem. Weight Watchers is one of the oldest and most successful of the group programs, and it now has chapters throughout the United States.

Increased physical activity is almost as important as reduced food intake, and again, group exercise programs usually are more successful than solitary efforts. Sadly, many overweight women are embarrassed to join exercise classes or programs because they feel ungainly and out-of-place among their slim fellow exercisers. To help overcome this shyness, the YWCA and many other organizations are setting up special exercise programs specifically for overweight women. Simply recognizing that you are not alone, losing weight and adopting a healthier, more active life-style in the company of others can be a major step toward lifelong weight control.

ANOREXIA NERVOSA/BULIMIA

Anorexia nervosa and bulimia are distressingly common eating disorders that have only recently been brought to widespread public attention. Most of the victims are young women—usually above-average in intelligence and socioeconomic background. Their bizzare eating behavior disrupts families and often leads to death through self-starvation.

Although most people think of anorexia as a modern disorder, it actually was first described in the medical literature in 1689 by Dr. Richard Morton. He told of a seventeen-year-old girl with "nervous consumption" who was "like a skeleton only clad with skin." In the 1930s, an American, Dr. J. M. Berkman, reported on his experience in treating 117 women with anorexia nervosa, concluding that they suffered from a mental disorder.

Today, doctors are uncertain as to what causes anorexia, but most experts agree that the extreme life-threatening nature of the disease involves serious emotional problems. Some researchers have theorized that a disorder involving the hypothalamus may cause anorexia nervosa, but this has not been proved. In some instances, the young woman is found to be schizophrenic or suffering from serious paranoia or obsessive behavior, but again, this is not a common denominator.

Deep-seated family problems have been implicated in

various eating disorders such as anorexia, bulimia and obesity. Dr. Daniel Foster, writing in *Williams Textbook of Endocrinology*, notes that these eating disorders seem to stem from troubled family behavior patterns in which both parents and children seem to be constantly involved in each other's problems. "A paralyzing sense of ineffectiveness" seems to dominate the lives of many eating-disorder victims, and food refusal or abuse becomes a means of self-expression and control. ("Eating Disorders: Obesity and Anorexia Nervosa," by Daniel W. Foster, *Williams Textbook of Endocrinology*, 7th ed., W. B. Saunders Co., Philadelphia, 1985, p. 1101.)

In a simpler sense, both anorexia and bulimia may be learned behaviors, usually during the teenage years. Anorexia is becoming more common, especially among upper-class young women in developed countries. For unexplained reasons, a disproportionate number are Jewish. It is estimated that up to five percent of postpubescent young women may suffer from anorexia and/or bulimia. Occasionally a young man will develop anorexia, but this is unusual — less than six percent of cases are males. However, young male athletes may take to compulsive exercising so they can eat huge amounts of food.

Anorexia and bulimia may occur independently or together. Since our society prizes thinness, and large numbers of young women seem to be constantly trying to lose weight, it is sometimes difficult to distinguish between obsessive dieting and true anorexia nervosa. Frequently, the early stages may go unnoticed by family and friends; they may notice that the young woman is losing weight, but they often do not associate it with illness. Often, the young woman may appear to be overly concerned with health and fitness. Many anorexics turn to excessive, compulsive exercise to increase weight loss, a move that may be misinterpreted as healthy.

Typically, the first visit to a doctor is for failure to menstruate, caused by the hormonal changes accompanying weight loss. The classic symptoms used by physicians to diagnose anorexia nervosa include:

1. A loss of one-fourth or more of original body weight. No physical illness can be found to explain the weight loss.
2. A distorted body image and obsessive fear of being fat. The young woman will insist that she feels or looks fat, even though she may be very emaciated.
3. Distorted preoccupation with food and eating. Anorexics will often spend hours preparing elaborate meals or obsessively collect recipes. But they will then decline to eat what they have prepared, or will take a taste or two and insist that they are full.
4. Signs of starvation. Doctors frequently use terms like "she looked like she had been in a concentration camp" or "I thought I was examining one of the Ethiopia famine victims" to describe the physical appearance of an anorexic patient. The extreme thinness often is not apparent when the young women are clothed because many, paradoxically, tend to wear clothes that make them look fatter, such as long-sleeved, full-cut styles that disguise their emaciated bodies.

Other common symptoms, all of which are associated with extreme malnutrition, include a low body temperature (hypothermia), low heart rate (bradycardia) and low blood pressure (hypotension). Extreme sensitivity to cold is common; when exposed to low temperatures, the women will experience numbness or tingling in their hands and feet. This is caused by constriction of the peripheral blood vessels as the body tries to conserve as much heat and energy as possible. Swelling from an accumulation of fluid, another hallmark of starvation, also is common.

In investigating the family history of anorexic patients, doctors frequently find that the mothers, and occasionally sisters as well, are markedly underweight. This is contrary to the popular notion that a young woman will starve herself because she has an obese mother or other family members and wants to avoid becoming fat herself. A study of 102 anorexic patients found that only ten had family members who were overweight; in contrast, twenty-nine had family members who were markedly underweight.

In some instances, mothers who themselves have a history of anorexia impose strange eating patterns on their children. For example, a mother may underfeed a baby or withhold many foods from older children in a mistaken notion that they are helping the youngsters by keeping them thin.

CONSEQUENCES OF ANOREXIA

Anorexia nervosa should be recognized for what it is—a very serious chronic disease with a high death rate. These unfortunate young women have such a distorted body image that they would rather die than gain weight, even though they may be little more than walking skeletons. Many die of fatal heart arrhythmias, caused by deterioration of the heart muscle. Breathing also becomes difficult because of weakened respiratory muscles.

Extreme malnutrition has numerous effects on the endocrine system, in addition to the most obvious consequence—cessation of menstruation. Everything slows down in an attempt to conserve as much energy as possible. Production of the pituitary's gonad-stimulating hormones drops, as does production of the sex hormones. The thyroid lowers production of its hormones in an effort to slow metabolism.

Treatment involves hospitalization and often forced feeding. After the immediate danger of starvation passes, intensive psychiatric treatment can begin. The treatment process is lengthy; sometimes psychiatric counseling must continue for years. The disease also has a high relapse rate, and many women who have recovered from anorexia nervosa say they are still uncomfortable with eating or their body image.

Follow-up studies of anorexic patients have found that within two years, about half achieve normal weight, twenty percent gain but are still underweight, twenty percent remain unchanged, six percent die and five percent become obese. Half to three-fourths resume menstruation with weight gain, but irregularity is common. Half continue to have psychiatric or emotional problems serious enough to require treatment.

BULIMIA

Bulimia, which means "ox hunger," is marked by a voracious, uncontrolled appetite. It often accompanies or follows anorexia—after periods of self-starvation, the woman becomes so hungry that she consumes a huge quantity of food. Because of her extraordinary determination to stay thin and the fact that gorging is contrary to her compulsive food denial, she then feels she must take action to purge herself of the food. This usually involves induced vomiting, either by stimulating a gag response or by training the body to vomit at will. With some bulimics, the vomiting becomes almost ritualistic.

Some bulimics attempt to compensate for a food binge by consuming huge amounts of laxatives. Diuretic abuse also occurs among bulimics, and some, especially young people with poorly controlled diabetes, may control weight through insulin abuse, decreasing their dose, causing the ingested sugar to pass into the urine. All of these are very risky practices that can cause serious medical problems. And, ironically, measures like laxative and diuretic abuse do not prevent weight gain when massive amounts of food are consumed.

Unlike anorexia nervosa, bulimia is a new disorder. It is particularly common among college students and young career women who are driven to succeed. As with anorexics, young women with bulimia are obsessed with a fear of getting fat, but they also have an irresistible urge to overeat. Some can engage in self-starvation, but they will eventually succumb to a food binge, usually when they are alone so no one can observe their compulsive eating. Some bulimics can consume almost unbelievable quantities of food—up to 50,000 calories a day.

A recent study reported in the *American Journal of Psy-*

chiatry described the bizarre eating patterns of forty bulimics. Invariably, they binged alone. The women binged an average of twelve times a week, but one admitted gorging forty-six times in a single week. The mean number of calories consumed per sitting, which ranged from one to eight hours, was 3,415, but some could eat more than 11,000 calories at a time. Ice cream was the favored food—some could consume more than a gallon, accompanied by cookies, candy, doughnuts, soft drinks and other high-calorie foods.

Bulimics have been found to be more antisocial than anorexics. One study found that twelve to fourteen percent admitted stealing, usually food, but the actual figure was thought to be even higher. Drug and alcohol abuse also is relatively common among bulimics. Self-mutilation and suicide also are relatively common in this group. In contrast, women with anorexia nervosa without bulimia tend to be models of good behavior, and suicide (other than through self-starvation) is rare.

CONSEQUENCES OF BULIMIA

Aside from the emotional and eating problems, bulimia does not have as many physical consequences as anorexia. The women are usually thin, but some are overweight and the kind of emaciation seen in anorexia nervosa is rare. The repeated vomiting and diarrhea from laxative abuse causes disturbances in body chemistry, particularly potassium depletion. This can cause convulsions, muscle spasms and weakness, but usually not to a serious extent.

Lack of menstruation sometimes occurs, but it is not as common as in anorexia. One study of twenty-eight bulimics found that eleven had menstrual irregularities.

Impaired taste and tooth decay are common among bulimics. These are thought to result from the frequent exposure of the teeth and taste buds to gastric acids when vomiting. Sometimes the salivary glands enlarge.

Depression and other emotional disorders are particularly common among bulimic patients. In recent years, a number of clinics and self-help groups for both anorexics and bulimics have been established. Although many women with bulimia tend to have deep-seated emotional problems, group therapy with patients who share similar eating disorders has been helpful.

SUMMING UP

Obesity, anorexia and bulimia all are rooted in poorly understood eating disorders, and all can have serious consequences on emotional and physical health. Many experts believe these eating disorders can be traced to childhood, and although this has not been proved, a prudent approach of instilling sensible eating habits at an early age is advised. Using food as either a reward or punishment should be avoided, and parents of teenage daughters should be particularly aware of weight loss, preoccupation with food and thinness and other warning signs in their children.

Chapter 14

How Hormones Affect
Your Skin and Hair

Every woman, no matter what her age, is concerned about the appearance of her skin and hair. Although most people think of skin in terms of how it looks rather than its importance to health, it actually is a vital organ that not only provides the body with its essential protective covering, but also serves as a sensory organ and performs a variety of metabolic and other functions. Indeed, the skin is our only readily visible vital organ, and physicians have observed and kept records of skin diseases since prehistoric times. Hair, often referred to as a woman's crowning glory, is mostly dead tissue derived from the skin, but it can be an important indicator of endocrine and other diseases.

Misconceptions abound concerning what the skin can and cannot do. Many of these mistaken notions are rooted in customs and old wives' tales that have persisted through the ages. Others are promulgated by the cosmetics industry, which reaps billions of dollars each year from convincing women that beautiful skin needs a mind-boggling array of "foods," cleansers, moisturizers, hormones and chemical concoctions. Of course, this is hardly new; through the ages women (and men, too) have used everything from milk and honey to dissolved pearls and mud to beautify their skin.

Much of this emphasis on skin and hair beauty attests to their sexual attractiveness. Primitive men and women used body paints and oils not only to make themselves more attractive to the opposite sex but also to ward off evil spirits and frighten their enemies. Ten-thousand-year-old eye makeup has been unearthed by archeologists in Egypt; the use of perfumes to camouflage or change our natural odors is even older.

Our preoccupation with beautifying skin and hair begins at an early age. As soon as a little girl is aware of herself in a mirror, she starts experimenting with her mother's makeup, and she is likely to use it throughout her life. Every now and then, an anticosmetics faction emerges to denounce makeup as immoral or as evidence of woman's subjacency to male domination, but there is little likelihood that women will ever cease using makeup and other beauty aids. What is important, however, is that women select cosmetics, deodorants, shampoos, skin cleansers, lotions and other such products with correct information and a clear understanding of what they can do.

SKIN ANATOMY AND FUNCTION

The skin is composed of two layers—the outer epidermis and the underlying dermis—both of which have several subdivisions. The epidermis gives rise to the nails and hair and also contains the sweat glands' pores, or openings.

Except on the palms of the hands and soles of the feet, the epidermis is paper-thin, even though it is made up of five layers of different cells or tissue in most places. About ninety-five percent of cells in the epidermis are keratinocytes, which form the body's protective outer layer, keeping harmful substances out and preventing the loss of vital body fluids. The other five percent of cells are melanocytes, the pigment cells that give skin its color and protect the underlying tissue from the sun's ultraviolet rays.

The outermost layer of the epidermis is called the stratum corneum, or horny layer, and it is composed mostly of keratin, a tough, opaque protein. The outermost skin cells contain soft keratin, while the protein that makes up the nails and hair is harder. But all are actually dead cells that are constantly being worn off and replaced by cells moving up through the underlying layers. These cells originate in the basal layer, or stratum germinativum. This basal layer functions as a cell factory, constantly producing new skin cells. The rapidly dividing keratinocytes are pushed up into the prickle cell layer, so named because the cells look like they have tiny spiny projections. After the cells reach this layer, they stop dividing and begin to produce keratin. As the cells are pushed out of the prickle cell layer and into the granular layer, they accumulate a granular substance that is a precursor to keratin. The cells lose their differentiation and become clearer and take on a semifluid substance, forming a clear, translucent layer immediately underlying the outermost horny layer. By the time the cells are pushed to the surface, they too are flat, flaking cells of dead keratin.

The process is never-ending; the five layers that make up the epidermis completely renew themselves every fifteen to thirty days.

The dermis, which is much thicker than the epidermis, contains numerous nerve endings, blood and lymph vessels, sebaceous and sweat glands, hair follicles and tiny muscles. This is the living layer of skin, where most problems, including acne, arise. It is also the layer where the many varied metabolic, sensory and other functions of the skin take place. For example, the eccrine sweat glands and the network of tiny blood vessels in the dermis are essential in controlling body temperature. These are the blood vessels that suddenly dilate, producing the rush of heat that a woman experiences during a menopausal hot flash.

A layer of subcutaneous tissue underlies the dermis; it contains fat and the fascia that connects the skin to the muscle. The layer of fat provides insulation, as well as reserve of energy that can be drawn upon when needed. This peripheral fat also helps convert androgen manufactured by the adrenal glands into estrogen.

HAIR

We usually think of humans as being relatively hairless; in reality, however, we have as many hair follicles as our distant cousins, the gorillas and other apes. Most of the human hair follicles produce only vellus hairs, the colorless, downlike hairs that cover the entire body except for the soles, palms and skin around various body openings and the nails. The more visible and thicker terminal hairs are found on the scalp, eyebrows and eyelashes.

With the hormonal stimulation of puberty, vellus hairs on specific parts of the body, such as the armpits and genital area, develop into terminal hairs. Men also develop terminal hairs on their face, chest, arms and legs. Women have the same number of hair follicles in these places as men, and many develop a few coarse terminal hairs on their upper lips, chin, around the nipples and other parts of the body. The extent of this hairiness is usually hereditary, but extreme hirsutism also may be sign of hormonal imbalance and serious disease.

Hair follicles are formed early in fetal life; by the end of the first trimester of gestation, the developing fetus has all of its hair-forming structures. Located at the bottom of the hair follicle's bulblike structures is the germinal matrix, which is analogous to the basal layer of the epidermis. The germinal matrix produces rapidly dividing cells that are pushed upward to the outer surface of the skin. As they grow further away from the nourishing blood vessels of the dermis, these cells produce keratin and become harder. The cells are differentiated into the middle cortex, which contains pigment cells, and the outer cuticle, which is made up of scaly dead cells. Some hairs also have a medulla in their center, which is made up of softer keratin, similar to that of the outermost layer of skin. The visible part of the hair, the shaft, is composed of dead cells; the root, which is in the follicle, contains the only living hair cells.

Hair growth is a cyclic rather than a constant process.

During the growing, or anagen, phase, the cells in the germinal matrix divide rapidly, and as the new cells are pushed upward through the hair shaft, the visible hair becomes longer. Generally, hair on the scalp and face grow the fastest and longest. The *Guinness Book of Records* claims that the longest hair measured was five feet five inches long on a five-foot-tall woman. Hair on the arms grows slowly and for a shorter period. The growing phase usually lasts for two to four years, after which the hair goes into its catagen stage. In this phase of the cycle, which lasts for only a few weeks, cells at the root's base become keratinized and club-shaped. This results in reduced blood supply to the root, and it eventually withers and dies. The hair then enters the resting, or telegen phase, marked by a shedding of the old hair as a new hair bulb forms in the follicle bottom. At any given time, about a third of the hairs are in a growing phase, another third are resting, and a third are in the process of being shed. But since the hairs in their different phases are evenly distributed over the body, we are not aware that some are growing while others are resting or being shed.

The length of time that a single scalp hair survives varies from person to person, and may be anywhere from two to six years. Since hair grows from the bottom up, there is no truth to the myth that cutting the ends of hair will stimulate new growth. Similarly, shaving will not cause hair to grow faster or coarser; nor will shaving stimulate down hair to become coarser terminal hairs. (If this were true, men who shave their scalps could grow a new head of hair.)

As both men and women grow older, there is a certain amount of thinning of scalp hair. Following menopause, most women notice that their hair is thinning, but the type of baldness that is common in men is rare in women. Hormones play a major role in hair distribution. The androgens that are responsible for stimulating the growth of pubic and body hair in boys are responsible for male-pattern balding in men who are genetically susceptible. The lower level of estrogen is responsible for the increase in facial hair experienced by many women after menopause.

FINGERNAILS AND TOENAILS

The nails also are formed early in fetal life, and develop from a plate of hard, translucent keratin. Nails get their pink coloration from capillaries in the underlying dermis, but like the hair and outer epidermis layer, the visible part of the nail is made up of dead cells. On the average, nails grow about 0.5 mm, or .020 in. per week. The nail on the middle finger grows the fastest; the little nail the slowest. For reasons that are not completely understood, nails grow faster in the summer than in the winter.

SEPARATING FACTS FROM MYTHS

We are constantly being extolled to "feed thirsty skin" or to let it breathe, rest, or perform any number of other impossible functions. Since visible skin is made up of dead cells, obviously any "food or drink" that we apply to its surface will not be consumed. Oils, moisturizers and other emollients may soften and soothe, but they do not feed the skin; all of its nourishment comes from the tiny blood vessels in the dermis. Diet does play an important role in maintaining healthy skin. Foods high in vitamins A and C help maintain skin, and a deficiency of either results in dry, rough skin.

Some substances with small molecules can be absorbed through the skin; in fact, a number of medications, including estrogen, can be taken by applying them to the skin. But the skin itself does not consume any of these products. Similarly, cosmetic manufacturers' claims that collagen—a substance that can be injected into the skin to make wrinkles, pitting and other deformities less apparent—can be absorbed into the skin are false; the molecule is simply too large to pass through the densely packed epidermal cells.

As we grow older, the skin loses some of its elasticity and moisture, causing sagging, wrinkling and a loss in resiliency. A number of factors—heredity, climate, cigarette use, sun exposure, hormonal balance and overall health, among others—determine how quickly skin ages. Women whose mothers had soft skin with little wrinkling can anticipate similar good luck. The British and others who live in damp climates with little sun are doubly blessed as far as their skin is concerned, since both a dry climate and sun can make skin leathery and wrinkled. Women who smoke often have very pronounced wrinkling at an early age; the reason for this is unknown, but it is believed to be related to the fact that smoking lowers estrogen levels.

While some of these factors can be controlled and minimized, all of the moisturizers and creams in the world cannot erase wrinkles and prevent the toll of time on the skin. Claims that hormone creams, which usually contain small amounts of estrogen, can restore the skin's "youthful glow" are patently false. The glow of youth comes from sebum; an excess of this in adulthood is simply oily skin. Estrogen creams will not effect sebum production, nor will they maintain collagen and the elastic reticular fibers which give the skin its resiliency. A face-lift to remove sagging excess skin can erase wrinkles and give a more youthful appearance, but the effects are not permanent. The same is true of collagen injected into the wrinkles.

Applying oils, creams or lotions to dried, cracked skin will not restore its normal balance, despite cosmetic manufacturers' claims that "thirsty skin soaks up" these products. Skin oil (sebum) comes from within; oils applied to the surface will not replenish those lost from the skin. What is needed is rehydration, which entails restoring water or moisture to the skin. This can be accomplished by soaking the skin in water and then applying petroleum jelly or some other oil-based barrier to prevent evaporation. Thus, applying a moisturizing lotion or skin cream to wet skin will help it retain more water.

Myths also abound as to what should be used to cleanse the skin. Dermatologists agree that a mild soap and water is all that is needed by the vast majority of women. Despite manufacturers' claims (and huge prices), most soaps are a combination of fats and lye, adjusted for the proper pH balance. Which soap is used is largely a matter of personal preference; all will cleanse the skin and remove dead cells and other debris, as well as bacteria that can cause odor.

Hair care is as fraught with misconception and misleading claims as is skin care. Since hair, like skin, is dead, it does not need to be fed, conditioned or subjected to any of the other body-building treatments so popular today. Hair is naturally strong and durable; archeologists have found intact hair in tombs thousands of years old.

The less that we do to hair, other than keep it clean and tangle-free, the better off it is. But given today's fashions for permed and colored hair, and exposure to a variety of chemicals, sun and other elements, hair can suffer damage.

Looking at a shaft of hair under a microscope, one sees its structure of tightly overlapping cuticle cells, the tips of which point upward. The hair is covered by a thin coating of oil. Split ends are caused by a separation of cell layers; back-combing, blow-drying, and the use of chemical dyes and permanent waves lifts or swells the overlapping cuticle cells. Since hair gets its shine from the even reflection of light off the oil-coated cells, changing the contour of the shaft can make it look dull and dry. Conditioners that return the cuticle cells to their original position and coat the hair with oil will make it look shiny. But these conditioners do not "feed" the hair or restore its natural protein.

Most of today's shampoos contain detergents rather than soap, which is difficult to completely rinse out if the water has a high mineral content. Although most shampoos are basically the same, they may produce different results for different people—one person may find a brand that leaves his or her hair limp, while the same shampoo will make another person's hair dry and fluffy.

People with psoriasis or some other skin condition may require a special shampoo, but the so-called antidandruff formulations have little value except for people who do not want to wash their hair very often. Everyone's scalp flakes to varying degrees; some people cannot go more than a day or two between shampooing without flaking, while others can go longer. If dandruff is a problem, more frequent shampooing and thorough rinsing will take care of it, unless psoriasis or seborrheic dermatitis is the cause. The addition of beer, eggs, protein and other substances to shampoo to give hair "body" may work for some people, but these ingredients also may lessen the shampoo's cleansing properties, which, after all, is its main purpose.

Hair gets its color from melanocytes—cells that deposit their pigment in the hair cortex. The pigment melanin, which is brown-black, predominates in hair that is dark or ash-hued. Phaeomelanin, which is yellow-brown, predominates in hair that is red, auburn or golden-hued. Graying is caused by a gradual reduction in pigment production; when it ceases completely, the hair is white. Although accounts abound of people whose hair "turned white overnight" after an illness or stressful event, this is impossible. Stress or illness can cause a reduction of pigment production and hasten the graying process, but it does not happen overnight. Stress also can force more hair into a resting phase, causing an accelerated loss of the older, pigmented hair. This may make it seem that a person has turned white overnight, but the night is more likely to be several months long.

Nothing can restore the hair's natural color. Sometimes when all the hair falls out, as during cancer chemotherapy, it may grow back with a color, even if it was white before. Often the color will be different than what the person had originally. But no amount of vitamins or topical preparations can cause the production of natural pigment cells.

Contrary to popular belief, nails are not made stronger or more supple by consuming gelatin or other protein products. Similarly, oils or other substances applied to nail surfaces to "feed" them cannot be consumed. Dry, brittle nails may be caused by aging, exposure to chemicals or drying agents, including excessive use of nail-polish removers and adhesives. Diseases also can cause a variety of nail problems, including grooving, changes in shape, brittleness and loosening.

HORMONE-RELATED DISORDERS
OF SKIN AND HAIR

Acne

Acne is by far the most common hormonal disorder affecting the skin. It is estimated that at some point in their lives, three out of four people suffer from acne, and some dermatologists put the figure even higher, maintaining that no one passes through puberty without having acne. Some people have acne for only a few months, and others suffer from it throughout their lives (although this is relatively rare).

Acne is primarily a disease of adolescence, but adults also may have it. In fact, some women go through adolescence with very little acne, and then develop it as young adults. Sometimes it starts in adolescence and comes and goes until menopause. While acne is not regarded as a serious medical condition, it can have profound psychological effects which are compounded by the fact that it usually appears at a time when a young person is particularly self-conscious about his or her appearance.

Although hormones play a role in acne, it is not known exactly how they cause it. Studies have been unable to identify any specific hormonal excess or imbalance that causes acne, although it is generally believed that androgens are somehow implicated. In women who are particularly susceptible to acne, any hormonal change seems to provoke a flare-up—menstruation, the use of birth control pills, pregnancy, menopause, even stress. Heredity also appears to be a factor.

Even today, many myths persist about acne, which can add to its adverse emotional effects. Young people with acne are often exhorted to wash their faces more often, implying that they are to blame for their skin problems because of inattention to personal hygiene. Cleanliness, or a lack of cleanliness, has nothing to do with acne—the process starts deep in the dermis.

Similarly, parents often blame their youngsters' acne on eating greasy foods, chocolate, sugary soft drinks and other so-called "junk foods." There is no evidence that diet causes acne, although there is some evidence that certain substances, such as large amounts of iodine or bromides, may provoke a flare-up in people who already have acne. Other practices that have wrongly been associated with causing acne include masturbation and other sexual activity, too much or too little sleep and constipation, among many others. There is no evidence that any of these can cause acne, although the stress (and resulting hormonal changes) associated with such factors may cause skin eruptions among susceptible people.

Acne arises in the sebaceous glands that are linked to hair follicles—structures referred to as philosebaceous units. It is most common in areas of the skin that have large philosebaceous units and mostly vellus hairs—in particular, the face and upper back. The sebaceous glands produce sebum, a waxy substance made up of fatty acids, cholesterol and dead cells. It carries dead cells to the skin surface and also lubricates the skin and hair.

Although it is not known what triggers acne, two factors—hormones and bacteria—are instrumental in its course. Sebum is secreted in response to hormonal stimulation (acne very rarely occurs before the onset of puberty). The sebaceous glands are particularly sensitive to androgens, and many experts feel that acne usually appears during puberty and is more common in boys than girls because of the surge in androgens. People with oily skin and hair are more prone to acne, but this is not absolute. Some people with dry skin develop severe acne, while others with oily skin are free of it. *Corynebacterium acnes*, a microorganism that is found in the hair follicle, is instrumental in the more severe types of acne.

In the initial stages of acne (see Figure 22), the pores that serve as sebum passageways become blocked with sebum, dead cells, keratin and bacteria that normally live in the hair follicles. This causes the formation of a comedo or

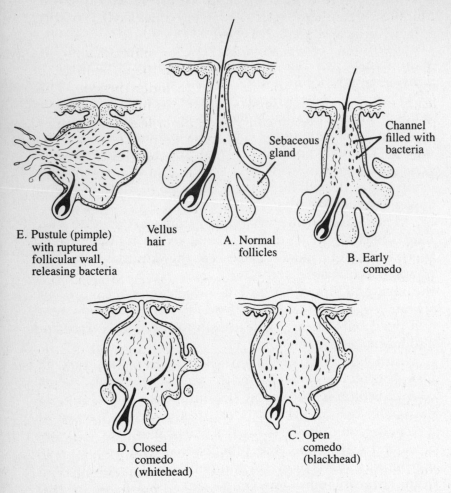

E. Pustule (pimple) with ruptured follicular wall, releasing bacteria

Vellus hair

A. Normal follicles

Sebaceous gland

Channel filled with bacteria

B. Early comedo

D. Closed comedo (whitehead)

C. Open comedo (blackhead)

How Acne Develops

plug, which blocks the duct through which sebum is carried to the skin surface. There are two types of comedones: closed comedones, or whiteheads, and open ones, better known as blackheads. In a closed comedo, the duct opening is blocked at the skin's surface and the underlying comedo is whitish or skin colored. If the comedo expands enough to poke through the pore opening, a blackhead will form. Blackheads get their dark color from pigment cells, not dirt, as many people commonly believe.

Acne may be noninflammatory or inflammatory. In more severe acne, pressure builds within the comedo, causing it to rupture and spill its contents under the skin. This leads to inflammation, infection and pus-filled pustules or pimples. Severe inflammatory acne often leads to scarring, but this is genetically determined; some people with widespread acne heal without scars, while others may develop deep and permanent blemishes from minor pimples.

In recent years, more effective means of treating acne have been developed, greatly reducing the incidence of disfiguring acne. Sometimes mild acne can be controlled by frequent washing with soap and "buffing" the skin with a slightly abrasive pad or cleanser. This helps dry the skin and also promotes scaling of the outermost layer of cells. One should avoid squeezing and picking, which can actually make the problem worse.

The most common acne treatment involves using irritating substances called exfoliants. These cause an inflammatory response in the upper layers of skin, resulting in peeling of the outer layer. Benzoyl peroxide in five or ten percent strengths is one of the most effective exfoliants (available in nonprescription form under a number of brand names). Dermatologists recommend starting with the five percent strength, and, if this is not strong enough to control the acne, moving up to the ten percent formulation. If oily skin and hair are contributing to the problem, frequent cleansing of the skin and shampooing is advised to help keep the skin dry.

If benzoyl peroxide alone is insufficient, antibiotics—either applied to the skin in a cream or taken orally—may be added to the regimen. Tetracycline or erythromycin are the most commonly prescribed antibiotics. They may be used long-term, but tetracycline should be avoided during pregnancy, especially in the second half, since it causes mottled tooth enamel in the baby.

The strongest anti-acne medications are derivatives of vitamin A, which are available only by prescription. The older of these is retinoic acid or tretinoin, which provokes a marked irritating and peeling action. It often is used in conjunction with benzoyl peroxide, with one medication used in the morning and the other in the evening. This strategy can be very effective, but not everyone can tolerate the irritation caused by using both drugs.

A newer drug is isotretinoin, sold under the brand name of Accutane. This is derived from a synthetic form of vitamin A and works by inhibiting the production of sebum. It is highly effective, but should be used only under close medical supervision since it is associated with a number of side effects. Among the most serious side effects are birth defects. Women are advised to have a pregnancy test before starting Accutane if there is even a remote chance they may be pregnant, and to use an effective contraceptive until at least a month after discontinuing the drug.

Patients using any vitamin A anti-acne drug should avoid sun exposure. Laboratory studies have found that animals given retinoic acid and then exposed to sunlight developed skin tumors that continued to grow even after the drug was stopped. These studies have led researchers to caution that the drugs may increase the cancer-causing potential of sun.

Since hormones play a role in acne, hormone manipulation may help in some instances. Many women taking birth control pills experience improvement in their acne. At one time, the pill was prescribed to treat acne. This is no longer common, since there are now other more effective anti-acne medications. But if a woman elects this form of contraception, a clearing up of her acne may be an added bonus. There are, however, women for whom birth control pills have an opposite effect and actually provoke a flare-up of acne. This is seen most often with the progesterone-only pill, or mini-pill. Switching to a combination that contains estrogen usually helps, although a trial of several months may be needed to see results.

Many women are troubled by premenstrual acne. Some researchers have observed that the high levels of progesterone in the premenstrual phase seem to affect the follicle ducts by making their surface openings smaller, which could promote their blockage and a flare-up of acne. This cyclic acne can be treated with benzoyl peroxide, or it can be prevented by taking birth control pills if a woman elects this method of contraception.

Excessive use of skin creams, lotions, moisturizers and oily cosmetics is associated with acne cosmeticus, a term coined by two prominent dermatologists, Drs. Arnold Kligman and O. Mills. It usually occurs in women who have been bothered by acne since adolescence, but sometimes it appears in middle-aged women who have enjoyed clear skins throughout adulthood. The use of exfoliants and switching to water-based or oil-free cosmetics usually will clear up this type of acne. Finding cosmetics that do not provoke acne may involve considerable trial-and-error, since even those promoted as water-based may contain fatty acids or other ingredients that trigger acne in susceptible women.

Other Hormone-Related Skin Problems

The skin can serve as an early warning sign for several hormonal disorders. Thyroid disorders, which alter the body's metabolism, affect the skin, hair and nails in several ways. An underactive thyroid causes the skin to become thickened, rough and dry, while an overactive thyroid causes a thinning of the skin and increased sweating.

Vitiligo, white patches of skin that have lost pigment, sometimes occurs with both overactive and underactive thyroids. The unpigmented areas are generally small and barely noticed, but in some people, they are quite extensive and require treatment by a dermatologist. Drugs called psoralins, which are applied to the skin and then exposed to the sun or ultraviolet rays, often help repigment the skin.

Generalized itching frequently accompanies thyroid disorders. Any kind of skin irritation, including something as simple as a hot shower, may produce hives and itching.

Pretibial myxedema is a rarer thyroid-related skin condition which involves development of a raised reddish rash or lumps on the front of the legs and top of the feet. It is not known why only these parts of the body develop the lumps, which are usually painless. The condition usually can be cleared up with cortisone creams.

Premature graying, defined as hair that turns gray before the age of thirty, is more common among people with thyroid disorders than the general population. Hair thinning is also common with both an overactive and underactive thyroid. Typically, the hair loss is evenly distributed, but sometimes it is patchy, causing bald spots on any part of the body that normally has hair. This condition, known as alopecia areata, is usually temporary, and the hair regrows after a few months. In some cases, however, the bald patches are permanent.

An overactive thyroid can cause nails to grow rapidly and with uneven margins that are difficult to keep clean. An underactive thyroid can cause dry, brittle nails with grooves.

Adrenal disorders also may affect the skin. People with Addison's disease, a disorder characterized by underproduction of adrenal hormones, often have increased skin pigmentation; in extreme cases, the skin may become very tanned, with black freckles over the forehead and upper body, and the pigmented areas, such as the areolas around the nipples or the mucous membranes of the lips, mouth and vagina, may turn bluish-black. There also may be white patches of unpigmented skin.

Cushing's syndrome, an adrenal disorder in which there is an overproduction of corticosteroid hormones, causes the skin to become thin and to bruise easily. One of the early signs of Cushing's is often the appearance of purple stretch marks on the abdomen. (For a more detailed discussion of both Addison's and Cushing's diseases, see Chapter 12.)

HIRSUTISM

Through the ages, people have been both fascinated and repelled by abnormal hair growth in women. Old circus posters invariably feature a bearded woman, witches invariably have hairy chins, and literature is full of horror stories of hair-covered women.

As noted earlier, men and women have an equal number of hair follicles, with the exception of Oriental women, who do not have as many facial hair follicles. Androgen—or more specifically, testosterone—is presumed to stimulate the conversion of the downlike vellus hair to the darker and coarser terminal hair in characteristic sex-linked places—namely, the face, armpits, chest, and pubic area. Thus boys begin to grow beards and hair on their chests and other parts of the body when the level of testosterone rises during puberty. (Ironically, high levels of androgen later in life are responsible for male balding.)

Since women have a much lower level of circulating testosterone, they do not develop as many terminal hairs as men, especially on the face and chest. Most women may have a few coarse, dark hairs on their upper lip, chin or nipples, and some may have a distinct moustache. Usually this is a hereditary characteristic; often a woman or her doctor can tell if her hairiness is normal simply by looking at other women in her family. This type of hairiness is particularly common among Mediterranean women, who are likely to have dark hair and skin and more facial and body hair than their fair-haired, light-skinned counterparts from northern Europe.

For most women, hairiness is more of a cosmetic problem than a medical one. Unless there is a hormonal imbalance or other medical problem causing the hairiness, it can be dealt with by simple removal. Electrolysis will remove hair permanently by destroying the follicle; shaving, depilatories or waxing are temporary measures.

Hairiness that is related to a hormone imbalance requires medical investigation to pinpoint the cause and determine what treatment should be undertaken. Warning signs that tell a woman she should see her doctor include: increased hairiness accompanied by loss of periods; any signs of masculinization, such as deepening of the voice, increased muscularity, lengthening of the clitoris, male-pattern balding, etc.; sudden and extreme abdominal swelling; and fertility problems.

Laboratory tests to measure the total circulating testosterone usually find no difference between normal and hirsute women, but those with abnormal hair growth will have almost twice as much free, or active, testosterone which can be readily used by the body. Testosterone circulates in the bloodstream attached to proteins called globulins. Less than one percent of testosterone circulates unattached or "free." It is only this free hormone that stimulates hair growth by converting vellus to terminal hair in the sex-linked areas of the body. Estrogen increases the amount of testosterone bound to protein, and therefore a low level of estrogen results in a low level of the carrier protein or globulin and more hormone circulating in the free form. Thus the total testosterone level does not reflect the amount of active hormone.

Numerous disorders—most of them relatively rare—can alter a woman's testosterone balance. The most common involve changes in ovarian function. Women who are very attuned to their bodies will note that, at certain times of their menstrual cycle, they need to shave their legs and underarms more often. This is a natural aspect of normal hormonal fluctuations, when testosterone is slightly elevated and estrogen is low. Women who stop ovulating will notice a greater increase in hairiness. A typical example might be a woman who starts vigorous exercise training or goes on a crash diet. If her percentage of body fat declines enough for her to stop ovulating, she will notice that she is more hairy than usual because her estrogen levels drop and free testosterone levels go up.

Women who are very overweight also may develop hairiness because the excessive fat tissue can alter hormonal balance and lead to failure to ovulate. Similarly, women going through menopause often notice an increase in facial hair due to their lack of ovulation.

Other possible causes of ovarian failure include polycystic disease, ovarian cancer and a variety of tumors. Disorders of the adrenal glands also can cause a rise in testosterone. These include Cushing's disease, congenital disorders, cancer and other tumors. Drugs containing androgens, progesterone and cortisol also can cause increased hairiness. Other medications which can cause hairiness include the antiseizure medicine phenytoin (Dilantin), the antihypertensive drugs Minipress and Hyperstat and antipsychotic medications such as Thorazine.

Correcting the cause of excessive testosterone will not solve the problem of hairiness: the conversion of a vellus hair to a terminal one is permanent, and it will remain dark and coarse for life. If the woman wants to rid herself of the unwanted hair, electrolysis is the most efficient method. But electrolysis alone will not solve the hairiness problem; if the underlying hormonal imbalance remains uncorrected, the active testosterone will simply convert more terminal hairs, and the electrolysis will be unable to keep up with the constantly emerging new growth.

ABNORMAL LOSS OR LACK OF HAIR

With age, women experience a certain amount of hair thinning or loss. But there are situations in which a person may experience widespread hair loss unrelated to age or hormonal imbalances. As explained earlier, hair growth is cyclic, and not all hairs are in the same growth phase at the same time. A condition that forces all hair into the same cycle—for example, a high fever can "shock" all hair into the resting phase—can cause it to be shed at the same time. Certain drugs, especially those used for cancer chemotherapy, X rays, freezing and burns are other examples of conditions that can force hair into a resting and shedding phase.

Occasionally, a child will reach the age of puberty and fail to develop the characteristic armpit and pubic hair, even though she may develop breasts. This may be a sign of a chromosomal abnormality in which the woman is lacking normal reproductive organs. Fortunately, these chromosomal abnormalities are rare, but when one is suspected, it should be checked by a doctor promptly, since hormone treatments may help correct some of the problems. These disorders are described in detail in Chapter 4.

SUMMING UP

All of us are very conscious of our skin and hair. Most skin or hair problems are cosmetic rather than serious medical disorders, but there are a number of hormonal imbalances and other disorders that are reflected in the skin and hair. Since the skin and hair are so visible, symptoms involving them often prompt a visit to the doctor more readily than perhaps more serious but less visible signs.

Glossary

Abortion: The termination of pregnancy through expulsion of the fetus before it can survive on its own. An abortion may be either induced (also called therapeutic) or spontaneous (also called miscarriage).

Acne: A hormone-related skin disorder characterized by inflammation of the sebaceous glands and hair follicles. Typically it occurs during puberty; comedones, either closed or open, form. The face, neck, and upper part of chest and back are the most common sites.

Acromegalia, acromegaly: A chronic disease in which certain bones enlarge or grow longer after a person is fully grown. Most commonly affects the arms and legs, and the frontal bones of the skull and jaws. The nose and lips also may grow and there is often a thickening of soft tissues of the face. It is caused by too much growth hormone and treated by X rays to shrink the pituitary, or part of the pituitary gland is removed.

Addison's disease: A relatively rare disorder characterized by a lack of adrenal hormones. The adrenal glands are gradually destroyed, usually by an autoimmune disorder or by other diseases, such as tuberculosis. Symptoms include fatigue, abdominal pains, lack of appetite, nausea, dizzy spells, a darkening of the skin, and an increased susceptibility to infection or physical stress.

Adipose tissue: Fatty tissue.

Adolescence: The period from the beginning of puberty until maturity.

Adrenal cortex: The outer part of the adrenal or suprarenal gland. The adrenal cortex makes three kinds of steroid hormones that are vital to the body: corticosteroids, mineralocorticoids, and the sex steroids.

Adrenal glands: Endocrine glands that rest just above the kidneys and which secrete several important hormones including cortisone and other steroid hormones, which are produced in the outer portion of each gland. The "stress" hormones, such as norepinephrine and epinephrine, are secreted by the inner portion of the gland.

Adrenal medulla: The inner part of the adrenal gland which secretes epinephrine and norepinephrine, the "stress" hormones that are responsible for the fight-or-flight response in the face of perceived danger.

Adrenocorticotropic hormone (ACTH): A hormone produced by the pituitary gland that controls the adrenal gland's secretion of corticosteroids.

Aldosterone: The major mineralocorticoid produced in the adrenal cortex. It helps maintain the body's balance of fluids by helping the kidneys conserve sodium; it also controls levels of potassium in the blood.

Aldosteronism: A condition caused by excessive aldosterone production. As a result, the body retains too much salt and excretes potassium, leading to high blood pressure, altered pH of the blood, muscular weakness, muscle contractions, and numbness. If untreated, it can lead to kidney disease and heart failure. Also called hyperaldosteronism.

Amenorrhea: Lack of menstruation. Primary amenorrhea refers to the failure of menstruation to ever occur, while secondary amenorrhea refers to cessation of periods in women who have menstruated.

Amino acids: The nitrogen-containing building blocks of protein used by the body to form muscle and other tissue. Some essential amino acids must come from the diet, while others are manufactured in the body.

Amniocentesis: An examination that is carried out during pregnancy, usually in the second trimester, in which a small amount of the amniotic fluid is withdrawn via a hollow needle and analyzed to detect certain genetic, chromosomal, or biochemical disorders in the fetus.

Amnion: The thin transparent sac which holds the fetus and the amniotic fluid during pregnancy.

Amniotic fluid: The fluid surrounding the fetus contained in the amniotic sac.

Androgen: Sex hormones that are secreted by the testes and adrenal glands that produce secondary male characteristics, such as beard growth, muscular development, and deepening of the voice. Testosterone and androsterone are the major androgens. Women also produce small amounts of androgen.

Androstenedione: An androgen that is secreted by the adrenal glands and which is converted by fat cells into a form of estrogen.

Androsterone: One of the male sex hormones (androgens). *See also* testosterone and androgen.

Angiotensin: A substance in the blood that causes blood vessels to narrow or constrict, thereby raising blood pressure. It also prompts the adrenal glands to secrete more aldosterone. In women, the levels of angiotensin rise following ovulation, which may account for some of the fluid accumulation that occurs during the premenstrual phase of the monthly cycle.

Anorexia nervosa: A serious disorder in which a person, most commonly an adolescent girl or young woman, embarks on extreme self-starvation. Victims have a markedly distorted body image, and a morbid fear of becoming fat. If allowed to progress, it causes a severe loss of weight, amenorrhea in women, and arrested growth among older children. Anorexia nervosa is believed to be a psychiatric illness, but its true cause has not yet been established.

Anovulatory cycles: Menstrual cycles in which there is menstrual flow without ovulation. They may occur in young women who have only recently started to menstruate but in whom regular ovulation is not yet established, and in older women who are approaching menopause. Other causes include hormonal imbalances. Also called anovular menstruation.

Anterior pituitary (adenohypophysis): The front (anterior) lobe of the pituitary gland, which is at the base of the brain. It secretes growth hormone as well as hormones that control the thyroid, gonads, adrenal cortex, and other endocrine glands. Hormones from the hypothalamus gland control the anterior pituitary.

Arrhythmia: Any change in the normal pattern of the heart beat.

Basal metabolic rate (BMR): The amount of energy or calories required to perform basic bodily functions like breathing, circulation, maintenance of body temperature, digestion, metabolism, and so forth.

Beckwith-Wiedemann syndrome: A growth disorder, present at birth, which is attributed to an overproduction of insulin. Babies with this syndrome tend to be very large and fat. They have very large tongues and often have an umbilical hernia.

Beta cells: Specialized cells within the islets of Langerhans in the pancreas whose major function is production of insulin.

Biopsy: The microscopic examination of a small sample of tissue. A biopsy is usually used to determine if a growth is cancerous.

Bradycardia: A slow heart rate, usually less than 60 beats per minute. Mild bradycardia may not cause problems, but if the heart rate is very slow, circulation is reduced, leading to dizziness, fainting, and, in extreme instances, a collapse of circulation.

Braxton Hicks contractions: Painless contractions of the uterus before the actual onset of labor.

Breakthrough bleeding: Vaginal bleeding between menstrual periods. This is a common side effect of low-dose or progesterone-only birth control pills.

Breech delivery: Delivery of a baby in which either the feet or buttocks, instead of the head, emerge first.

Bromocriptine: A drug that suppresses production of prolactin. It is generally given to women who fail to ovulate because of prolactin overproduction. The drug is also used to treat Parkinson's disease.

Bulimia: A disorder marked by insatiable appetite, often resulting in binges of uncontrolled continuous eating. This is followed by periods of depression and self-denial, and in some cases, forced vomiting and laxative abuse to avoid weight gain. Bulimia is thought to be a psychiatric illness, but its true cause has not yet been established. The most common victims are young women, often college students or professionals.

Calcitonin: A hormone released by the thyroid gland to control blood levels of calcium.

Calcium: This is a silver-white mineral essential to building and maintaining bones and teeth. It is also instrumental in blood clotting; proper function of muscles, nerves, and the heart; the activation of certain enzymes; and maintaining the permeability of membranes.

Calorie: A unit of energy. The amount of energy or heat required to raise the temperature of one gram of water one degree centigrade.

Cancer: A general term referring to the uncontrolled reproduction and growth of cells. There are more than 100 different types of cancers.

Candidiasis: A yeast infection caused by the candida fungus. Many common diseases, such as vaginitis and thrush, are caused by candida infestations. A warm, moist environment will aid the growth of candida. (Also called moniliasis.)

Catecholamine: A group of chemicals that work as important nerve transmitters and, among other functions, are instrumental in the body's fight-or-flight response. The main catecholamines made by the body are dopamine, epinephrine (adrenaline), and norepinephrine.

Celiac disease: An intestinal disorder characterized by failure to absorb digested food, especially foods containing gluten. Symptoms include diarrhea, malnutrition, bleeding tendency, and low blood calcium. Treatment consists of avoiding foods that contain gluten.

Cervix: The neck, or the narrow part of the uterus that extends into the vaginal cavity.

Cesarean section: Surgical delivery of the fetus by means of an incision through the abdominal wall and into the uterus. It is done when it appears that a vaginal birth will be dangerous for mother or baby.

Chlamydia: A family of microorganisms that live as parasites within the cell, and which have characteristics of both viruses and some bacteria. Two species of *chlamydia* have been recognized; both cause diseases in humans. The most common is *Chlamydia trachomatis*, which is found in the membrane lining the eye (conjunctiva) and the lining of the urethra and the cervix. The latter is respsonsible for one of the most common sexually transmitted diseases in North America and can cause pelvic inflammatory disease and fertility problems in severe cases. *Chlamydia psittaci* infects birds and causes a type of pneumonia in humans.

Cholesterol: A crystaline fatlike substance that is instrumental in forming cell membranes in all animals. It is particularly abundant in the brain, nerves, liver, blood, and bile. Cholesterol is made in the liver and is essential in the production of sex hormones, nerve function, and a number of other vital processses. Excessive consumption of dietary cholesterol (found only in animal products, particularly organ meats, egg yolks, etc.) and/or saturated fats (i.e., those found in red meats, coconut or palm kernel oils) raises blood cholesterol levels.

Chorionic villus sampling: The removal and examination of cells shed by the fetus in the early stages of pregnancy in order to determine genetic and other chromosomal disorders. This test is still experimental, but is available at a number of research institutions and major medical centers in the United States.

Chromosome: A microscopic rod-shaped body that develops from the nuclear material of a cell. Chromosomes contain the genes that determine hereditary characteristics.

Clomiphene (Clomid): A nonsteroidal drug used to stimulate ovulation in women whose pituitary and ovaries are capable of normal functioning. Women who become pregnant while taking this drug have an increased chance of multiple births.

Collagen: A protein consisting of bundles of tiny fibers which form connective tissue including the white inelastic fibers of the tendons, the ligaments, the bones, and the cartilage. Collagen also makes up most of the dermis skin layers, and collagen ir ections are sometimes used to fill in wrinkles, acne scars, and other small skin deformities.

Colostrum: A thick, yellowish substance that is secreted from the breast before the onset of true lactation two or three days after delivery. Colostrum is believed to be important in conferring the mother's immunity to certain diseases to the newborn baby.

Comedo. Comedones: The greasy plug blocking the opening of the sebaceous gland. Often called a blackhead because of the dark coloration which comes from discoloration of the blocked sebum, not dirt, as is commonly believed. An infected comedo may develop into a pustule or pimple.

Computerized tomography scan (CT): A painless scanning procedure using multiple X-ray images and computer processing to map internal organs and structures. The X-ray beam is rotated around the part of the body being examined, and the computer processes these images to produce a complete picture of a thin slice of the organ. CT produces a highly accurate picture that shows relationships of structures to each other. The technique is used to detect tumors, blood clots, bone displacement, and fluid accumulations. It is used mostly to examine the brain, chest, stomach, and pelvis.

Conception: The union of the male sperm and female ovum, or egg; fertilization.

Congenital: A condition that is present at birth.

Conjugated estrogen: A form of estrogen, either natural or artificial, that can be prescribed to relieve symptoms of menopause, such as hot flashes or vaginal thinning, as well as the bone loss that frequently occurs in older women. Conjugated estrogen also may be used to treat failure to ovulate; it also provides relief in advanced cancer of the prostate and some kinds of breast cancer.

Conn's syndrome: *See* aldosteronism.

Contraception: Prevention of conception; birth control.

Contraceptive: An agent or device used in preventing conception.

Corpus leteum: A small yellow body which develops within a ruptured ovarian follicle. It is an endocrine structure secreting progesterone, a hormone responsible for changes in uterine endometrium in the second half of the menstrual cycle. It is also important in the development of the placenta.

Corticosteroid: Any one of the hormones made in the outer layer of the adrenal gland (adrenal cortex). They are instrumental in a number of important body functions including the proper metabolism of carbohydrates and proteins, and the working of the heart, lungs, muscles, kidneys, and other organs. Corticosteroid production increases during stress, especially in anxiety and severe injury. Too much of these hormones in the body is linked with various disorders, such as Cushing's syndrome.

Corticosterone: A hormone produced by the adrenal cortex which is important in metabolism of carbohydrates, potassium and sodium. It is also essential for normal glucose absorption and storage.

Cortisol: The principal corticosteroid hormone in humans. Its many functions include countering the effects of insulin by increasing the liver's output of glucose and increasing conversion of amino acids to glucose; regulating blood pressure by controlling microcirculation; and countering inflammation. It also stops growth in children and adolescents by causing the skeletal bones' growth plates to close. Also called hydrocortisone.

Cortisone: A hormone isolated from the cortex of the adrenal gland and also prepared synthetically. Its effects are similar to those of cortisol and can be converted to cortisol in the body.

Cretinism: A congenital condition caused by severe lack of thyroid in the baby or serious thyroid or iodine deficiency of the mother during pregnancy. Signs of cretinism include dwarfism, mental retardation, puffy facial features, a large tongue, navel hernia, and lack of muscle tone and coordination. Early treatment with thyroid hormone can restore normal body growth, but it may not prevent mental retardation. The use of iodized salt dramatically reduces the incidence of cretinism in a population whose food is lacking in iodine.

Crohn's disease: A chronic bowel disease characterized by swelling and inflammation of the lower part of the small intestine and the colon. The cause is unknown, but it is thought to be an autoimmune disorder. Frequently, the diseased parts may be separated by normal sections of bowel. (Also called regional enteritis.)

Cushing's syndrome: An overproduction of glucocorticoid hormones often caused by an ACTH-producing tumor, usually of the pituitary gland. People with Cushing's syndrome develop a distinctive moon-shaped face and redistribution of fatty tissue to form a "buffalo" hump on the upper back, a portly trunk, and thin legs. Symptoms include muscular weakness and wasting, a thinning of the skin, excessive hairiness, weight gain, high blood pressure, increased vulnerability to infection, and in later stages, the development of diabetes. Cushing's syndrome can also be caused by taking large doses of steroid drugs over a prolonged period, as might be the case in severe asthma.

Cyclic adenosine monophosphate (cyclic AMP): A chemical compound important to the action of many peptide hormones and the transmission of nerve impulses.

Cyst: A closed sac or pouch that contains fluid, semifluid, or solid material. Many women develop fluid-filled breast cysts; cysts also may result from obstructed ducts or from parasitic infection.

Cystic fibrosis: An inherited disorder of the glands that secrete through ducts (exocrine glands), causing the release of a thick mucus that can block or damage the pancreas, lungs, and sweat glands. The sweat is excessively salty and bitter to the taste—an important clue in proper diagnosis. The disease is usually diagnosed in infancy or early childhood; it is eventually fatal, but with improved treatments of recent years, a growing number of cystic fibrosis children are living into adulthood, and some are surviving into their thirties.

Cystosarcoma phyllodes: A rare breast tumor which is usually benign, but sometimes malignant. The tumors tend to grow very rapidly and may occupy the entire breast.

Danazol (danocrine): A drug that suppresses the action of the pituitary gland through androgen-like action.

Deoxyribonucleic acid (DNA): A nucleic acid present in the chromosomes of the nuclei of cells that is considered the chemical basis of heredity and the carrier of genetic information.

Diabetes insipidus: An uncommon disease caused by inadequate secretion of vasopressin, a hormone that helps the body retain water. It is marked by excessive thirst and overproduction of urine, and is more common in the young.

Diabetes mellitus: A complex disorder caused by the failure of the beta cells in the pancreas to produce adequate insulin, a hormone essential for proper carbohydrate metabolism and a number of other important body functions. It is characterized by high blood sugar (hyperglycemia) and sugar into the urine (glucosuria). Early symptoms include excessive thirst, unexplained weight loss, mood swings, and a general unwell feeling.

Diencephalon: The portion of the brain that includes the thalamus, metathalamus, epithalamus, and hypothalamus. It is the seat of many basic drives or instincts essential to survival, such as hunger, thirst, sleep, procreation, and the instinct to fight for survival.

Diethylstilbestrol (DES): A synthetic estrogen hormone once given to pregnant women to prevent miscarriages. Its use is believed to have resulted in a higher risk of a rare form of vaginal cancer and other reproductive abnormalities, including difficulty in achieving or maintaining a pregnancy among daughters born to women who took it. DES is also used to prevent conception if given promptly after unprotected intercourse (the "morning-after" pill). DES alters the uterine lining and thereby prevents implantation of a fertilized egg should conception take place. It is also used in the treatment of certain cancers.

Dilation and curettage (D&C): A procedure in which the opening to the uterus (cervix) is widened and the lining (endometrium) of the uterus is scraped with a curet. A D&C is done to diagnose diseases of the uterus, remove polyps and other small growths, or to correct heavy vaginal bleeding. It also may be used as an abortion technique, or to remove remnants of pregnancy left behind in an incomplete spontaneous abortion, or miscarriage.

Diuretic: Popularly called water pills. Any drug or other substance that promotes increased fluid removal from the body via increased urine production. Diuretics are commonly used to treat high blood pressure, congestive heart failure, edema, and other disorders characterized by excessive water retention.

Down's syndrome: A congenital condition marked by mental retardation and physical deformities caused by a chromosomal abnormality called trisomy 21. The incidence of Down's syndrome increases among babies born to women over 35 years of age. The disorder was formerly called Mongolism because of the characteristic shape of the eyes and face.

Dysfunctional uterine bleeding: The term refers to uterine or vaginal bleeding that occurs in the absence of ovulation. Sometimes the bleeding may resemble normal menstruation; more often, however, it is irregular and may be heavier than in normal menstruation. Causes include tumors, both benign fibroids or cancer, and hormonal imbalances in which ovulation does not take place. It also occurs in adolescent girls or women approaching menopause, the times of a woman's life in which ovulation may be irregular or absent.

Dysmenorrhea: Painful or difficult menstruation; menstrual cramps. In about ten percent of women, dysmenorrhea is severe enough to interfere with normal activities, and may even be incapacitating. In most women, a specific organic abnormality cannot be found, in which case it is called primary dysmenorrhea. Excessive prostaglandin activity is now assumed to cause the pain, and taking anti-prostaglandin drugs (ibuprofen and other anti-inflammatory drugs commonly used to treat arthritis) will relieve the cramps for most women. Secondary dysmenorrhea is menstrual pain that is caused by specific pelvic abnormalities, such as endometriosis, an abnormal tissue growth of endometrial tissue outside the uterus; long-term pelvic infection; chronic pelvic congestion; or fibroid tumors.

Eclampsia: A serious complex of problems seen only in pregnancy which includes high blood pressure, swelling or edema, kidney damage, protein loss, and a tendency toward seizures. Toxemia of pregnancy can develop as a consequence of the high blood pressure.

Ectopic pregnancy: Implantation of the fertilized ovum outside of the uterus, usually in a fallopian tube. If undetected in its early stages, an ectopic pregnancy may cause a tubal rupture and serious abdominal bleeding.

Edema: Swelling of body tissue caused by a buildup of fluid.

Embryo: The early stage of fetal development during which the various organ systems are formed. In humans it occurs between the second and eighth weeks following conception.

Endocrine system: The body's ductless glands and other structures that secrete hormones into the blood stream, affecting virtually every organ system and bodily function. Endocrine glands include the thyroid and the parathyroid, the pituitary, the pancreas, the adrenal glands, and the gonads. A number of other organs, such as the kidney, small intestine, lungs, and heart also produce hormones and have endocrine functions.

Endometriosis: A common disorder in which some of the endometrial cells that normally line the uterus escape into the pelvic cavity and form clusters of endometrial tissue. These clusters may become attached to the uterus, ovaries, tubes, colon, and other abdominal structures. In rare instances, they may migrate to the lungs or other internal organs. These cells respond to hormonal stimulus during each menstrual cycle and grow and become engorged with blood, as does the normal endometrium. The tissue bleeds and forms scars which can cause pain and fertility problems.

Endometrium: The lining of the uterus in which the fertilized ovum is implanted and which is shed during menstruation if conception has not taken place.

Epinephrine: One of the stress, or catecholamine, hormones produced by the adrenal medulla. Also called adrenaline, it acts to constrict blood, thereby raising blood pressure, and stimulates the heart to beat faster. It also speeds up the release of glucose stored as glycogen in the liver to provide fast extra energy. The body secretes extra epinephrine and other catecholamines in response to danger; they are instrumental in the body's fight-or-flight response, which occurs in the face of stress or perceived danger.

Episiotomy: An incision made in the final stages of childbirth from the vagina downward toward the rectum to prevent tearing of the skin and help shorten the second stage of labor.

Erythropoietin: A hormone that controls the bone marrow's production of red cells. Erythropoietin production rises following a serious bleeding episode, which lowers the number of red blood cells. The hormone is also increased when a person goes to a high altitude and needs more red blood cells to get enough oxygen from the thinner air.

Estradiol: The most potent form of natural human estrogen. It is secreted mostly by the ovarian follicle, and also by the placenta, and perhaps by the adrenal cortex. It is responsible for development of secondary sex characteristics in adolescent girls; it also promotes the growth of the endometrium during the first part of the menstrual cycle.

Estrogen: One of a group of steroid hormones responsible for the development of female secondary sex traits (such as breast development). Human estrogen is produced in the ovaries, adrenal glands, testicles, and both the fetus and placenta. Estrogen prepares the wall of the uterus for fertilization, implantation, and nutrition of the early embryo.

Exocrine glands: These glands release secretions through a duct to the target organ or tissue. Examples of exocrine glands include the sweat glands of the skin or the saliva glands. The kidney, digestive tract, and breasts all contain exocrine glands.

Fallopian tubes: The two tubes or ducts in the female reproductive system that extend from each side of the uterus and end near the ovaries. After ovulation, the egg enters one of the fallopian tubes and travels through it to the uterus. (Also called oviducts.)

Fascia: Layer or sheet of connective tissue that separate muscles and various organs or other structures of the body. It also surrounds many muscles and helps hold them together.

Fat necrosis: The death of fat cells. The dead cells may eventually become calcified, with fibrous tissue growing around them forming a hard, irregular lump.

Fertilization: Union of male sperm and female ovum to form a zygote from which the embryo, and eventually the fetus, develops. The process of conception.

Fetal alcohol syndrome: A series of birth defects caused by heavy alcohol consumption, especially during the early part of pregnancy. The defects include small head size, facial deformities, mental retardation, heart defects, poor coordination, crossed eyes, and other problems.

Fetus: In humans, the child in utero from the third month to birth. Prior to that time it is called an embryo.

Fibroadenomas: A relatively common benign breast condition that manifests itself as a lump—usually round, firm, and painless. Typically, a fibroadenoma will move freely when examined with the fingers. Although fibroadenomas are benign, it is not always possible to tell one from a cancer by physical examination alone. Therefore a needle or surgical biopsy should be done to rule out a malignancy.

Fibrocystic disease: A condition in which cysts, normally fluid-filled sacs, develop thick fibrous tissue, forming benign tumors.

Fibroid tumor: Uterine tumors made up of smooth muscle cells, which are most common after the age of thirty or thirty-five. Most are small and slow-growing, and they very rarely develop into cancer. Large, fast-growing fibroids, or tumors that interfere with fertility, bladder function, or that cause excessive menstrual bleeding may require surgery, either removal of the tumors or, if indicated, a hysterectomy.

Fibrosis: A gradual replacement of glandular tissue by inert fibrous tissue. Commonly occurs in the breast, but is not associated with breast cancer.

Fluorine, fluoride: A mineral that helps to form the bones and teeth. In small amounts, such as fluoridated water, it helps to prevent tooth decay.

Follicles, ovarian: The egg-forming cells in the ovaries.

Follicle stimulating hormone (FSH): A hormone secreted from the anterior lobe of the pituitary that prompts the ovaries to ripen an egg each month and is also instrumental in making sperm in the male. (Also called menotropins.)

Gastrin: A gastrointestinal hormone that stimulates secretion of gastric acids in the stomach. Eating stimulates its release.

Gene: The basic unit of heredity. Each ultramicroscopic gene occupies a specific place on a chromosome, and is, under certain circumstances, capable of giving rise to a new characteristic, a process called mutation.

Gestation: Period of intrauterine fetal development from conception to birth.

Gestational diabetes: High blood sugar that occurs during pregnancy, then disappears as soon as the baby is born. It is a result of a genetic predisposition to diabetes and the stress of pregnancy. Because of the high levels of glucose in the mother's blood, the fetus produces extra insulin, which acts as a growth hormone. Many of these babies are over-sized at birth, often weighing nine or more pounds. After birth, the baby may be unable to stabilize its own blood glucose levels, and suffer life-threatening drops in blood sugar. Gestational diabetes is the major cause of stillbirths in the United States.

Gland: Any organ that produces and secretes a chemical substance used by another part of the body. Ductless, or endocrine, glands secrete into the bloodstream. Examples are the thyroid and the pancreas. Exocrine glands are located near their target organs, and have ducts that permit secretion directly to a particular location. Examples are the sweat and the salivary glands.

Glucagon: A hormone secreted by the alpha cells of the pancreas. It stimulates the liver's release and conversion of glycogen into glucose, thereby raising blood sugar and supplying needed energy.

Glucocorticoid: Any of the steroid hormones that promote the conversion of protein to glucose and glycogen. Cortisone is a major example of a glucocorticoid. When used as drugs, glucocorticoids treat inflammation and temper the body's immune response.

Glucose: Blood sugar. The most common monosaccharide (simple sugar) and the main source of energy for humans. It is stored as glycogen in the liver and can be quickly converted back into glucose.

Glucosuria (also called glycosuria): Abnormal levels of glucose in the urine. Common causes include diabetes and kidney disease.

Glycogen: The major carbohydrate stored in animal cells. It is made from glucose and stored chiefly in the liver and, to some extent, in muscles. Glycogen is changed to glucose and released into circulation as needed by the body for energy. *See also* Glucose.

Goiter: An overgrown thyroid gland, usually seen as a swelling in the neck. Depending upon whether the cause is too much or too little thyroid hormone, treatment may involve giving antithyroid drugs or radioiodine, surgery, or giving thyroid hormone.

Gonad: Primary sex gland. Ovaries in the female; testes in the male.

Gonadotropins: Gonad-stimulating hormones which promote the testes or the ovaries to perform their biological functions.

Graves' disease: A disorder characterized by an overactive thyroid and excessive thyroid hormone production. Obvious signs include a goiter and, if untreated, bulging eyes (exopthalmos). Graves' disease, which is five times more common in women than in men, occurs most often between the ages of twenty and forty and often follows an infection or physical or emotional stress.

Growth hormone (GH): A hormone instrumental in regulating growth. It is secreted by the anterior pituitary and its release, which occurs in bursts mostly during sleep, is controlled mainly by the central nervous system. A lack of GH causes dwarfism; an excess results in gigantism or acromegaly. (Also called somatotropic hormone.)

Hashimoto's disease: An autoimmune disorder that damages the thyroid gland, or affects proper thyroid growth. It strikes women more frequently than men.

Hermaphroditism: A rare condition in which a person has both male and female sex organs. It is caused by a chromosomal abnormality.

Herpes simplex: Recurring infection caused by the herpes virus. Type 1 involves blisterlike sores usually around the mouth and referred to as "cold sores" or "fever blisters." Type 2 usually affects the mucous membranes of the genitalia and can be spread by sexual contact. In unusual circumstances, either type can cause damage to other parts of the body such as the eyes or brain. Also, the distinctions between type 1 and type 2 herpes is not as clear as once thought; either virus can cause genital or oral sores.

Hirsutism: Excessive body and facial hair. In women, the hairiness occurs in a masculine pattern, and is particularly noticeable on the face, chest, and lower abdomen. Common causes include heredity, diseases characterized by hormonal imbalance, and as a side effect of medication.

Hormone: A chemical that is produced by the endocrine glands or tissue which, when secreted into body fluids, has a specific effect on other organs. Hormones are often referred to as chemical messengers, and they influence such diverse activities as growth, sexual development and desire, metabolism, muscular development, mental acuity, behavior, and sleep cycles. Hormones are also instrumental in maintaining the proper internal chemical and fluid balance.

Hormone-receptor assay: A test that measures the sensitivity of cancer cells to hormones, commonly used in breast cancer treatment. The test measures the sensitivity of cancer cells to estrogen, and to a lesser degree, progesterone. The test aids in the treatment of certain breast cancers with hormonal manipulation.

Human chorionic gonadotropin (hCG): A hormone released by cells in the placenta—the tissue connecting the mother and fetus. After fertilization, hCG prompts the corpus luteum to continue to secrete estrogen and progesterone to establish and maintain the pregnancy. Early pregnancy can be detected by measuring a rise in hCG.

Human growth hormone (hGH): A hormone secreted by the pituitary which is the major hormone controlling growth after birth. A failure of the pituitary to produce adequate hGH results in pituitary dwarfism, in which the person has a normal body conformation, but is abnormally small.

Human placental lactogen (HPL): A hormone produced in the placenta which stimulates the breast to begin milk production.

Hydrocortisone: *See* cortisol.

25 Hydroxycholecalciferol: The precursor to the active form of vitamin D, which assumes hormonal function by promoting the absorption of dietary calcium from the intestines and also increases the kidneys' reabsorption of the mineral.

Hyperaldosteronism: An overproduction of aldosterone which causes excessive sodium retention and high blood pressure, as well as a depletion of potassium, which can cause irregular heart beats, muscular weakness, and cramps. (Also called aldosteronism.)

Hypercalcemia: An excessive amount of calcium in the blood. Causes include bone cancer and other bone disorders, excessive parathyroid and thyroid hormones, or overdoses of vitamin D.

Hyperplasia: An overgrowth of tissue due to excessive proliferation of normal cells. Common examples include cervical hyperplasia, which is an overgrowth of cervical tissue.

Hyperthyroidism: Overactivity of the thyroid gland leading to excessive production of thyroid hormone. Symptoms include weight loss; restlessness; signs of Grave's disease, such as abnormal bulging of the eyeballs (exopthalmos); constant hunger; fatigue; rapid and irregular heartbeat; and, sometimes, a goiter.

Hypertrophy: An increase in an organ's size, independent of normal growth, that is caused by an increase in cell size rather than number.

Hypocalcemia: Abnormally low blood calcium.

Hypoglycemia: Abnormally low levels of blood sugar as a result of taking too large a dosage of insulin or excessive release of insulin by the pancreas. Symptoms include weakness, headaches, hunger, problems with vision, loss of muscle coordination, anxiety, personality changes, and if untreated, delirium, coma, and death.

Hypospadias: A structural defect in which the opening in a man's penis is on the underside, preventing his depositing the sperm deeply enough in the vagina, causing fertility problems.

Hypotension: Blood pressure that is too low for normal functioning.

Hypothalamus: The part of the brain just above the pituitary gland. It works in concert with the pituitary to control other endocrine glands and is instrumental in a number of body functions.

Hypothermia: Abnormally low body temperature (below 95° F or 35° C), which can lead to a failure of vital organ systems.

Hypothyroidism: Underactive thyroid, characterized by inadequate production of thyroid hormone, which results in a slowing down of almost all body functions. It is sometimes caused by surgical removal of all or part of the thyroid gland, an overdose of antithyroid medicine, or a shrinking of the thyroid gland itself. It also can stem from a pituitary problem, in which that gland secretes an improper amount of thyroid stimulating hormone. Common symptoms of hypothyroidism include weight gain, sluggishness, dryness of the skin, constipation, increased sensitivity to cold, and a general slowing of body processes.

Hysterectomy: Removal of the uterus.

Insulin: A hormone secreted by the beta cells of the islets of Langerhans of the pancreas. The hormone is essential for proper metabolism, especially of carbohydrates, and for maintenance of the proper blood sugar level.

Interstitial cell-stimulating hormone (ICSH): An anterior pituitary hormone that stimulates the testes to produce male hormones.

Ischemia: A marked drop in blood flow to an organ or body part, often marked by pain and inability to function normally. A common example is ischemic heart disease, in which a portion of heart muscle does not get enough blood —usually because of atherosclerosis in the artery supplying that area—resulting in chest pain and even a heart attack. Prolonged ischemia can result in tissue death, as is the case in a heart attack.

Islets of Langerhans: A group of cells (alpha, beta, and delta) in the pancreas that secrete endocrine hormones; the alpha cells produce glucagon, the beta cells produce insulin, and the delta cells produce somatostatin. Destruction or impairment of function of the islets of Langerhans may result in diabetes.

Kallmann's syndrome: A disorder in which the pituitary fails to secrete the hormones that stimulate the production and release of gonadotropins. Boys with this disorder may have undescended testicles and lack normal male sex characteristics; girls do not develop breasts or other female characteristics. It also is associated with the loss of the sense of smell.

Ketone bodies, ketones: Highly acidic substances produced in the body as a result of normal fat metabolism in the liver. Ketones provide fuel for muscles; excessive production of ketones, as may happen in poorly controlled diabetes, leads to their excretion in urine and a potentially dangerous build-up in the blood. (Also called acetone bodies.)

Ketosis: The buildup of ketones, which are highly acidic substances, in the body. This condition is often associated with poorly controlled diabetes and can lead to a fatal coma.

Klinefelter's syndrome: The most common of the male gonadal abnormalities. Men with this disorder will have small, hard testes and impaired sperm production. Some fail to develop secondary male characteristics, and instead, develop breasts and have little or no body hair. They also suffer from mental retardation or psychological problems. The underlying defect is the presence of an extra X chromosome.

Lactase: An intestinal enzyme important in the digestion of lactose, or milk sugar.

Lactose: A complex sugar found in milk and milk products. It is converted to glucose and galactose by lactase, a digestive enzyme.

Lactose intolerance: Intolerance to milk caused by a deficiency of the enzyme lactase which is essential to the absorption of lactose from the intestinal tract. Symptoms include abdominal cramps, intestinal gas, and discomfort. It is more common almong blacks and Orientals than whites, and frequently develops as a person grows older, although it also can be present from birth.

Laurence-Moon-Biedl syndrome: A developmental disorder associated with low levels of gonadotropin hormones and characterized by retinitis pigmentosa, a progressive eye disorder; mental retardation; obesity; extra fingers and toes; and undeveloped gonads.

Luteinization: Process of development of the corpus luteum within a ruptured follicle following ovulation.

Luteinizing hormone (LH): A hormone secreted by the anterior pituitary that is instrumental in reproductive function. In men, it stimulates the testes to produce testosterone, the male sex hormone which acts with the follicle stimulating hormone (FSH) in prompting the testes to produce sperm. In females, luteinizing hormone, working together with FSH, stimulates the ovary to secrete estrogen. High levels of estrogen cause a surge of LH, which stimulates the release of an egg from the ovary (ovulation).

Luteinizing-hormone releasing hormone (LHRH): A substance secreted by the hypothalamus that controls the release and synthesis of two pituitary hormones—the luteinizing hormone and the follicle stimulating hormone.

McCune-Albright syndrome: A disorder affecting the central nervous system resulting in precocious puberty. The syndrome is characterized by development of brownish cafe-au-lait spots, facial asymmetry, or skeletal deformity.

Marfan's syndrome: An hereditary condition of connective tissue, bones, muscles, ligaments, and skeletal structures. Typically, people with Marfan's syndrome are taller than average and have very long limbs with very narrow, spider-like hands and feet. They also may have weakened sections of the aorta, which can rupture unexpectedly. Lincoln is said to have been afflicted with Marfan's.

Mastectomy: The surgical removal of breast tissue. Part or all of a breast may be removed, together with muscle and lymph tissue.

Mastitis: Breast inflammation which may occur most commonly among women who are breast-feeding, but it may also be caused by an obstructed milk duct or a bacterial infection.

Melanin: A black or dark brown pigment that occurs naturally in the hair, skin, and in the iris and choroid membrane of the eye.

Menarche: The onset of menstruation during puberty.

Menometrorrhagia: Irregular and excessive menstrual bleeding.

Menopause: The end of a woman's ability to reproduce, marked by a gradual cessation of menstrual periods. Menopause occurs between the ages of 40 and 58, with 51 being the mean age. Typically, as a woman approaches menopause, menstrual periods become more irregular, and the flow may be lighter or heavier. Ovulation become more erratic and there may be hot flashes, night sweats, mood changes, and other symptoms, most of which can be relieved by hormone replacement therapy.

Menstrual cycle: A woman's monthly cycle that begins with menarche and ends with menopause. Each cycle is characterized by hormonal changes that thicken the endometrium, the lining of the uterus, and which prepare the body for pregnancy. If conception does not take place, the endometrium is shed during menstruation and a new cycle begins. The average length of the cycle is 28 days, but this can vary from 20 to 35 days or even more, depending upon the individual woman.

Menstruation: A period of uterine bleeding accompanied by shedding of the endometrium. Averages 4 to 5 days in duration.

Metabolism: The combination of chemical and physical changes in the body essential to convert food to energy and other substances needed to maintain life.

Metastasis: The spread of disease—usually cancer—from one body part to another, usually via the blood or lymph.

Mineralocorticoid: A class of steroid hormones secreted by the adrenal cortex that affect sodium and potassium balance. Aldosterone is the primary example.

Mitosis: The process of cell division.

Mittleschmerz: Pain experienced during ovulation which may range from a mild twinge to severe cramping.

Myomectomy: The surgical removal of a fibroid tumor, most often from the uterus.

Myxedema: A severe form of thyroid deficiency which, if untreated, may lead to coma and death.

Nipple papillomas: Wart-like growths in a milk-duct lining near the breast nipple. They usually produce a bloody discharge, and may be felt as a small lump near the nipple. They occur most often in premenopausal women.

Nipple polyps: Small benign growths that form on the nipple skin. They often resemble tiny mushrooms, with a thin stalk and rounded head. They are not cancerous.

Nisidioblastoma: A growth disorder, present at birth, in which babies tend to be very large and fat; they also have very large tongues and often have an umbilical hernia. The excessive growth is attributed to overproduction of insulin due to a pancreatic tumor. Once the tumor is removed, they usually grow normally.

Nonsteroidal antiinflammatory drugs (NSAID's): These drugs are used in the treatment of arthritis and are effective in preventing or relieving menstrual cramps for up to 90 percent of women who suffer from dysmenorrhea. A common example is ibuprofen, which is available in both prescription and nonprescription strengths.

Norepinephrine: A stress hormone produced by the adrenal medulla that is similar to epinephrine. It increases blood pressure by narrowing the blood vessels.

Oral contraceptive: An oral steroid drug for birth control. The two major steroids used are progestogen only (the "mini pill") and a combination of progestogen and estrogen.

Orthostatic hypotension: Unusually low blood pressure that occurs when a person stands after sitting or lying down, causing dizziness and light-headedness. In some people, the sudden drop in blood pressure may cause the person to faint. (Also called postural hypotension.)

Osteomalacia: Softening of the bones due to a lack of mineralization. The disease is marked by increasing softness of the bones, so that they become flexible and deformed. It is often seen in people with kidney failure.

Osteoporosis: A condition in which bones become thin and porous as a result of calcium loss. It occurs most frequently in postmenopausal women, especially those who are small-boned, of northern European extraction, and who smoke. It usually can be slowed or prevented by estrogen replacement therapy, along with adequate calcium intake.

Ovaries: The female reproductive glands whose function is to produce the eggs (ova) and the sex hormones estrogen and progesterone.

Ovulation: The periodic ripening and rupture of the mature follicle and the discharge of the ovum, which is then ready for fertilization by the male sperm.

Oxytocin: A pituitary hormone that stimulates the uterus to contract, thus inducing labor. It also acts on the breasts to stimulate the release of milk.

Pancreas: The gland situated behind the stomach which has both endocrine and exocrine functions. Its secretion of enzymes and pancreatic juices plays an important role in digestion. Specialized clusters of endocrine cells (the islets of Langerhans) secrete insulin and glucagon, hormones that are essential in the regulation of carbohydrate metabolism and blood sugar levels; and somatostatin, a hormone important in regulating growth.

Pap smear or test (also called Papanicolaou test): The microscopic examination of cells or mucus shed from organs such as the cervix or bronchi to detect cancer and precancerous conditions. The technique allows early diagnosis of cancer and has helped lower the death rate from cervical cancer.

Parathyroid glands: Small endocrine structures, usually four in number, that lie on the back and sides of each thyroid lobe. Their parathyroid hormone is instrumental in regulating the level of blood calcium.

Parathyroid hormone (PTH): A hormone released by the parathyroid glands that acts to keep a constant level of calcium in body tissues. This hormone controls the movement of calcium in the body and controls its excretion in the urine. Loss of the parathyroid glands results in low blood calcium, leading to muscle spasms, seizures, and death if the hormone is not replaced.

Pelvic inflammatory disease (PID): A serious infection of the reproductive organs that can damage a woman's fallopian tubes, uterus, and ovaries. Causes include sexually transmitted diseases, especially gonorrhea and chlamydia. Use of the IUD by a woman with multiple sex partners also increases the risk of pelvic inflammatory disease.

Pergonal: A trademarked drug made from menotropins (LH and FSH hormones) that is sometimes used to induce fertility when other less-potent fertility drugs fail. It acts directly on the ovaries, stimulating them to produce and ripen eggs.

Pheochromocytoma: A relatively rare benign tumor of the adrenal gland or, less commonly, the urinary bladder that secretes epinephrine and norepinephrine, two of the major stress hormones. It causes persistent hypertension; other symptoms may include headaches, sweating, high blood sugar, nausea, vomiting, and fainting spells. Treatment is by surgical removal or drug therapy to lower the hormone levels.

Pineal body: A small, cone-shaped gland located on the back of the midbrain. It is often listed as an endocrine gland, but no hormones or definite function have been associated with it.

Pituitary dwarfism: A disorder in which the pituitary gland does not secrete growth hormone, producing an abnormally short child. Sexual development may eventually take place if the pituitary produces the necessary gonadotropins. Some growth usually can be achieved by treatment with growth hormone.

Pituitary gigantism: A rare disorder characterized by a very rapid growth spurt during childhood and a change in features—namely, an overgrown lower jaw, a thickening of the hands and feet, and an overgrowth of soft tissue. It is usually caused by a tumor that secretes growth hormone.

Pituitary gland: The pea-sized gland located at the base of the brain. It is controlled by the hypothalamus and it, in turn, controls the hormone production of many other endocrine glands.

Placebo: An inert substance that has no medicinal properties, but which may be given for psychological benefit or as part of a clinical research study.

Placenta: The structure that develops on the uterine wall during pregnancy and which links the mother's circulation to that of the developing fetus. Through the placenta, the fetus receives nourishment and oxygen and eliminates waste products. It is expelled from the mother as the afterbirth following delivery of the baby.

Placenta previa: Placenta which is implanted in the lower uterine segment and covers part or all of the cervical opening. If the placenta covers all or most of the cervix, a cesarean delivery is usually performed to prevent excessive bleeding during labor.

Polycystic ovary syndrome: A disorder characterized by a complex of hormonal imbalances, resulting in failure to ovulate and infertility. During the monthly cycle, one or more ovarian follicles will swell, but no egg is released. Women with polycystic ovaries also may develop abnormal growth of body hair and weight gain. (Also called Stein-Leventhal syndrome.)

Precocious puberty: Puberty before the age of 9 years in boys and 8 years in girls. Precocious puberty has a number of causes, the most common being a tumor affecting the hypothalamus. Other causes include a variety of hormonal imbalances and disorders affecting the central nervous system.

Prednisone: A potent anti-inflammatory drug derived from a synthetic glucocorticoid hormone. It is used to treat many diseases characterized by inflammation and/or an immune response. Severe asthma is a common example.

Premenstrual syndrome (PMS): A variety of symptoms, both physical and emotional, associated with the menstrual cycle, usually occurring in the week before menstruation.

Pretibial myxedema: A rare thyroid-related skin condition —usually a part of Grave's disease—which involves development of a raised reddish rash or lumps on the front of the legs and top of the feet. The lumps are painless and are usually cleared up with cortisone creams.

Progesterone: A steroid hormone secreted by the corpus luteum, adrenals, or placenta. It rises during the second phase of the menstrual cycle and is responsible for preparing the endometrium to support a pregnancy. If conception does not take place, progesterone production drops and the endometrium is shed in the menstrual flow.

Progestin, progestogen: Any of a group of hormones, natural or synthetic, released by the corpus luteum, placenta, or adrenal cortex. They have progesterone-like effects on the uterus and are now used in conjunction with estrogen in postmenopausal hormone replacement therapy.

Prolactin: Hormone produced by the pituitary gland that is responsible for initiating and sustaining the production of breast milk. It also has other metabolic functions that are not completely understood.

Prostaglandins: A group of fatty acid derivatives present in many tissues including the prostate gland, menstrual fluid, brain, lungs, kidney, thymus, seminal fluid, and pancreas. Prostaglandins are extremely active substances that affect the cardiovascular system, smooth muscle, and stimulate the uterus to contract, among many other functions. They are also instrumental in carrying out many other hormone-mediated functions.

Pseudohermaphroditism: A condition in which a person has the body traits of both sexes, but has either male testicles or female ovaries (not both).

Puberty: The developmental stage during which secondary sex characteristics appear and reproductive organs become functionally active. In girls, puberty is marked by breast development, the onset of menstruation, and ovulation. In boys, it includes growth of the penis and testes, increased muscle mass, and deepening of the voice. Both sexes experience rapid growth, changes in body conformation, and growth of pubic and axillary hair.

Relaxin: A hormone secreted during pregnancy which acts on the pelvic ligaments during labor, enabling the birth canal to widen so a baby can be born.

Renal erythropoietic factor (REF): A hormone produced by the kidneys that helps control the production of red blood cells in the bone marrow.

Ritodrine (Yutopar): A drug that stops premature contractions.

Secondary sex characteristics: Any of the visible bodily features of sexual maturity that develop as a child enters puberty and matures. In women, they include growth of breasts and increased fatty tissue and the growth of pubic and axillary hair.

Somatomedins: Insulin-like growth factors believed to control the action of the pituitary's growth hormone. Their precise role is not fully understood, but these growth factors are thought to be important in a number of diseases.

Somatostatin: A hormone that controls growth and helps to control the release of certain other hormones. Also called growth hormone release inhibiting hormone.

Somatotropic hormone, somatotropin: *See* Growth hormone.

Soto's syndrome: Also referred to as cerebral gigantism, this rare disorder, whose cause is unknown, is present at birth. Children with Soto's syndrome are taller than average at birth, and grow rapidly during the first few years of life. Puberty occurs early. Other characteristics of this disorder include a large, elongated head and jaw, large ears, prominent forehead, slanted eyes, below normal intelligence, and poor coordination.

Spermatozoa: The mature male sex or germ cell that is formed within the seminiferous tubules of the testes. When it unites with the female ovum, fertilization takes place.

Stein-Leventhal syndrome: See polycystic ovary syndrome.

Steroid hormones: The sex hormones and hormones of the adrenal cortex. These include corticosteroids (i.e., hydrocortisone), the mineralocorticoids (i.e., aldosterone), androgen, estrogen, and progesterone.

Stilbestrol: *See* Diethylstilbestrol.

Tamoxifen: A drug that counters the effects of estrogen. It is used to treat advanced breast cancer in premenopausal women whose tumors are estrogen-dependent. It also may be given to women with fibrocystic breasts to reduce lumpiness and relieve the swelling and pain.

Testicles, testes: The pair of primary male sex glands enclosed in the scrotum. They produce the male sex hormone testosterone and spermatazoa.

Testosterone: The male sex hormone which induces the secondary sex characteristics.

Thelarche: The beginning of breast development at puberty.

Thymus: A gland that lies behind the breast bone and which is instrumental in immune system function during early life. Its function is not fully understood, but as a child approaches maturity, the gland shrinks and is only a remnant in adults.

Thyroid: A butterfly-shaped gland that lies over the windpipe and just below the larynx. Thyroid hormones are essential to numerous metabolic processes and are essential for early growth, regulation of the heart beat, temperature control, and other functions.

Thyroid stimulating hormone (TSH): A substance released by the front lobe of the pituitary gland which controls the release of thyroid hormone. (Also called thyrotropin.)

Thyrotropin releasing hormone: A substance of the hypothalamus that stimulates the release of thyroid stimulating hormone from the pituitary gland. (Also called thyrotropin releasing factor—TRF—and TSH releasing factor.)

Trophic hormones: These hormones have no direct action of their own; instead, they stimulate other endocrine glands to go into action and secrete their hormones. Gonadotropins which stimulate the ovaries or testes to release their hormones are major examples of trophic hormones.

Turner's syndrome: A chromosomal disorder in women that is characterized by short stature, failure to mature sexually, and depending upon the chromosomal pattern, a variety of birth defects that may include mental retardation.

Uterus: The female organ, commonly called the womb, in which the fetus develops from the time of conception until birth.

Varicocele: A varicose vein in the testes which can block the passage of sperm or promote male infertility by raising the temperature within the scrotum.

Vasomotor instability: Hot flashes caused by changes in hormone levels affecting the temperature-regulating center of the hypothalamus. They are a common symptom of menopause; they also may occur when taking certain drugs, such as high-dose niacin to lower blood cholesterol.

Vasopressin: A posterior pituitary hormone that controls the muscle tone of blood vessels and acts as an antidiuretic hormone to conserve body fluids.

von Recklinghausen's disease: A disorder affecting the central nervous system and characterized by development of brownish cafe-au-lait spots, overgrowth of the sheaths encasing the nerves and other fibrous tissue, seizures, visual defects, and mental retardation. Puberty may be either premature or delayed.

Selected Bibliography

Bolinger, Robert E. *Endocrinology: New Directions in Therapy.* New York: Medical Examination Publishing Co., 1977.

Crouch, James E. *Functional Human Anatomy,* third edition. Philadelphia: Lea E. Febiger, 1978.

Ezrin, Calvin, John O. Godden, and Robert Volpe. *Systematic Endocrinology.* New York: Harper & Row, 1979.

Moor, Mary Lou. *Realities in Childbearing.* Philadelphia: W. B. Saunders, 1978.

Wilson, Jean D., and Daniel W. Foster (editors). *Williams Textbook of Endocrinology,* seventh edition. Philadelphia: W. B. Saunders, 1985.

Yen, Samuel S. C., and Robert B. Jaffe. *Reproductive Endocrinology: Physiology, Pathophysiology and Clinical Management.* Philadelphia: W. B. Saunders, 1978.

Index

abortion, 22, 98, 137
  spontaneous, *see* miscarriage
Accutane, 320
acetaminophen, 132, 253
acini, 197
acne, 73, 100–101, 208, 231, 268, 276, 309, 316–321
acromegaly, 44
Addison's disease, 14, 276–277, 322
adenyl cyclase, 20
adolescence, 47–64, 159, 189, 194, 199, 268, 316
  amenorrhea in, 84–86
  anorexia nervosa in, 39, 56, 60–61, 86, 88, 285, 301
  gender-linked differences in, 39, 49–50, 52
  pregnancy in, 49, 54
  psychological changes in, 53–55, 60–61
  sexual activity in, 54
  sleep in, 32, 50
  see also puberty
adrenal cortex, 12, 13, 271, 272, 274, 275, 276
adrenal glands, xiii, 12–16, 49, 50, 52, 62, 116, 126, 143, 193, 216, 217, 225, 253, 309
  disorders of, 271–283, 322, 325
  location of, 12, 271

stress and, 13, 257, 271, 272–273, 280
adrenaline (epinephrine), 12, 15–16, 271, 280
adrenal medulla, 12, 15, 271, 280–281, 283
adrenocorticotropic hormone (ACTH), 7, 13–14, 20, 41, 126, 225, 272, 273, 276, 277, 279, 282
Advil, 80
alcohol consumption, 54, 55, 74, 76, 91, 110, 117, 123, 163, 184, 189, 204, 253, 305
  for premature contractions, 143
aldosterone, 13, 14, 19, 20, 21, 126, 226, 271, 272, 273, 274, 277, 278
allergies, 13, 132
allupurinol, 195
alopecia areata, 322
alpha cells, 16
aluminum, 185, 194
amenorrhea, 9, 56, 57, 59, 60, 69, 84–91, 226–227, 301, 303, 305, 324
  post-pill, 90, 101–102
  primary, 84–86, 226–227
  secondary, 84, 85, 86–91
American Cancer Society, 201, 213–214, 220
American College of Radiology, 110

LOIS JOVANOVIC, M.D., is currently a senior scientist at the Sansum Medical Research Foundation in Santa Barbara, California, and a clinical associate professor at the University of Southern California, Los Angeles. Dr. Jovanovic received her M.D. from the Albert Einstein College of Medicine. She completed her internship and residency training in internal medicine as well as her fellowship in endocrinology and metabolism at The New York Hospital–Cornell Medical College where she stayed on as a faculty member and chief of their Diabetes Clinic. She is board certified in both internal medicine and in endocrinology. Dr. Jovanovic was recently elected president of the Diabetes and Pregnancy Council of the American Diabetes Association and is on the editorial boards of eight medical journals. She is the author of scores of professional articles and has written or edited six medical books. She currently lives in Santa Barbara, where she is continuing her research in the field of diabetes and pregnancy.

GENELL J. SUBAK-SHARPE is the author or editor of over twenty books in the field of medicine, including the bestselling *Columbia University College of Physicians and Surgeons Complete Home Medical Guide*. She has worked on numerous newspapers and was formerly on the news staff of the *New York Times*. Ms. Subak-Sharpe lives in New York City with her husband, Dr. Gerald Subak-Sharpe, and their three children.

17